FIFA (Fédération Internationale de Football Association)

Founded in 1904 by representatives of the sporting organisations of seven European nations, then expanding into the Americas, Asia and Africa, FIFA has developed into one of the most high-profile and lucrative businesses in the global consumer and cultural industry. In recent years, however, a series of crises have left the organization open to critique and exposure, and have created a soap-operatic narrative of increasing interest to the global media.

In this critical new account of one of the world's most important sporting institutions, Professor Alan Tomlinson investigates the history of FIFA and the underlying political dynamics of its growth. The book explores the influence of the men who have led FIFA, the emergence of the World Cup as FIFA's exclusive product, FIFA's relationships with other federations and associations, the crises that have shaped its recent history, and the issues and challenges that are likely to shape its future. Particular attention is given to selected moments in the post-Havelange administration and the way in which FIFA, its current president Joseph Blatter and some close key colleagues have responded to and survived successive scandals. The book provides a foundation for understanding the growth and development of what is widely accepted as the world's most popular sport; sheds light on the shifting politics of nationalism in the post-colonial period; and reveals the opportunistic drive for personal aggrandizement which is shaping an increasingly media-influenced and globalizing world, in which international sport was a harbinger of these trends and forces.

Fascinating and provocative, this is essential reading for anybody with an interest in soccer, sport and society, sports governance or global organizations.

Alan Tomlinson is Professor of Leisure Studies at the University of Brighton, UK. His most recent roles have been Director of Research &

Development (Social Sciences) and Director of Postgraduate Studies (Arts). His research interests are in the sociology and socio-cultural study of sport and leisure cultures and the sociology of consumption, in particular the politics and culture of the sport spectacle. Recent books include the *Dictionary of Sports Studies* (Oxford University Press), *The World Atlas of Sport* (Myriad/New Internationalist), *Watching the Olympics: Politics, Power and Representation* (Routledge, edited with John Sugden), and *Understanding Sport: A Socio-cultural Study*, second edition (Routledge, co-authored with John Horne, Garry Whannel and Kath Woodward).

FIFA (Fédération Internationale de Football Association)

The Men, the Myths and the Money

Alan Tomlinson

Routledge
Taylor & Francis Group

LONDON AND NEW YORK

First published 2014
by Routledge
2 Park Square, Milton Park, Abingdon, Oxon OX14 4RN

and by Routledge
711 Third Avenue, New York, NY 10017

Routledge is an imprint of the Taylor & Francis Group, an informa business

British Library Cataloguing in Publication Data
A catalogue record for this book is available from the British Library

Library of Congress Cataloging in Publication Data
Tomlinson, Alan.
  FIFA (Fédération internationale de football association) /
Alan Tomlinson.
    pages cm.
  Includes bibliographical references and index.
  1. Fédération internationale de football association--History.
2. Soccer--Management. 3. Soccer--Economic aspects.
4. Soccer--International cooperation. I. Title.
  GV943.55.F43T65 2014
  796.334--dc23
                                        2013035463

ISBN: 978-0-415-49830-2 (hbk)
ISBN: 978-0-415-49831-9 (pbk)
ISBN: 978-0-203-71040-1 (ebk)

Typeset in Bembo
by Taylor & Francis Books

Contents

Illustrations

Figures

Tables

Acknowledgements

I first wrote on the history and the politics of FIFA in the mid-1980s, when there was little if any scholarly or academic material on the organization, at least from historical, sociological or political perspectives. This was a decade into Dr João Havelange's reign as FIFA president, and before Sir Stanley Rous, president from 1961–1974, died. Throughout these years, and up to 1998, the current incumbent of FIFA's presidential position, Joseph S. Blatter, was general secretary of the organization. I am grateful to FIFA and its personnel in the 1980s for answering telephone queries, sending me materials and, a further decade into my researches, welcoming me to FIFA House. I never managed to meet Rous, but since beginning work on his biography I have, supported superbly by his family descendants and his former personal assistant Rose-Marie Breitenstein, begun to feel that I have an authentic, and unprecedented, grasp of the character, aspirations and accomplishments of the man. I finally interviewed Havelange, with my then co-author Professor John Sugden, in Cairo, Egypt, in September 1997. I last saw him at close quarters walking around the Hotel Adlon Kempinski, just by Berlin's Brandenburg Gate, during the 2006 men's World Cup; he was accompanied by a companion, and was window-shopping, stopping to peruse the hotel's luxury goods. He was clearly comfortably in the bosom of his FIFA family eight years on from the end of his 24 years as president, though in 2013 he resigned his honorary presidency of FIFA just days before the publication of a report confirming his dubious financial conduct during the years of his presidency. I have observed Blatter for many years now, and spoken to him in hotel lobbies, bars and lounges, congress halls and press conferences. For several years I have written to him requesting an interview, and never been explicitly refused; his personal assistant explains that he is away, busy, on the move, immersed in urgent business, always not quite available. As I put the finishing touches to this book, I made one final effort to secure an interview with him, offering him the chance to tell his side of the FIFA story, to make the case for FIFA's claims, achievements and integrity.

Of course FIFA's story is not just about single individuals such as its presidents. But grasping their presidential styles, evaluating their institutional missions and personal ambitions is central to understanding how FIFA has developed and operated, particularly in the more contemporary period of increasingly globalizing and globalized media, and the commodification of the sporting spectacle. Havelange and Blatter have always been unerringly courteous to me, and it is appropriate to clarify this in these opening acknowledgements. At the same time, like many in their world, they can choose to cut you off like a fragile twig.

Conducting this research has required close attention to available documents, and I am eternally grateful to those who have made such documents available to me. This includes people in FIFA itself, and in all of the six continental confederations that are recognized by FIFA. Access to events, people and places has also been vital; for this, I thank FIFA and those confederations that generously afforded me accredited status for particular events, not primarily to see the game but to gain access to particular individuals whose lifeblood and career adrenaline flow through, and are sustained by, those events. I am especially grateful to all those who have, over the years, been willing to speak to me and share their experiences, observations and views on the world of football and FIFA's place in that world. Some people ask me – particularly radio or television interviewers – "Why do you go on doing this kind of work? Why does understanding how FIFA works matter, next to the drama of the sporting encounter, the thrill of the game?" This book looks to answer such questions, and for their encouragement and continuing support I am grateful to those who have found the topic of sufficient interest and importance to stimulate me to keep chasing the sources. This of course includes editors and publishers, and I owe special thanks here to Andy Lyons and his colleagues at *When Saturday Comes*.

I owe a particular debt to researchers, both journalistic and academic, who have led by example and encouraged me to keep ferreting around the institutional and organizational world of the international game. Special thanks must go to Andrew Jennings, for never allowing the imperative of the investigative to flag; and to John Sugden, my collaborator on work on FIFA that led to three co-authored books. He and I have also taught together at the University of Brighton since 1996, testing ideas and interpretations on generations of students, and presented our work and ideas at other hospitable host institutions such as the University of Montpellier; many thanks to Dr Charles Pigeassou for his untiring support in slotting us in as one of his European initiatives. I have sat at desks and in archives of several continental confederations, and received warm – if sometimes cautious – receptions; it is perhaps over-cautious or even discourteous to refrain from naming these people individually, but they will know who they are.

My work over this 26-year period has been sustained by the University of Brighton, and more recently by the British Academy, which has funded archival work and interviews with key people related in particular to the expansion of football as spectacle, and its commercial development. Thanks go too to colleagues in International Programmes, Pembroke College, Cambridge, where the Pembroke/King's Programme has allowed me to exercise some of my interpretations on sharp and responsive cohorts of students over the last decade.

Simon Whitmore, at Routledge/Taylor & Francis, has stimulated or overseen five of my previous books. I am grateful for his continuing support, in particular his faith in the investigative model of research in which this study is rooted. Kate Manson proved the most assiduous of copy editors. Thanks also to Sarah Douglas for meticulous attention to detail in the production process.

Finally, my thanks go again to the home team, my wife Bernie and the four girls: Alys, Rowan, Jo and Sinead. They have all, in one way or another, contributed materials, analyses and most of all support at various points during the conduct of the long programme of research that underpins this book.

Alan Tomlinson, August 2013
Brighton, East Sussex, UK and Campillergues, L'Hérault,
Languedoc, France

Abbreviations

AFC	Asian Football Confederation
CAF	Confederation of African Football (Confédération Africaine de Football)
CBF	Brazilian Football Confederation (Confederação Brasileira de Futebol)
CONCACAF	Confederation of North, Central American and Caribbean Association Football
CONMEBOL	South American Football Confederation (Confederación Sudamericana de Fútbol)
ECA	European Club Association
EU	European Union
ExCo	FIFA Executive Committee
FA	The Football Association
FIFA	Fédération Internationale de Football Association
IAAF	International Association of Athletics Federations (formerly International Amateur Athletics Federation)
IFAB	International Football Association Board
IOC	International Olympic Committee
ISL	International Sport and Leisure
OFC	Oceania Football Confederation
UEFA	Union of European Football Associations (Union des Associations Européenes de Football)
UN	United Nations

Introduction
FIFA's *Annus Horribilis* and its Aftermath

In all of its history, FIFA had rarely occupied the global media spotlight more prominently than during president Joseph "Sepp" Blatter's manoeuvrings at the end of 2010 and in the first half of 2011, dispensing World Cup hosting rights on behalf of his Executive Committee (ExCo), and manipulating institutional politics to ensure his re-election and retention of presidential power for a fourth term. Blatter was trained as a young man by Swiss timepiece giant Longines, pedigree watchmaker since 1842. He must have learned a lot about longevity in business and organizational life. But maybe not enough about timing: switching the FIFA Congress to May–June 2011, a year on from FIFA's main showcase, the World Cup, was supposed to take FIFA business matters such as presidential elections away from the limelight and the media glare, a policy adopted in 2007. But that backfired in 2011, with the storm stemming from the 2018 and 2022 World Cup decisions in December 2010. Nevertheless, he survived once more. Blatter was also a protégé of legendary Adidas sport boss Horst Dassler, groomed for the business in the 1970s and 1980s, when world football finances were transformed by Dassler's dealmaking, and FIFA made exclusive partnership deals with Dassler's organizational baby, International Sport and Leisure (ISL). Dassler trained Blatter up at his Adidas headquarters in Landersheim, in Alsace, France. Blatter speaks of Dassler as a father figure, with unusual respect and awe. Picked out by Dassler, mentored by FIFA president João Havelange, at the heart of FIFA for a third of a century, Blatter knows the art of survival in the double-dealing world of international football governance.

Here, I look at several Blatter moments from December 2010, on the way to 1 June 2011, when Blatter secured his fourth term as FIFA president, and into early 2012.[1]

Zurich, early December 2010 In Tokyo in 1964 FIFA's president, Englishman Sir Stanley Rous, was busy organizing the Olympic football competition. He had other matters on his mind too. FIFA's membership was expanding, and at the FIFA Congress of that year 62 national associations cast their votes for a revolutionary plan for allocating and scheduling World Cup finals. By 55 votes to seven the Congress authorized that in future the Executive Committee (ExCo), rather than the Congress, would allocate World Cups.

In Rous's view, leaving the decision to Congress was putting a "strain on friendships" and basing the choice of the hosts "on not wholly relevant issues". In the cosier climate of world football politics of the time, few saw anything at all odd in the change. Veteran administrator and respected patrician Rous could be trusted, and in London's Royal Garden Hotel two years later his committee confirmed that West Germany (1974), Argentina (1978) and Spain (1982) would be future hosts.

Dr João Havelange changed many things when he seized the FIFA presidency from Rous in 1974, promising much to emerging football federations in Asia, Africa and the Caribbean, in particular. But the power of the Executive Committee to award hosting rights remained intact until May 2013, when at its 63rd Congress in Mauritius FIFA approved the transfer of the responsibility for selecting host nations/associations back to the Congress – effectively, the Congress took the power for itself. Rous had thought that canvassing for votes would end once the big decision lay in the hands of a few honourable committee members. Havelange, his successor Sepp Blatter and their bloated Executive Committees have had no such qualms, actually encouraging the likes of the FA to spend lavishly within the bidding process.

In 2000, this bought England's bid for 2006 a respectable five votes in the first round, though this dwindled to two in the second-round knockout stage. A decade later, the UK's prime minister, heir-to-the-throne-but-one and most glamorous and famous footballer – "two toffs and a twerp," wrote Max Bell in a letter to the *Guardian*,[2] in reference to David Cameron, Prince William and David Beckham – flattered the ExCo members at breakfasts and lunches in the swishest hotels in town; they might as well have been blinded by the blizzards blowing outside by the lake. England's first-round elimination with just two votes was a much worse performance than in 2000: with the vote of one low-profile English Executive Committee member (who unlike his successful counterparts from Russia and Qatar took no part in the final presentation) already in the bag, England's ill-advised bid for the 2018 World Cup finals garnered just one further vote. A relatively conservative estimate of the cost of that vote is £15 million. England's presentation pitched royalty, politics and celebrity to FIFA, and during its presentation its chief executive oleaginously – or was it sarcastically? – congratulated FIFA general secretary Jérôme Valcke and his colleagues for the "superb way they've managed this complicated bidding process." The England delegation wasn't congratulating FIFAcrats when Russia's name came out of Blatter's envelope. Vladimir Putin was soon en route to Zurich to thank FIFA, and no doubt his faithful mover and shaker Roman Abramovich, who had been with the bid team. When asked which win pleased him most – getting the 2014 Winter Olympics for Sochi or this World Cup – Putin simply smiled and said how much he likes to win. Russia's bid prioritized development and new football markets, in a post-communist climate, in the biggest country in the world. It fitted a mission that was laid out in Havelange's manifesto of 1974.

England's bid was patronizing in at least two ways: offering national associations help from English clubs during the finals; and proposing a "Football United" scheme to match FIFA monies that had been committed to grassroots and world football development, in effect an economic partnership with much-maligned FIFA. The England bid looked even sillier as ExCo "promises" were counted. "Given the promises that were made to us," the England bid boss asked, "how could the vote have turned out the way it did?" You couldn't get much more naive than this, in the world of FIFA politics; it's not a gentleman's club. Executive Committee members have said to me that you always accept a bit of bad to go with all the good, and former International Sport and Leisure (ISL) executive and architect of UEFA's Champions League Jürgen Lenz told me: "FIFA's now so corrupt that it no longer knows that it's being corrupt." English prime minister Cameron's charm and courteousness don't work in this world. Heir to the British throne Prince William was out of his depth in far-from-neutral Switzerland. These ambassadors for the England bid could never match Machiavelli's star pupil Blatter. A "wise prince," recommended Machiavelli, makes sure that his citizens "are always and in all circumstances dependent on him and on his authority," so that they will "always be faithful to him."[3] Insiders reckon that Blatter has at least 150 faithful dependents among FIFA's 209 national associations and many of these are represented by long-serving ExCo men from the continental confederations. Russia was always in the driving seat and a Russian victory would keep the rhetoric intact and the accounts books closed. How could a three- or four-day England charm offensive have ended any other way than it did on that ice-cold Thursday afternoon?

Wales, 14 March 2011 "Fayre and Square" isn't the motto of FIFA. It's the bargain slogan of the pub chain that includes the New Inn, Langstone, just off the M4 at Newport in south Wales. There's a Wacky Warehouse kids' area, two dinners for a tenner all day and every day, and rooms at £49 a night for as many of the family as you can squeeze in. The International Football Association Board (IFAB) was in town for the first weekend in March, but it wasn't patronizing the New Inn.

Just along the road and up the hill is the Celtic Manor Resort, sprawled across 1400 acres. There, you don't see many kids and it's nearer £152 a night for a hotel room. That's where the International Football Association Board (IFAB) gathered for the much-awaited decisions on goal-line technology and player attire, the main items on the agenda of its 125th Annual General Meeting. Football's *Laws of the Game* are actually the product of (and authorized by) the IFAB, a body made up of the four UK football associations and FIFA. The board began in 1886, FIFA joined it in a fragile alliance in 1913, and in 1958 current voting rights were approved. In decision-making terms, it's one vote apiece for the UK associations and four for FIFA; for a proposal to carry, a three-quarters majority must be achieved: six out of eight. So while the guest list at Celtic Manor numbered 61, for whom Friday night fireworks at Cardiff Castle provided a dazzling welcome, just eight men were deciding on whether the game would be better for the introduction of goal-line technology. It was no great surprise when FIFA president Sepp Blatter confirmed that tests with selected companies had as yet proved inconclusive. Turning to new FA chair David Bernstein, Blatter expressed much sympathy for the "blatant" injustice of Frank Lampard's disallowed goal at South Africa 2010 but, pressed by a Sky Sports News reporter claiming to speak for the wronged England fan, asked for "just a little bit of patience" – what actually amounted to another full year's testing.

David Bernstein was smiling diplomatically, saying that the outcome was not perfect but that the principles supporting the introduction of goal-line technology were wholly accepted by the IFAB; we could be positive about its future. Not imminently though. Any IFAB decision cannot take effect until 1 July following the date of the decision, so a 2012 IFAB decision in February or March was already too late for Euro 2012 in Poland and Ukraine. Blatter conceded that Brazil 2014 could herald the end of the over-the-line, in-or-out debates and legends concerning what might have been. Of ten companies, including the FIFA president's former employer Longines, three "have a good chance," said Blatter, in the extended test period in live games themselves. And a newcomer, Hawk-Eye, was also now among the invited companies.

IFAB also ruled on snoods: not allowed, quite simply not permitted in the *Laws of the Game*. I thumbed through Law 4, looking for what would permit the caps of goalies, or gloves for anybody; neither is included in the "basic compulsory equipment of a player." Blatter and IFAB were a bit quick off the mark here, the FIFA president even suggesting that snood-wearers were endangering their lives by risking strangulation.

At such absurd moments you can only wonder how IFAB–FIFA cooperation has survived so long. You have to look at the rituals and protocol of the board. Blatter sits amid generally silent and acquiescent football administrators from the British associations, and guests and partners are well catered for – the Ladies' Day Agenda took in museums, the Millennium Centre and a tour of the Welsh National Opera. All gathered together again for the Gala Dinner on the Saturday night in Celtic Manor's Beaufort Suite, where the SFA (Scottish Football Association) president, George Peet, toasted the Queen and Heads of State; the IFA (Irish Football Association) president, Jim Shaw, toasted the Ladies; David Bernstein of the FA toasted the IFAB; and host president Phillip Pritchard of the Welsh FA toasted FIFA. The UK men had five minutes each for their speeches; maybe there was a proportional principle based on status, with Blatter then allotted 20 minutes for his response.

Whatever their private thoughts on FIFA's *modus operandi*, the UK men weren't going to rock this lawmaking boat. Blatter ranged wide in the IFAB press conference, confirming his determination to lead FIFA for a fourth presidential term: "I'm not tired at all … just to make it clear, for my next four years I will dedicate my work to the social and cultural impact of football in society." Nobody laughed. The IFAB is seen as the guardian or custodian of the long-established laws of football. It's a pseudo-independent body that operates essentially as Blatter and FIFA's lapdog, but allows Blatter to control access to it from within FIFA. It's the president and the general secretary who are routinely the FIFA men turning up with voting rights, plus two others – the chair of the referees' committee and a senior vice-president were the lawmakers this time round. There's no transparent route to these positions, they're effectively in the FIFA president's gift. The FIFA president flatters the UK associations and their historical legacy, bankrolls the IFAB and does, for the most part, exactly what he wants.

Zurich, 1 June 2011 Three months later, back in Zurich, and Blatter has done it again. Faced with what commentators and pundits, and innumerable opponents, were calling FIFA's biggest ever crisis, his Congress gave him his strongest mandate yet, 186 national associations backing him for his fourth term. The Football Association (England) mustered just 16 allies in its clumsy attempt to postpone the election, in the wake of allegations and counter-allegations about corruption emerging from within the FIFA ExCo, and the withdrawal of Blatter's rival in the presidential contest. Main sponsors issued soft slaps on the wrists to FIFA, and image-cleaning was soon in progress as Blatter marched on.

In a FIFA "FACT Sheet" issued by the presidency itself, the president is confirmed as "the supreme leader of FIFA."[4] There's mess to mop up, spin to get right. The sponsors might disapprove of the practices of some senior FIFA personnel and committee members, but does Visa really want the global spotlight on how it replaced MasterCard to become a primary World Cup sponsor? Wouldn't Adidas be a little embarrassed were its close dealings with FIFA ExCo personnel past and present – including outgoing committee member Franz Beckenbauer – subjected to close scrutiny? There was work to be done to deal with the allegations of corruption, without alienating powerful interests within the football "family," or constituencies of continental confederations whose presidents were facing investigation by FIFA's ethics committee; Trinidadian Jack Warner of CONCACAF had already withdrawn from all his positions in international football administration; Qatari Mohamed Bin Hammam, AFC president and Blatter's principal rival for the presidency, was banned for life by FIFA's ethics committee. But, to quote Machiavelli again, the wise prince operates in ruthless and effective fashion, and recognizes that "it is far better to be feared than loved if you cannot be both."[5] Blatter may look like a bit-part actor in a comic opera; underestimate him, though, to your cost and possibly at your peril.

Surrey, 3 March 2012 At the Celtic Manor Resort in March 2011, the drawn-out saga of GLT (goal-line technology) had been the main item on the IFAB agenda, though Blatter had been bushwhacked by journalists keen to pin him down on the nitty-gritty of his forthcoming re-election campaign, mired as it was in waves of corruption revelations. Safely re-elected in June 2011 and promising reform to core FIFA practices and processes, at the beginning of March 2012 Blatter breezed into the plush Pennyhill Park Hotel in the home counties region of England, the upmarket venue chosen by the FA as host of the 126th Annual General Meeting of the IFAB.

IFAB decisions often reflect bloc voting. But the UK associations are not automatically on each other's side. In the Ascot Bar on the morning of the AGM, six grey-suited, white-haired Welshman were huddled in animated discussion. The most vociferous of these veteran football administrators was adamant that the Welsh delegation should follow its instincts and long-held principles. "There's nothing wrong with what we've got now ... . We're not happy with it. If all we've got to do is agree with other countries we might as well not come here."

Happy or not, such delegations routinely turn up for the two meetings that the IFAB has each year. And it's not surprising that they do. At Pennyhill, the Ascot Bar has a Connoisseurs Club that offers a range of champagnes from Perrier Jouët Grand Brut at £54, to £595 for a 1995

Louis Roederer Cristal Rosé. The meeting room names echo British privilege: Balmoral, Blenheim, Sandringham, Windsor. The social agenda sandwiches the meetings nicely, and the British associations certainly don't want any big run-in with FIFA that might jeopardize the autonomy and independence of their "national" status. The birth of the IFAB predated that of FIFA, in 1904, by 18 years, and as long as no boat is rocked too much the reciprocal interests of FIFA and the four British associations sustain the collusive collaboration.

"I would die," Blatter responded on the eve of the meeting, as he was asked by Sky News whether there could ever be any repeat of the Frank Lampard goal-that-never-was at the 2010 World Cup. He also reaffirmed his determination to carry the IFAB with him on the issue. He didn't get to the Pennyhill press conference himself, but briefed his general secretary Jérôme Valcke to transmit FIFA's positive support for GLT, alongside representatives of the UK associations. The FA's Alex Horne, as host, summarized the outcome of the main items on the IFAB agenda: GLT would enter its second phase of testing – it would be "tested to destruction," Horne added melodramatically, with two companies (Hawk-Eye and GoalRef) left from an initial eight contenders; unlimited numbers of substitutes would be allowed for "amateur players" of all ages in "recreational football" to boost participation; and, after a highly praised presentation by FIFA Executive Committee member Prince Ali of Jordan, the hijab would be permitted in women's football, again boosting participation.

GLT dominated the agenda, though, and Valcke acknowledged that FIFA might introduce it in its own competitions as early as the 2012 Club World Cup in December. It was left to national associations to see if they, their clubs and leagues would be able to afford it, and to decide on when it might be implemented. The GLT must be restricted to goal decisions, must be as accurate as technologically possible, must answer the "goal or not" question within one second, and communicate this decision to the match officials only. It would be what Alex Horne whimsically called a "private moment" for the referee.

Asked whether the poorer UK associations and leagues of Northern Ireland, Wales and Scotland would be able to afford installation, the chief executives of those associations conceded that they would adopt a wait-and-see strategy, based on the declining costs of established technologies and increased competition in the GLT market that could bring in alternative approved providers and licence holders. The elite of world football would get the benefits first; the poorer the football culture, the longer the old arguments will be destined to go on. But this didn't undermine the harmony of the IFAB spokesmen. No dissenting voices or views were reported from the IFAB meeting. So the Welsh rebellion looked muted. The GLT experiment would be continued to a promised resolution at a special meeting of the IFAB in Ukraine's capital Kiev on 2 July, which no doubt the reluctant Welshmen made room and time to turn up to, the day after the final of Euro 2012, which in all probability they would dutifully have attended. On 13 January 2014 in Zurich, IFAB relaunched at a "Foundation Meeting", FIFA hailing "the beginning of a new era for the board as an autonomous organization" registered as "an independent association under the Swiss Civil Code, with its own statutes". IFAB was being given all the trappings of a mini-FIFA. Version 1 of the Statutes confirms IFAB's associational status within the Swiss Civil Code, places the FIFA secretary general as *ex officio* chair of a Board of Directors and confirms FIFA President "Joseph S. Blatter" as "Founding chairman."

Putting FIFA under the microscope

The IFAB meetings are small-scale events in FIFA's calendar. The annual Congress operates at a different level, and in May 2013 1300 "guests" attended the 63rd Congress at the Swami Vivekananda International Convention Centre in Mauritius. A small country like Mauritius seizes such an opportunity, and the Mauritius Football Association's Rooben Armoogum, project manager for the event, observed that: "For a small country like ours, organizing such an event and hosting 1300 delegates is a fantastic opportunity ... an incredible opportunity to show them our country, and it can definitely be a springboard for our tourism industry."[6] The Mauritius Football Association brought 450 children to the event, from football academies in disadvantaged areas of the island, to act as flagbearers, and Armoogum expressed his pride at his country's pioneering contribution to FIFA's "11 for Health" and "Grassroots" programmes. Although the business of the Congress would be dominated by reform issues, the Mauritius hosts appeared more than satisfied with the presence, profile and image of FIFA.

FIFA's relationship with such member associations has been cultivated carefully over recent decades, so that the FIFA machine motors on smoothly enough despite widespread external criticism. Exploring how this self-perpetuating capacity of the organization works is a primary aim of this study, which is motivated by three points of critical social scientific principle.[7] First, the level of hypocrisy underlying the gap between FIFA's rhetoric and its practices must be challenged. Any institution or organization appealing to ideals of international friendship and cooperation, including in the spheres of youth and "football development," must be called to account and seen to be above board in its fundamental claims.

Second, the money generated on behalf of the global peoples' game – at the end of 2010, FIFA's reserves stood at more than US\$ 1.2 billion[8] – surely needs monitoring. Much might be doled out to needy national associations, but there is no accepted process of review, no guarantee that these sums do not go to individual bank accounts or private businesses, no examination of unmonitored accounts of self-serving associations. And third, bodies such as FIFA cannot be immune from consideration in any global debate about the nature of corporate governance. FIFA may be based in the land of neutrality, international tolerance, hush-hush bank accounts and Nazi gold, but as businesses such as Enron, WorldCom and Xerox are exposed for their dubious accounting practices, and prestigious banks damned for their direct influence on the 2008 global financial crisis, bodies such as FIFA can no longer be allowed to hide behind idealist hyperbole and a rhetoric of global goodwill, veiling a bogus organizational democracy.

The new millennium began with FIFA claiming that it still stood, in its 1996 slogan, "For the good of the game." A few years on, FIFA aimed higher, replacing this in 2007 with "For the game. For the world." In this book I explore the historical roots and the sociological and political realities of a FIFA that in its own pithy slogan claims a worldwide mission and significance. Such exploration must of necessity be an interdisciplinary project, framed by the imperatives of an investigative sociological approach. At the same time, when the whistle blows and the game kicks off, people's passions – understandably, given the widely recognized force of sport as a form of positive collective cultural expression and identity – often override their interest in that other kind of whistle-blower. So this book is not only about the bad apples in the FIFA applecart, or the corrupt FIFAcrats in the tumbrel. World Cups are cosmopolitan parties; international football provides a kind of Esperanto of sport. I recognize these positive cultural dimensions of the game, and the FIFA achievements that have contributed to them. These positive elements have been a factor in the capacity of FIFA to survive, reproduce itself and continue to prosper in spite of the revelations of corruption and malpractice during the tenures of Blatter and his predecessor Havelange.

In Chapter 1, "Origins," I present an overview of the history and development of FIFA in its first few decades, tracking the organization's emergence, its relationship with the British associations and its increasing internationalization. This follows the story from the founding date of 1904 to the challenge in the 1920s to the Eurocentric bases of the organization, and a consequent gradual expansion, including the introduction of the first World Cup in 1930 and the lessening importance of the Olympic Games as a world football competition.

Chapter 2, "Workings," covers how FIFA actually conducts its business: its mission, rationale, membership, organizational and committee structures and processes, innovations. Here I seek to balance the achievements with the excesses, the accomplishments with the allegations. This breaks any linear, diachronic narrative in the book, as it is important to clarify what FIFA looks like and claims to do before reviewing particular dimensions of its past and present dealings, goals and objectives.

Chapter 3, "Leaders," picks up on the historical legacy of the particular sets of ideals and institutional and personal ambitions of the first seven FIFA presidents. Chapter 4, "The Supreme Leader," concentrates on the career of FIFA's eighth president. Chapter 5, "Moneyspinners," considers the extraordinary story of the growth and escalation of the political economy of the sport.

Chapter 6, "Cash Cow," focuses on the men's World Cup, its transformation from small beginnings into the financial bonanza for FIFA and its partners that it has become, and on Africa's first World Cup host, South Africa, as well as outlining the spheres of positive intervention and development that FIFA has sought – or claimed – to develop in lower-profile and subsidized events and initiatives.

Chapter 7, "Crises," maps the scandal-hit first decade of the current century, as FIFA's Supreme Leader became increasingly unable to curb – or cover up – the ambitions and abuses of numerous highly placed people and individuals in the organization. Chapter 8, "Futures," reviews current challenges and challengers, mapping out scenarios for how FIFA might develop or be changed.

Chapter 9, in an analytical and theoretical conclusion, considers what is perhaps the most important question to answer when studying FIFA: How, given increasing and widespread awareness and knowledge of its corrupt practices and self-serving *modus operandi*, does FIFA continue to have such a hold on the controls of global football governance?

I have been researching and writing on FIFA since 1985, and locating key sources used to be a cumbersome task. It is simpler now in the age of electronic media and digitization of documents and materials, yet there remains surprisingly little work of academic substance that seeks to provide a balanced overview of the organization: what it is, where it has come from, what it does, and how it works. In this study I draw upon three of my previous books, to establish historical and political contexts;[9] where this is the case, sources and data have been expanded and updated, and this book is informed by dozens of new interviews and previously unpublished data, along with more than a decade of continuing fieldwork and observation, and document analysis.

FIFA is not an abstract entity; it is peopled, and in the earlier books many voices of prominent actors in the FIFA story were quoted from original interviews. One reviewer considered that this sort of treatment was some-times too detailed, the coverage of the subject at times too arcane;[10] this is a just criticism, but I have persisted in seeking to people my analysis by describing the key actors, probing the views of the dominant figures in the FIFA story, citing from my observations of and encounters with them, and attempting to capture the cultural world in which such global operators and political players have moved. Some of these voices are anonymized – out of respect for privacy, when requested, or fear of legal consequences – but many are not. This is a book seeking to account for the fascinating rise and phenomenal expansion of a global body that has served individual interests as well as the collective passion of the world's fans. It is therefore based on a commitment to a not-always-fashionable investigative social scientific approach, one that is nevertheless indispensable to any realistic or credible account of FIFA's growth, expansion, survival and potential reform.

Notes

1 These pieces were initially written for the *When Saturday Comes* "WSC Daily": "FIFA's executive committee unimpressed by celebrity," 6 December 2010; "Sepp Blatter's archaic British lapdog does his bidding," 14 March 2011; and "Over the line? IFAB moves towards GLT," 6 March 2012. See www.wsc.co.uk.
2 "Some of the crowd are on the pitch … ," *Guardian*, 4 December 2010.
3 Niccolò Machiavelli, translated with an introduction by George Bull, *The Prince* (Harmondsworth: Penguin, 1961), 71.
4 FIFA, "FACT Sheet," FS-110_01E_President, http://www.fifa.com/mm/document/fifafacts/organisation/52/00/03/fs-110_01e_president.pdf, consulted 18 November 2013.
5 Machiavelli, *The Prince*, 96.
6 Fifa.com, "Mauritius all set for FIFA Congress," 29 May 2013, http://www.fifa.com/aboutfifa/organisation/bodies/Congress/new/newsid=2086301/index.html, consulted 14 July 2013.
7 This methodological rationale is adapted from "FIFA and the men's World Cup: The expansion of the global football family," in Alan Tomlinson, *Sport and Leisure Cultures* (Minneapolis: University of Minnesota Press, 2005), 53–75.
8 FIFA, "FIFA Financial Report 2010: 61st FIFA Congress, Zurich, 31 May and 1 June 2011" (Zurich: FIFA, 2011), 14, http://www.fifa.com/mm/document/affederation/administration/01/39/20/45/web_fifa_fr2010_eng[1].pdf, consulted 18 June 2013.
9 John Sugden and Alan Tomlinson, *FIFA and the Contest for World Football: Who Rules the Peoples' Game?* (Cambridge: Polity Press, 1998); John Sugden and Alan Tomlinson, *Great Balls of Fire: How Big Money is Hijacking World Football* (Edinburgh: Mainstream Publishing, 1999); John Sugden and Alan Tomlinson, *Badfellas: FIFA Family at War* (Edinburgh: Mainstream Publishing, 2003).
10 Leslie Sklair, "Book reviews: *FIFA and the Contest for World Football: Who Rules the Peoples'. Game?*", *International Journal of the History of Sport*, 16/1, 1999: 184–185.

1   Origins

FIFA was founded by seven European footballing nations in 1904. More than a century later, it boasted a membership of 209 national associations. The story of this growth is testimony to FIFA's remarkable impact on international sport and on cultural relations around the world. The growth of association football itself (and many other modern sports) was coterminous with the rise of industrial society and nation states; sport was an ideal vehicle through which internal – often urban, male and working-class – communities could organize their own collective culture,[1] and countries symbolize their prowess and world superiority; Eric Hobsbawm called football "the child of Britain's global economic presence."[2] The power of football to express national identity in both internal and external forms has propelled the game to gaining the status of the world's most popular sport. International sport, in its turn, has contributed to the making of societies, through the symbolic expression of the sense of national identity. The nation, imagined as a community, "conceived as deep, horizontal comradeship,"[3] has found its fullest expression in two spheres: tragically in conflict and war; less harmfully in competition and sport. The early phases in FIFA's history established a dynamic between the global and the national that has continued to frame relationships between FIFA and its worldwide constituencies; this inbuilt contradiction and recurring tension between national interests and international aspirations has underpinned the story of FIFA's development, as from its beginnings it offered more and more nations a vehicle for the articulation of national distinctiveness, national belonging and cultural superiority.

From its roots in a Eurocentric initiative, world football has come to represent a global passion, capable of mobilizing national sentiment and pride in unprecedentedly dramatic and, more recently, increasingly sophisticated mediated, and digitalized, forms.[4] The balance between national interests and claimed idealist internationalism, though, has continued to be contested in the FIFA story, and is discussed at the end of

Table 1.1 The growth of FIFA: member associations 1904–1959

Year	Number of associations in FIFA
1904	7
1914	24
1923	31
1930	41
1938	51
1950	73
1954	85
1959	95

Source: Meisl, 1960

this chapter in the context of the process of globalization. Prior to that, the growth of the world governing body is traced up to the 1950s and 60s, to the period during the presidency of the Englishman Sir Stanley Rous (from 1961 to 1974) that culminated in FIFA's recognition of five new continental confederations – from UEFA in 1954 to the newest, Oceania, in 1966 – by which time FIFA had 126 member associations. Table 1.1[5] shows the incremental growth of FIFA during this period, and the explosion of membership in the post-World War II period and through the 1950s, when newly independent nations in the post-colonial era sought membership of FIFA as a statement of their national autonomy and political and social aspirations.

FIFA's origins

The founding nations of FIFA were Belgium, Denmark, France, the Netherlands, Spain, Sweden and Switzerland. In some cases, these nations were looking for guidance from the longer-established British associations. Robert Guérin, of the French USFSA (Union des Sociétés Françaises des Sports Athlétiques) approached Frederick Wall, the secretary of the English Football Association (FA).[6] The Englishman offered a diplomatic but uncooperative response: "The Council of the Football Association cannot see the advantages of such a Federation, but on all such matters upon which joint action was desirable they would be prepared to confer."[7] Wahl relates how Guérin became the first president of FIFA, helped by the phlegmatic and haughty English response, "for lack of interest of the British."[8] Guérin met Wall twice in 1903, and also the FA president Lord Kinnaird on one occasion, but, "tiring of the struggle, and recognizing that the Englishmen, true to tradition, wanted to wait and watch, I undertook to unite delegates from various nations myself." Guérin wrote that dealing with the English/British was like "slicing water with a knife."[9] England had effectively been offered the leading role, but showed a haughty disregard for the initiative. In the founding moments of the world body's history, the British – the English in particular – displayed an indifference and insularity that was a mystery to its continental suitors.

The 1904 initiative proved a false start, though. A planned international tournament did not materialize. By 1906 Guérin had stepped down from the leadership. The FA, meanwhile, had considered it wise to become involved, and a special FA committee invited continental nations to a conference on the eve of the 1905 England–Scotland match in London. Though this was in reality a means of undermining FIFA's authority, the outcome of the meeting was that the British associations accepted FIFA's general objectives and expressed willingness to cooperate. An English/British delegation to Berne in the same year responded more and more positively to the international initiative, if still in a tone of patronage and *hauteur*. D.B. Woolfall reported that:

> it is important to the FA and other European Associations that a properly constituted Federation should be established, and the Football Association should use its influence to regulate football on the continent as a pure sport and give all Continental Associations the full benefit of the many years' experience of the FA.[10]

England joined the fledgling organization, then, once the FA felt sufficiently respected. The FA had been approached by Belgium in the late 1890s and by the Netherlands in 1902, both suggesting that the formation of an international association would benefit the European game; England had been seen as an obvious leader of such developments. Thus even when FIFA was formed without England or the FA, it was clear that its experience would offer benefits: France had played its first international match a mere three weeks before the meeting at which FIFA was formed, and Denmark was not to play an international until 1908, at the Olympics in London, the same year in which Switzerland played its first international match. Three of FIFA's founding members (Sweden, France and Spain) had not actually formed a football association in their own country at the time at which the international body was founded, and Spain was represented by a delegate from a club, FC Madrid. Paradoxically, in these cases, the international initiative was the spur to the founding of national associations. In France's case this leads to the bizarre entry, in one reference source, "Fédération Française de Football ... Year of Formation: 1918 ... Affiliation to FIFA: 1904."[11]

FIFA's founding fathers were novices, then, and it is unsurprising that the FA was drawn into the leadership role. In 1905, FIFA considered the FA to have joined the international federation, and the English proceeded to take the presidency at the third FIFA Congress in Berne in 1906, ushering other British associations into membership; the English stayed until 1920, joined again from 1924 to 1928, leaving over disputes concerning payments to amateurs, and then rejoined in 1946. In these early years of English leadership the vexed question of eligibility arose repeatedly. The first article of the FIFA statutes (dated 1 September 1905) stated unambiguously that: "Ces fédérations se reconnaissent réciproquement comme les seules fédérations régissant le sport du football association dans leurs pays respectif et comme les seules compétentes pour traiter des relations internationals."[12] ("These federations recognize each other reciprocally as the sole federations regulating the game of association football in their respective countries, and as the only ones competent to negotiate international relations" – author's translation.) Of course much could be disputed at the beginning of the century in relation to the status of a "country," and the FA could hardly claim to speak for a single nation state. Where, then, would the Welsh, Scottish or Irish football associations fit into the emerging world order of football?

At the Vienna Congress in 1908, Scotland and Ireland were rejected as members. Should Scotland and Ireland have been accepted, Austria and Germany had planned to request membership for their confederate states, numbering 26 and 12 respectively. Withdrawing this threat, Austria nevertheless accomplished the expulsion of the Bohemian FA, on the basis of the status of Bohemia as an Austrian territory. In 1909 a breakaway federation, the Union Internationale Amateur de Football Association, was founded, comprising French, English and Bohemian organizations. But the FA's leadership of FIFA, and increasing domination of the international agenda, was demonstrated at the 1910 Milan Congress in "the admittance, against the statutes, of Scotland, Ireland and Wales."[13] South Africa joined in 1909/10, Argentina and Chile in 1912, the USA in 1913. Holland's C.W. Hirschman, serving FIFA as secretary and honorary treasurer through to 1931, could with increasing credibility claim FIFA as the authentic head of "a universal game," though the laws of the game were still the prerogative of the four British associations that made up (from 1886) the International Football Association Board (IFAB). In 1911 Germany's representatives suggested tentatively that FIFA should in time become the regulatory body controlling the laws. The English FIFA president and the FA rejected the idea outright, and also responded negatively to a request that a member of FIFA be invited to sit on the IFAB. But by 1913, at the Copenhagen Congress, it was announced that two FIFA members would be invited onto the IFAB, and the following year it was confirmed that FIFA could nominate these representatives. Here, the foundation was laid for a long-term cooperation between, and alliance of, the FIFA administration and the top administrators of the British associations, despite the in–out dynamics of the UK bodies in terms of formal membership of the international federation.

British intransigence

FIFA administration continued throughout World War I, and membership expanded with the provisional acceptance of Brazil, Paraguay and Uruguay. The British associations withdrew from FIFA in 1920, on a matter of principle, as the only associations continuing to refuse recognition to football associations authorizing matches against defeated nations. The Football Association of Wales in its Consultative Committee decided that "the Association should agree with the English and Scottish Football Associations in refusing to recognize the Central Powers in football matters."[14] FIFA was negotiating sensitive territory here, and though Jules Rimet was provisionally named as new president in 1920 and officially approved in the position in 1921 it was not until 1923 that a full Congress was held. The Football Association of Ireland, from the newly independent Irish state, was accepted, prompting a hostile response from the FA; though in 1924 the British were accepted back into FIFA. But this *rapprochement* was not to last long.

In 1924 Uruguay won the Olympic Games football tournament, and what was in effect the world football championship, in the absence of any coherent initiative from FIFA, became mired in controversy and debate concerning the nature of professional and amateur status in football. British amateur teams had a record of success at the Olympics, taking the title at the three Europe-based Games before World War I. But they did not compete in 1920, in the immediate aftermath of the war, and watched from the sidelines again as an accomplished Uruguayan side took the gold medal in Paris in 1924. But it was clear that the Uruguayan players were not only accomplished, they were also essentially full-time. At the 1925 Congress FIFA took the decision to allow individual associations to rule on the amount of money that could be paid to amateur players for their loss of earnings. This was the context of the British stance that led to the 1928 decision of the UK associations to once more withdraw from FIFA; it was more than anything else the outcome of exchanges with other national associations concerning the distinction between amateurs and professionals. In July 1925, A. Verdyck, general secretary of the Union Royal Belge des Sociétés de Football

Association, wrote to FA secretary Frederick Wall, suggesting a meeting of those national associations opposed to FIFA's accommodating stance on what Verdyck called "sham amateurism," and he looked to muster the support of those associations most likely to join his own in "fighting to bring cleanliness in sport":

> We have noticed at the last FIFA Congress that some Associations do not desire to fight that evil and to take the necessary measures to outroot it.[15]

The UK associations showed no great willingness to meet with the Belgians, though they did attend a conference the following year in Brussels and so showed some support for the Belgian stance. Another year on, though, FIFA provided these defendants of pure amateurism with further provocation. In Paris in August 1927, FIFA and the International Olympic Committee agreed that players receiving "broken time" payments could play in the Olympics in Amsterdam in 1928. The 1924 Olympic football champions, Uruguay, had run what was in effect a full-time elite squad, a case no doubt of "sham amateurism," and the pressure was mounting for a liberalization of the IOC policy on pure amateurism. The UK associations would have none of this, and met in Liverpool in October of 1927 to respond. No deviation from the British Olympic Association's (BOA) definition of the amateur would be tolerated. Amateurs could claim "hotel and travelling expenses actually paid," but any training expenses – loss of earnings or wages for example – had to be borne by the players themselves.

At a meeting of its Commission in Lausanne on 31 October 1927, the IOC documented the decision taken by its executive in response to the British objections to the emerging liberalization of the amateur principle.[16] The BOA referred back to the meeting earlier in the year, on 8 August, at which the IOC agreed that FIFA was eligible to participate in the following year's Summer Games in Amsterdam. The British alleged that this decision was *ultra vires*, beyond the power of the IOC, and that such a precedent would arrogate the right of any member to annul an IOC decision. FIFA, in Rome in 1926, had approved the principle of covering players' loss of earnings, up to 90 per cent for a married player, 75 per cent for an unmarried one, for up to 20 days a year. The IOC resolution of August 1927 was a cautious, relatively pragmatic one, stipulating that "reimbursement would be made, in any due case, by the National Federation to the employer which requests it; athletes/players would not touch directly any of the compensation for lost earnings." The IOC minute stated that this would put on the same footing those players taking paid or unpaid leave, as the latter might, if claiming, be said to break the amateur code. Any other decision on the matter was put off for future discussion at Congress.

Just a few months later, in February 1928, in Sheffield, England, the UK associations passed the unanimous resolution that took British football nations out of FIFA again until 1946. Withdrawal was recommended on the basis that the British associations "should be free to conduct their affairs in the way that their long experience has shown to be desirable." Wall wrote to FIFA secretary C.A.W. Hirschman stating that the FIFA/IOC decision made it impossible for the United Kingdom to take part in the Olympic Games, and that the British experience of adapting rules to control the amateur/professional distinction was the only way to "remedy the mischief" of the rule-breakers. British know-how was presented here in British know-all fashion:

> The great majority of the Associations affiliated with the Federation International de Football Association are of comparatively recent formation, and as a consequence cannot have the knowledge which only experience can bring.[17]

The resolution concluded that "whilst desiring to maintain friendly relations with the Federation and its affiliated Associations, and to cooperate with them on all suitable occasions," the decision of the UK associations was to resign from the international federation.

At its executive meeting on the eve of the Amsterdam Games (on 24 July 1928) the IOC president Henri Baillet-Latour asked whether a vote was needed in relation to the attitude and position of the BOA. No vote was called for, and the resolution of the previous year was reaffirmed and supported. The British associations thus absented themselves from the international platform of a FIFA-based Olympic football tournament, and two years later from the biggest initiative in FIFA's history: the introduction of the World Cup in Uruguay.

FIFA marches on

The growth of FIFA's membership was not hampered by the British withdrawals. National associations that had held an affiliated status with the FA had already begun to switch their affiliations to FIFA, and Cuba and Costa Rica joined in 1927. South America's continental confederation was recognized by FIFA in 1928, and on the cover of the 1928–1929 FIFA handbook the previous year's image of a globe displaying Europe, Africa and Australasia was replaced by two interlocked globes, the additional one displaying the Americas; two sides of the globe symbolizing the inclusion of all continents.[18]

Expansion of FIFA produced the need for a stronger administrative base, and suggestions from members included appointing a permanent secretary based in Zurich. When in 1931 Hirschman was found to have embezzled and lost the bulk of FIFA's monies in financial speculation, he resigned, though retaining a lifelong FIFA pension. The Dutch association covered the losses, and FIFA established its base in Zurich in 1932, with a permanent appointment to the post of secretary. Much FIFA business of the 1930s – apart from the World Cups in Uruguay, Italy and France – was involved in ruling on the movements of international players, which replaced the amateurism issue as FIFA's major administrative concern. FIFA also found time to reject a proposal, from the newly admitted South American member of the Executive Committee, to create five autonomous continental confederations. Rimet believed that the Europe-based FIFA was best fitted to administer the game worldwide, and that the creation of continental power bases would undermine the authority of FIFA. It was in the post-Rimet years that the confederations were to emerge, reshaping FIFA's institutional basis by multiplying the membership of the Congress almost fourfold by the time of the organization's centenary in 2004. Nevertheless, Rimet's philosophy allowed an incremental internationalism to be nurtured in FIFA's inter- and post-war expansion.

Rimet was responsive to the claims of Central American, Asian and African associations for "a more equal treatment in the name of ... sporting universalism."[19] Much of his time in office was dedicated to negotiating, engaging with and adapting to sporting cultures and sporting politics of non-European regions. The Egyptian FA was the first African association to join FIFA, in 1923; in 1925, the Football Association of Siam (Thailand) was the first Asian member. Indeed, the inauguration of the World Cup in Uruguay in 1930 generated much-needed income for FIFA, even though only Belgium, France, Romania and Yugoslavia chose to travel from Europe to participate in the tournament.

The tensions between the established South American associations, emergent Central American ones and the Europe-based world governing body dominated FIFA business in the 1930s; a confederation for Central America and the Caribbean was formed in 1938, and lobbied along with the South American confederation for more representation within FIFA and guaranteed places in the World Cup finals. When Rimet attended the South American Congress in Buenos Aires in 1939, he argued for cooperation between the regions, stating that: "Mutual understanding is based on knowledge." His diplomatic efforts averted the threat of any breakaway body led by South America, and, despite some ambitions to lead the world body, South American CONMEBOL personnel helped sustain FIFA through the war years, rewarded by the recognition in 1946 of Spanish as one of FIFA's official languages.

FIFA's German general secretary, Schricker, sustained the organization's correspondence throughout World War II, from the neutrality of its Swiss base. But no Congress could be held. FIFA activity was at a standstill, its Swiss bank accounts – lacking subscriptions or match revenues – close to exhausted. The South American confederation supported FIFA but also sought to place its FIFA Executive Committee member in the presidential role, claiming that the mandates of all other members had expired. FIFA had seen its 1942 World Cup cancelled, and had no plans or resources for 1946. But the fragile international federation held firm, and was revitalized by a European initiative that generated start-up funds, brought the British back in, and cemented the cooperation between the IFAB and FIFA.

Stimulated by the belief of FA secretary Stanley Rous that sport would have an important post-war role, the UK associations were in close negotiation with FIFA about the prospect and terms of their re-entry. In 1944 Rous identified some "immediate measures" that should be considered "following the cessation of hostilities in Europe," including:

> That the relationship of the four British National Associations with the Federation Internationale de Football Association (F.I.F.A.) shall be reviewed, consideration being given to the advisability of a resumption of membership and/or that the representation on the International Football Association Board shall be extended to allow all countries to be more directly represented.[20]

In April 1946 a conference between the British associations and FIFA took place at FA headquarters in Lancaster Gate, London. Rous was there, with the FA's International Committee chairman Arthur Drewry (soon to become FIFA's fifth president) alongside him. Five FIFA officials were there: France's Rimet, the president; Rodolphe Seeldrayers, from Belgium, vice-president; D. Eie, president of Norway's federation; K.J.J. Lotsy, president of the Netherlands federation; and secretary Dr Ivo Schricker. Four of the eight individuals to hold the FIFA presidency from 1904 to 2014 were in this room, and between them accumulated 54 years in that position, from 1920 to 1974. They all knew that Europe needed to be united in the face of the South American challenge. The FA chaired the meeting and Rous was appointed to act as "Secretary to the Meeting." This was a new *entente cordiale*, and Secretary Rous celebrated this new beginning in recording the "hearty welcome" afforded the FIFA delegates. Rimet then invited the British associations to rejoin, the British affirmed the probability of their respective associations joining, and "the alterations necessary to the F.I.F.A. Statues [sic] and Regulations for this to become effective, were discussed."[21]

This sounds like dry bureaucratic business but it was historic and potentially explosive work. FIFA agreed to "prepare a draft embodying the proposed alterations." These were drawn up and put before the FA within five weeks. Duly accepted, they went off for ratification at FIFA's 25th Congress in Luxemburg Town Hall at the end of July 1946, where, regarding "affiliations," the "proposal that the four British Associations should be re-elected to membership was unanimously and enthusiastically received," and the "proposals by the Four British Associations ... were accepted."[22] At the same meeting FIFA expelled Germany and Japan from membership, confirmed the membership of Honduras and Syria, and rejected an application for membership from the Palestine Sports Association (on the grounds that the Palestine FA was already a member). By October, the FA and the Irish FA had rejoined, the Welsh association was intending to apply, and the Scottish FA was considering a further amendment. Arthur Drewry was confirmed as the British nomination for vice-president of FIFA.

What Rous had accomplished, in the rewording and reframing of key passages, was the confirmation of the special status – against the statutes – of the UK, giving it: four independent national associations within a single nation state; a permanent vice-presidential position on the FIFA executive for the British associations (matching the South American confederation; the rest of the member associations had to scramble over just two positions); and reaffirmation of the IFAB's autonomy and authority, so that the laws of the game would be those "settled by" and "promulgated by" the Board, with FIFA, or any other body, compelled to play the game only "according to the Laws of the International Board." FIFA representation in IFAB decision-making would be doubled in the ensuing decade, but the autonomy of the law-making Board was reaffirmed. It was not until the 63rd Congress in 2013 that the UK associations' right to a vice-presidential position was rescinded.

This pact between Rimet's FIFA and the post-war FA, along with the other UK associations, was cemented when in 1947 a Great Britain versus Rest of the World match was staged at Glasgow's Hampden Park, Scotland. A crowd of 135,000 saw the British coast to a 6–1 victory, and the £30,000 of receipts from the game were gifted to FIFA. The international federation was re-established in a hegemonic leadership role, with a modicum of financial security, and its inner circle would lead the organization for the next 28 years.

By the middle of the century Rimet had secured a degree of stability for FIFA, and the three European presidents following him were to build on that in negotiating the dramatic expansion of FIFA's reach and profile in a post-colonial world. In its origins FIFA was so Eurocentric that no need was seen for any separate European organization, or other continental confederations beyond the long-established South American body: Europe-based FIFA could speak for the world.

Rimet's concept of the world football family was deeply rooted in an entrenched, paternalistic colonialism. His successors would need to be aware of the dynamics of a post-colonial world if the football family was to hold together in the second half of the century. As soon as Rimet left his position, continental confederations were created to represent, and when appropriate contest, Rimet's ideal and conception of world unity: UEFA for Europe in 1954; the Asian and African confederations in 1954 and 1957 respectively. These were followed by the Central and North American and Caribbean confederation in 1961, and the minnow, Oceania, in 1966. The creation of these confederations both bolstered FIFA's legitimacy and created an administrative infrastructure from which FIFA hegemony could be challenged.

FIFA and globalization

Many early international sport federations were little more than what Barbara Keys calls "tiny organizations that for years foundered on the edge of obscurity and bankruptcy."[23] Some hung onto the coat-tails of the expanding IOC; some were formed in a later phase, in direct response to the IOC's demands for international organization in order to be deemed eligible for the Olympics, particularly after the retrospective inauguration of the Winter Olympics (in Chamonix, France, in 1924, the same year as the Paris Summer Olympics). The credibility of international bodies rested in part on the association with events, and so the quadrennial Olympic Games covering numerous sport disciplines could claim a form of moral leadership of the international sporting world. It was very different for the governing body of world football, FIFA, which spent the first 24 years of its existence seeking the legitimacy to lead the world game, in tension with countries and regions such as England and South America, which laid their own claims to leadership of sport in their own parts of the world, and beyond. It was not until the arguments over amateurism in the late 1920s led to the British associations leaving FIFA once again, following earlier periods of membership and withdrawal, that the way was cleared for the top international football nation of the day, double Olympic winners Uruguay, to offer FIFA a venue and a rationale for an inaugural competition. In 1930, the first FIFA World Cup was both hosted and won by Uruguay, and what was to become FIFA's major asset was established. FIFA now had something that all countries would want to be a part of, excepting England and its UK partners, all of which remained outside of FIFA until 1946. Developing a mega-event such as the men's football World Cup gave FIFA a genuinely international profile and an acknowledged remit, attracting the attention of international strategists and opportunist politicians.

In his seminal work on global culture and the globalization process, Roland Robertson identified five phases in the temporal-historical path to what, towards the end of the twentieth century, he described as "a very high degree of global density and complexity."[24] A "germinal" phase, from the early fifteenth to the mid-eighteenth century in Europe, saw the beginnings of national communities, challenging a mediaeval transnational system. A subsequent "incipient" phase, up to the 1870s, was characterized by the idea of a unitary state, which functioned within a recognized world order of international relations. The third phase, from the 1870s through to the mid-1920s, was one of "take-off." As we locate FIFA's early growth within the broader political and economic picture, it is worth quoting Robertson's prescient portrayal of a take-off phase in which:

> increasingly manifest globalizing tendencies of previous periods and places gave way to a single, inexorable form centred upon the four reference points, and thus constraints, of national societies, generic individuals (but with a masculine bias), a single "international society," and an increasingly singular, but not unified conception of humankind ... . [This phase included] development of global competitions – for example the Olympics and Nobel prizes.[25]

Relatively obscure and certainly bankrupt FIFA might have been for many of its early, formative years, but it was building, and can in retrospect be seen as without doubt a serious player in the remaking of the world order. Robertson's fourth phase, up to the end of the 1960s, was labelled the "struggle-for-hegemony," and the fifth, a long and enduring phase lasting up to the 1990s, was identified as a phase of "uncertainty," but one in which global consciousness increased and the number of global institutions and movements multiplied. FIFA's rise from its modest beginnings, its survival and consolidation on the basis initially of a Europe–South America alliance, and its continued growth, accommodating the dramatic increase in the number of national members in the post-colonial period, mark it as a more than merely peripheral player in the narrative of globalization. Its international growth was both an echo of the third, fourth and fifth phases of the globalizing process and a harbinger of the expanding profile of cultural–economic organizations claiming to speak, in Robertson's words, for "humankind as a species-community," and on behalf of a global citizenship. The balance would change between the four elements or focal points of Robertson's model: national societies would come and go; the composition (and motivations) of male-dominated groupings of generic individuals would vary; notions of the international society would be contested through simple questions such as "whose society?"; and any singular conception of humankind would prove impossible to agree upon and sustain. But how these focal points of the globalization process have interacted with each other has shaped in part the trajectory and degree of the globalizing process in any particular sphere of culture, and sport is no exception.

With whom do small, new national communities or societies ally themselves in the politics of FIFA? What drives particular individuals to seek to enter and stay in the FIFA "family"? Where does FIFA's sense of its worldwide constituency come from? Thomas Eriksen has observed that the "organization of football today involves many cross-cutting ties of loyalty, deterritoralized fandom and global governance (with considerable democratic deficit), but its 'global' dimension is limited."[26] It is often limited in this global dimension by the obduracy, revival or renaissance of the local, a process for which Robertson borrowed (from Japanese business thinking and practice) the term "glocalize."[27] FIFA has constantly had to balance the interests of the local and the global, in dealing with continental federations, national associations and intranational leagues. The very breadth and impossible-to-reach scale of this brief has allowed FIFA to abnegate responsibilities in particular areas, and to pick and choose the spheres of its interest and influence according to dominant sets of interests at a particular time.

In the name of football, the world, and international harmony, FIFA's profile grew exponentially as it passed through the globalization phases. To understand how this happened it is essential to have some grasp of how FIFA functions, organizationally and institutionally, in an increasingly global world order. In the next chapter, the organization's mission and the means whereby it seeks to achieve its goals and objectives are reviewed and evaluated, in the light of illustrations of the vulnerability of the institution to forms of sabotage by individuals and networks less committed to the claimed mission of the federation than to their own individual and personal interests.

Notes

1 Eric Hobsbawm, *Industry and Empire* (Harmondsworth: Penguin, 1969), 308.

2 Eric Hobsbawm, *Age of Extremes: The Short Twentieth Century 1914–1991* (London: Abacus, 1995), 198. See also James Riordan, "Sport in capitalist and socialist countries: A Western perspective," in *The Sports Process: A Comparative and Developmental Approach*, eds. Eric Dunning, Joseph Maguire and Robert Pearton (Champaign, IL: Human Kinetics, 1993), 261–262.

3 Benedict Anderson, *Imagined Communities: Reflections on the Origins and Spread of Nationalism* (London: Verso, 1983), 16. Applied to football in Alan Tomlinson, "Going global: The FIFA story," in *Off the Ball: The Football World Cup*, eds. Alan Tomlinson and Garry Whannel (London: Pluto Press, 1986), 98.

4 For a magisterial synthesis of the world history of the game, see David Goldblatt, *The Ball is Round: A Global History of Football* (New York: Riverhead Books, 2008).

5 Willy Meisl, "The F.I.F.A.," in *Association Football, Volume 4*, eds. A.H. Fabian and Geoffrey Green (London: The Caxton Publishing Company Limited, 1960), 304.

6 England's Football Association christened itself "The Football Association" in 1863, and has retained this assertive definitional distinctiveness through use of the definite article throughout its 150-year history. Hereafter in this study the English body is referred to as the FA.

7 Quoted in Meisl, "The F.I.F.A.," 299.

8 Alfred Wahl, "Le footballer français: de l'amateurisme aù salariat (1890–1926)," *Le Mouvement Social*, 35, April/June 1986: 12.

9 Quoted in Pierre Lanfranchi, Christiane Eisenberg, Tony Mason and Alfred Wahl, *100 Years of Football: The FIFA Centennial Book* (London: Weidenfeld & Nicolson, 2004), 99.

10 Quoted in Meisl, "The F.I.F.A.," 301.

11 Guy Oliver, *The Guinness Book of World Football: The History of the Game in over 150 Countries* (London: Guinness Publishing, 1992).

12 Lanfranchi et al., *100 Years of Football*, 60.

13 Ibid., 64.

14 Item 50, meeting of 20 August 1919, Archives of the Football Association of Wales, Cardiff, Wales.

15 Letter dated 29 July 1925, marked "Issued to Members of Council Only," in minutes of the Football Association of Wales, Cardiff, Wales.

16 The IOC documents drawn upon are the minutes of the IOC Commission, Lausanne, 31 October 1927 and Ordre du Jour de la Commission Executive, Amsterdam, 28 July 1928. Both documents are in the IOC archives, Olympic Museum, Lausanne, Switzerland.

17 *Report of the Conference of the Representatives of the Associations of the UK*, held at Clifton House, Sheffield, 17 February 1928; in the archives of the Football Association of Wales, Cardiff, Wales.

18 These handbooks are pictured in Lanfranchi et al., *100 Years of Football*, 68.

19 Paul Dietschy, "Making football global? FIFA, Europe, and the non-European football world, 1912–74," *Journal of Global History*, 8/2, 2013: 279–298, 281. The account here of the inter-war period is based on this article.

20 Rous drafted his report in a memorandum issued in May 1943, and presented his consolidated recommendations and proposals to the FA Council in *Post War*

Development – An Interim Report, October, 1944. This was visionary stuff, and in its initial form had met with unsympathetic and sometimes hostile responses from across the English/British football community. Sub-committees were established and the FIFA recommendation is presented as Immediate Measure (e) in the section from Sub-Committee 4 – International Relationships in Football, p. 6 (from FA Council document in the author's possession).

21 *Conference between the British Associations and the F.I.F.A., held at 22, Lancaster Gate, London W.2, on Monday, 29th April, 1946,* Reference Minute 82, The Football Association *Minutes of a meeting of the Council held at 22, Lancaster Gate, London, W.2 on Monday June 3rd, 1946.* Consulted in FA Archives, London, England.

22 Ibid.

23 Barbara J. Keys, *Globalizing Sport: National Rivalry and International Community in the 1930s* (Cambridge, Massachusetts: Harvard University Press, 2006), 42.

24 Roland Robertson, *Globalization: Social Theory and Global Culture* (London: Sage, 1992), 58.

25 Ibid., 59.

26 Thomas Hylland Eriksen, *Globalization: The Key Concepts* (Oxford: Berg, 2007), 83–84.

27 Robertson, *Globalization*, 173; see also John Tomlinson, *Globalization and Culture* (Cambridge: Polity Press, 1999), 195–196.

2 Workings

As an organization FIFA is in many respects a very simple body, comprising an Executive Committee and a Congress broadly representative of national football associations and continental federations across the world. To support its stated goals and mission, though, it is an expansive bureaucracy in its modern form – one estimate indicating 390 Zurich-based employees earning an average salary of US$172,677[1] – with staff numbers swelling when event managers and organizers are taken on for premier events such as the organization's showpiece, the men's football World Cup. It also establishes committees or commissions for key functions; these include refereeing, finance, media, marketing and, latterly, ethics. Such committees are commonly chaired by football officials from bodies outside FIFA, usually the affiliated confederations. In this overview of how FIFA functions, I also point to inbuilt dysfunctions in its structure, and to examples of such dysfunction crossing over into corruption. This is done with reference to factual occurrences and individuals' institutional positions in order to convey not just the abstract and general structures and procedures of FIFA, but the realities and institutional practices of its organizational culture.

FIFA's mission

FIFA's mission, as stated in 2012, is "to develop the game, touch the world, build a better future."[2] It is in essence a form of self-branding, describing football as a "symbol of hope and integration,"[3] prioritizing fair play and football development, in a blend of traditional sporting rhetoric and vague universalism:

WHAT WE STAND FOR

Our core values of authenticity, unity, performance and integrity are at the very heart of who we are.

Authenticity. We believe that football must remain a simple, beautiful game played by, enjoyed by and touching the lives of all people far and wide

Unity. We believe it is FIFA's responsibility to foster unity within the football world and to use football to promote solidarity, regardless of gender, ethnic background, faith or culture

Performance. We believe that FIFA must strive to deliver football of the highest quality and as the best possible experience, be it as a player, as a spectacle, or as a major cultural and social enabler throughout the world

Integrity. We believe that, just as the game itself, FIFA must be a model of fair play, tolerance, sportsmanship and transparency[4]

This statement is a vital backdrop to any study of the nature of the organization and its impact on football at all of the game's levels. It is in the light of this public declaration that the organization's working procedures and practices are considered in this chapter.

Commerce or charity?

Under Swiss law, FIFA is "an association registered in the Commercial Register in accordance with art. 60 ff. of the Swiss Civil Code."[5] Article 60 is in the second chapter of the Swiss Civil Code, on "Associations." Those associations "with a political, religious, scientific, cultural, charitable, social or other non-commercial purpose acquire legal personality as soon as their intention to exist as a corporate body is apparent from their articles of association … . The articles of association must be done in writing and indicate the objects of the association, its resources, and its organization."[6] In accordance with this Code, FIFA states its objective, pitching itself as a developmental body with a global reach:

> Pursuant to article 2 of its Statutes, FIFA's objective is to improve the game of football constantly and promote it globally, particularly through youth and development programmes. FIFA is a non-profit organization and is obliged to spend its reserves for this purpose. FIFA is taxed in Switzerland according to the ordinary taxation rules applying to associations. The non-profit character of FIFA and the four-year accounting cycle are thereby taken into account.[7]

At its Congress in Mauritius in May 2013, FIFA reaffirmed this principle still more emphatically, adding "results" and "funds" to the term "reserves" and confirming that: "As FIFA is an association, no dividends are paid."[8] In effect, then, FIFA is a non-profit making non-commercial organization, and shares certain privileged statuses with other international sport federations. As the then-deputy general secretary Michel Zen-Ruffinen stated in 1997, the main implication of the associational status in the Code is "that an association shall only pursue ideal purposes and it is deemed to be non-commercial in definition."[9] This status relates to the tax arrangements for non-Swiss employees, as well as confirming the organization's non-commercial rationale in its financial operations.

The confederations

FIFA recognizes six continental confederations, whose member association numbers in May 2012, when South Sudan became FIFA's 209th member, were as follows:

1 CONMEBOL, the South American Football Confederation, founded 1916: 10 members
2 UEFA, the Union of European Football Associations, founded 1954: 53 members from Europe, and Israel
3 AFC, the Asian Football Confederation, founded 1954: 46 members from Asia, and Australia
4 CAF, the Confederation of African Football, founded 1957: 54 members
5 CONCACAF, the Confederation of North, Central American and Caribbean Association Football, founded 1961: 35 members
6 Oceania, the confederation for the South Pacific region, founded in 1966: 11 members from New Zealand and the Pacific islands.

These confederations are independent and are not organizationally or institutionally part of FIFA, though in the practice of world governance of the game they work in partnership with FIFA and historically have gained their legitimacy by receiving recognition from FIFA. They are also pragmatically flexible in defining confederational affiliations according to political sensitivities or economic imperatives; thus Israel is in UEFA and not the AFC, and Australia is in the AFC and not Oceania.

What does FIFA do?

FIFA's Executive Committee (ExCo) meets at least twice a year. Along with the Financial Committee and other management activity and directors' meetings, the ExCo was supported by a budget of US$20.9 million in the 2009 cycle.[10] No woman had ever sat on the ExCo until May 2013.

The FIFA Congress meets annually, for its Annual General Meeting and to conduct business as appropriate in the cycle of the planning and staging of its events. The 209 member associations are predominantly national associations of single nation states, with exceptions including the United Kingdom's four "home" associations, Hong Kong since its absorption into mainland China, various territories or protectorates without autonomous nation state status, and contested states such as Palestine. For election as FIFA president, a candidate must gain two-thirds of the votes cast in Congress. To change the statutes, Congress must vote for, or approve, a proposal by simple majority.

The Congress has done little of serious substance beyond the acclamation or election of the president every four years, though at its May 2013 meeting it accepted responsibility for the selection of World Cup hosts. Its responsibilities have been a catalyst for much dubious lobbying of individuals and allegations concerning gift-making and inducements, when an incumbent president has been challenged or the presidency has been contested by candidates who have not previously been president. This was certainly the case in 1974 and 1998; infamously in Paris in 1998 one national association delegate who was absent from the Congress was unofficially replaced by an individual from a different country when it came to the presidential vote. No FIFA security process adequately checked on the identities of those entering the polling booth. Unlike the situation in the reformed IOC, there was still, in 2013, no limit to the number of four-year periods that a FIFA president can serve, nor any age limit for FIFA office holders, though within the continuing debates concerning institutional reform these two issues have been recognized as being in need of review and amendment.

FIFA's highest profile asset is the men's World Cup, and the rest of its portfolio is subsidized by the revenues that flow from the escalating value, in terms of marketing, broadcasting and media rights, of that single event. Chapters 5 and 6 consider these financial and economic aspects of FIFA's development and global influence, and review this wider portfolio in relation to its stated mission and objectives.

The rules of the game

The rules of football are dealt with not by FIFA's Congress but by the International Football Association Board (IFAB), the body featured prominently in the introduction to this book. Throughout its history, from its formation in London in 1886 when representatives of the four British associations met to establish an authoritative body for the standardization of the rules of football, the Board has had responsibility for monitoring and overviewing the rules of the game – the 17 sacrosanct laws defending the essential simplicity of the sport.

On FIFA's formation, IFAB cooperated and negotiated with, and latterly to some degree within, the international federation. The initial rules of conduct for the Board itself established the membership at two for each British association, with an annual meeting rotating between the four countries.[11] At its annual meeting in 1911, at the Station Hotel, Turnberry, Scotland, the FA's delegate C. Crump reported that the FA secretary, Frederick Wall, had received a letter from FIFA stating that: "The International Federation of Association Football had unanimously agreed, at their Annual Congress held in Dresden on 5th June, 1911, to ask for power to send a representative to The International Board."[12] This initiated exchanges and negotiations culminating in FIFA joining forces with the IFAB in 1913.

In 1925, though, the British Associations were still defending their domination of the Board. The annual meeting was held at 22 Rue de Londres in Paris, the offices of the French Football Association, where the Football Association of Wales proposed altering the rules to bar FIFA's secretary from having voting powers. In fact, FIFA was still marginal and seen as a junior partner in the IFAB rules of conduct, as starkly illustrated by Rule IV:

> The Board shall meet annually on the second Saturday in June. The meetings shall be held in rotation in England, Scotland, Wales, Ireland and Paris, at the invitation of each Association in order of seniority. The invitation for the year 1925 shall be given by the Fédération Internationale de Football Association and for 1926 by Scotland.[13]

Rimet, as FIFA president, having welcomed the Board to Paris, withdrew from the meeting, leaving just Henri Delauney to represent FIFA. At its 1926 meeting in the Grand Hotel, St Andrews, Scotland, the IFAB, with two FIFA delegates present, minuted Rimet's statement at FIFA's Rome 1926 Congress to the effect that "the Federation would never express its opposition to the authority of the International Board. Correspondence had been exchanged with the British football associations and there was no doubt, it was not the intention of the Federation to reduce the authority of the International Board as the highest authority in Association football. Mr. Rimet expressed satisfaction at being able to explain the misunderstanding."[14] These were status games and power plays, destined to recur over the succeeding decades, right through to 1958 when new voting rights were established, with Grimsby fish merchant Arthur Drewry now in the FIFA presidential chair. Initially, it seems, the formalization of FIFA's equal role in the IFAB, as a response to the growing internationalization of the game, was in practical terms a means of expanding British representation and control still further.

The IFAB comprises, in its modern contemporary form, eight voting members: a single member from each of the UK national associations, and four voting members from FIFA. This body meets twice a year, reviews and pronounces on the laws of the game and is wholly autonomous. Neither FIFA's ExCo nor its Congress can call the IFAB to account, though the FIFA president has in essence provided a generous form of patronage to the Board. It is routine practice for the FIFA president to decide who from FIFA attends the IFAB as a voting member.

Commissions and committees

ExCo

The FIFA Executive Committee (ExCo) has 24 voting members, comprising 24 officials representing or elected from the confederations. The president and the secretary general are also on the committee, and if a vote is tied the president can give a casting vote. In 2013, two women were also brought onto the ExCo, as "co-opted members for special tasks." The ExCo is routinely serviced by the General Secretary, formerly titled the Chief Executive. The ExCo members serve terms of four years.

The composition of the committee in November 2011 was as follows:

President:	Joseph "Sepp" Blatter (Switzerland)
Senior Vice-President:	Julio H. Grondona (Argentina, CONMEBOL)
Vice-Presidents:	Michel Platini (UEFA, France)
	Jimmy Boyce (UK associations, Northern Ireland)
	Issa Hayatou (CAF, Cameroon)
	H.R.H. Prince Ali Bin Al Hussein (AFC, Jordan)
	Ángel María Villar Llona (UEFA, Spain)
	David Chung (Oceania, Papua New Guinea)
	Vacancy (CONCACAF)

Members (15 + 1 vacancy):   5 from UEFA (Michel D'Hooghe,
Belgium; Senes Erzik, Turkey; Marios
Lefkaritis, Cyprus; Vitaly Mutko, Russia;
Theo Zwanziger, Germany)
2 from CONCACAF (Chuck Blazer,
USA; Rafael Salguero, Guatemala)
2 from CONMEBOL (Ricardo Terra
Teixeira, Brazil; Nicolás Leoz, Paraguay)
3 from AFC (Worawi Makudi, Thailand;
Jilong Zhang, China; V. Manilal
Fernando, Sri Lanka)
3 from CAF (Jacques Anouma, Côte
d'Ivoire; Mohamed Raouraoua, Algeria;
Hany Abo Rida, Egypt)

Suspension and resignation can undermine the stability of the membership. The vacancy for the CONCACAF vice-presidency occurred when
Jack Warner was suspended on the basis of bribery allegations; a CAF
place was unoccupied, also due to suspension. Within months, the
November list of members would lose Chuck Blazer (CONCACAF),
and Ricardo Texeira and Nicolás Leoz (both CONMEBOL), all accused
of financial improprieties in relation to their activities in their FIFA roles
and/or their federation positions. Replacements for these, and other
outgoing ExCo personnel, would include delegates from the Cayman
Islands (the offshore financial centre where Chuck Blazer had been storing
many of his financial assets) and Bahrain (where human rights atrocities
hardly match FIFA's developmental agenda), as well as Burundi (whose
delegate Lydia Nsekera became FIFA's first ever woman ExCo member).
The vice-presidential line-up would also change, with the decision at the
FIFA Congress in 2013 no longer to allocate one of these positions to
the four British associations, on expiry of the current incumbent's term
of office (though the position would stay within UEFA/Europe).

In 2013, then, excluding the president, the ExCo divided up, in terms
of confederational affiliation, as follows: CONMEBOL 3; UEFA 8;
CAF 5; AFC 4; CONCACAF 3; Oceania 1.[15] The European body
UEFA, with slightly over a quarter of the 209 members, is somewhat
over-represented, with a third of ExCo members. The historically long-
established South American confederation is also, in relation to its
number of member associations, disproportionately represented on the
committee.

In relation to Congress, the country that in 2013 was 197th in FIFA's
ranking table in terms of the national side's on-field performances –

American Samoa – wields just as much power as the top-ranked nation, Spain, or any of the other giants of international football.[16] San Marino, host to the powers of European football in World Cup qualifiers, and joint bottom of the rankings along with Bhutan and the Turks and Caicos Islands, could in principle wield as much influence in the FIFA Congress as any of its UEFA neighbours.

The ExCo has the responsibility of awarding its tournaments and events to countries bidding for the host role, most prominently in the case of the men's football World Cup. A decision can be made on the basis of a simple majority, or on a casting further vote of the president. As the composition of the committee shows, there is no single geopolitical interest bloc dominant within it. If all Europeans voted together, including the Swiss president, this would muster only nine of the available votes. ExCo operations have thus been dominated by alliances and deal-making, or, during the reigns of several of FIFA's eight presidents, by the imposition of the individual will of the president.

The ExCo should, in principle, make decisions on FIFA policy, but it is effective only insofar as it is informed and consulted on the matter and detail of the workings of the FIFA committees. The individual members are actually delegates from the continental confederations, as well as (in a historical anomaly having effect between 1946 and 2014) the four national associations of England, Northern Ireland, Scotland and Wales. But rather than paying attention to their federational constituencies, numerous individuals are prone to self-serving strategies; between Autumn 2010 and July 2011 four members were suspended (the member from Nigeria and three confederation presidents, from CONCACAF, the AFC and Oceania). Three were expelled from the committee and one resigned from all his positions in world football. Another ExCo member, the CAF president, was also at this time under investigation for alleged corruption by the IOC, of which he was also a member. A further member, the CONCACAF general secretary, was cautioned by FIFA's ethics committee for comments and allegations concerning the practices of fellow committee members' confederations, and later announced that he would resign from his positions at the confederation and on FIFA committees at the end of his current tenure.

This core committee could scarcely be said to have functioned with consistency or efficiency, and the workings of FIFA can hardly be said to operate with consistency, stability and integrity characterized by such a volatile and dubious membership of its primary executive body. Skilfully managed, cunningly and when necessary ruthlessly chaired, the ExCo has been open to manipulation by the president and the general secretary.

Standing committees, commissions, bureaux

In 1996, FIFA had 22 standing committees to support the work of the ExCo; in 2001, there were 29. In 2011, the number of committees, commissions or bureaux had risen to 35. Getting onto a FIFA committee was becoming an established, and widely perceived as rewarding, form of involvement in football governance and development. For some, it was an idealistic commitment to the mission of FIFA; for others it was a favour from the FIFA president and an entry point for making potentially lucrative international and business contacts; for everyone, it was a passport to a luxury lifestyle and global power-broking. In late 2011, 387 different individuals peopled the FIFA committee structure; of these, 326 sat on just a single committee, 38 on two, 22 on between three and seven committees, and one individual was on nine committees. Table 2.1 indicates FIFA's most active committee men.

Multiple committee membership could bestow on a single individual influence, power, status and personal benefits. David Chung, Malaysian-born but from the age of 23 a resident of Papua New Guinea, may be relatively unknown to most football administrators, let alone fans.[17] But he is one of FIFA's top committee men, sitting on nine committees. And these are not peripheral committees, boards or bureaux. Chung was on the all-powerful ExCo as a vice-president after taking over from the

Table 2.1 Influence and power in FIFA: the top 15 committee men, November 2011

Number of committees	Member	
9	David Chung	Papua New Guinea
7	Rafael Salguero	Guatemala
7	Ricardo Terra Teixeira	Brazil
6	Chuck Blazer	USA
6	Michel D'Hooghe	Belgium
6	Senes Erzik	Turkey
6	Issa Hayatou	Cameroon
6	Marios Lefkaritis	Cyprus
6	Michel Platini	France
5	Jacques Anouma	Côte d'Ivoire
5	Ángel María Villar Llona	Spain
4	Joseph 'Sepp' Blatter	Switzerland
4	Jiri Dvorak	Switzerland
4	Nicolás Leoz	Paraguay
4	Jilong Zhang	China

Source: Compiled from FIFA listings, Autumn 2011

disgraced Oceania president Raymond Temarii of Tahiti in 2010, and was confirmed in this position on his unopposed election as Oceania president in 2011. He was also Deputy Chair of the Marketing and Television Advisory Board, chair of the Organising Committee for the FIFA U-17 World Cup, sat on the powerful trio of the Finance Committee, Emergency Committee and Strategic Committee, and still had time to attend the Bureau for the 2014 Brazil World Cup, the Goal Bureau and the Organising Committee for the FIFA Club World Cup.

The Emergency Committee is briefed to deal with anything that the president wishes, and is made up of Blatter, as president, and just five others. In late 2011 four of these were confederation presidents: Chung, Michel Platini, Issa Hayatou and Nicolás Leoz, presidents of Oceania, UEFA, CAF (Africa) and CONMEBOL, respectively. The final member was Guatemala's Rafael Salguero from CONCACAF; the Asian confederation was the only one not represented on the Emergency Committee. Three of the six Emergency Committee members also formed half of FIFA's Finance Committee. Although 387 individuals shared 511 positions on FIFA's committees, a small number moved around the most important committees. David Chung, a football careerist, may be one of the most powerful and influential figures in world football governance and development. This is good for him, good for Oceania and potentially very good for Papua New Guinea.[18] The *Goal* project and FIFA's Financial Assistance Programme delivered a million US dollars into the developmental coffers of the national association, of which Chung was still president, before the handout of US$550,000 from FIFA (to each national association) from the revenues of South Africa 2010.

Chuck Blazer has always charmed his suitors, in his quintessential man-of-the-people fashion. When Blatter fled the room after his press conference at the IFAB in March 2011, Blazer allowed the newsmen to surround him to go over some of the questions that had been left in the air. He has shown endless patience in his role as general secretary of CONCACAF, covering the Caribbean and Central and North America. He has had a lot of practice listening to colleagues, as another of FIFA's experienced committee stalwarts. In early October 2011 Blazer announced that he would be withdrawing from his FIFA work at the end of his tenure, but at that point he still held six positions on FIFA committees: he was a long-term survivor on the ExCo; chairman of the Marketing and Television Advisory Board and of the Organising Committee for the FIFA Club World Cup; deputy chair of the players' status committee; a member of Bureau Special Projects; and consultant on the Committee for Club Football. You can see the focus here on media, markets and the top clubs.

FIFA president Blatter chaired Bureau Special Projects and Turkey's Senes Erzik was the deputy chair, their colleagues coming from South Korea, New Zealand, Uruguay and Morocco, representing the six continental confederations. But what does the Bureau do? There is little information on its brief, its responsibilities, its activities and its accomplishments. In Blatter's period in power, FIFA has increased dramatically its number of committees, and multiple committee membership can give individuals widespread influence over FIFA decisions, not only concerning technical aspects of the sport but also FIFA's core business deals in broadcasting and marketing rights.

Ethics

FIFA did not introduce an ethics committee until 2004 (its composition and terms of reference were revised in 2006 and several times thereafter), previously choosing to deal with any ethical matters within its disciplinary committee.[19] Its code of ethics could not be retrospectively applied "to facts that have arisen after it has come into force" (Article 2). Article 3 summarizes the three general rules of the code:

1. Officials are expected to be aware of the importance of their function and concomitant obligations and responsibilities. Their conduct shall reflect the fact that they support and further the principles and objectives of FIFA, the confederations, associations, leagues and clubs in every way and refrain from anything that could be harmful to these aims and objectives. They shall respect the significance of their allegiance to FIFA, the confederations, associations, leagues and clubs and represent them honestly, worthily, respectably and with integrity.

2. Officials shall show commitment to an ethical attitude while performing their duties. They shall pledge to behave in a dignified manner. They shall behave and act with complete credibility and integrity.

3. Officials may not abuse their position as part of their function in any way, especially to take advantage of their function for private aims or gains.

Article 5 deals with conflicts of interest, and demands that officials "disclose any personal interests that could be linked with their prospective function." Private or personal interests must not detract from officials performing their duties "with integrity": "Private or personal interests include gaining any possible advantage for himself, his family, relatives, friends and acquaintances." In many cases, FIFA has been able to pass responsibility for dealing with cases of conflict of interest to the official's own organization, typically the national association or the confederation. A closer consideration of individual cases of prominent current and former FIFA committee members will illustrate how the workings of the FIFA system are open to misuse, and how serial and endemic breaches of the ethical code have been tolerated throughout FIFA's modern history.

The man from Malta: "If someone should make a strange offer it should be declared"[20]

Dr Josef Mifsud is from Malta, and was a FIFA ExCo committee member for several years. Buoyed by his recent elevation to the top committee in world football administration, he responded eloquently to my questions about the stories and rumours that were swirling around Paris on the eve of Sepp Blatter's election to the presidency: "In my opinion there should be a code of ethics … one of the points should be that if someone should make a strange offer or something, it should have to be declared. Should bidding groups visit you at home? No, in fact in my opinion, representation should be made jointly." I asked him whether he felt pressurized by the offer of unsolicited gifts: "Yeah, yeah … . I think there should be an obligation for committee members to declare anything. I will, I will raise this point at a future executive meeting, because I think giving the World Cup should be a decision for the real good of football and not a decision from which one can personally gain. It should be outside our scope to gain personally from our position."

As we have seen, an ethics committee was put in place during Blatter's time as president. But however much Dr Mifsud campaigned on such principles and towards such an outcome, he showed no haste in telling colleagues about dynamics and economics underlying the prestigious football matches that he brought to his small country in the years preceding the 2000 decision for the 2006 men's World Cup. Germany's top team, Bayern Munich, arrived on his small island; the English national team turned up. Dr Mifsud had a vote to cast in 2000, and English and German football administrators were happy to collude in his demands in exchange for the prospect of his vote, looking for even the slightest hint that he might look favourably on their bid. Dr Mifsud was also silent on the monies that found their way into his personal bank account for some of these deals, and in no mood to respond to BBC *Panorama* journalist Andrew Jennings on this matter. Dr Mifsud is no longer at the FIFA top table, but is to be seen at significant UEFA meetings and events. Dr Mifsud, lawyer, long-term head of the Maltese Football Association and FIFA ExCo member 1998–2000, has been less effusive about ethical standards and expectations since the revelations about his own practices.

Thailand tales: "Human beings cannot be perfect"[21]

Worawi Makudi is an effervescent and personable character, who has bounced in and out of FIFA's Executive Committee in recent years. After Germany won the vote for the 2006 World Cup in dramatically controversial circumstances – the Oceania president Charles Dempsey abstaining/departing, and Germany pipping South Africa by a single vote, so saving the president from exercising the chair's casting vote – there were countless allegations that New Zealander Dempsey had been paid off (or threatened) not to vote for South Africa. Germany's government, it was then revealed, had concluded arms deals with the Saudis close to the decision day.

Worawi Makudi was one of those to cast his vote in the controversial ballot. I asked him about his relationships with the likes of Havelange, who had visited Thailand in his capacity as president: "When he came to visit us he offered us his personal help to send a coach to Brazil to take a coaching course there, at his own [Havelange's] expense. If you ask anything valid to him he will respond to you in the sense that he can." I asked about Havelange's leadership style: "90 per cent good, maybe 10 per cent a mistake or something. For me, personally, I think that it's acceptable, you have to balance the good and the bad. You don't pick up on the negative points, a lot of good people make mistakes, human beings cannot be perfect." In other words, turn a blind eye. And Makudi argued for the autonomy of his own confederation: "FIFA will never jump over the confederation. In terms of respect I think they have treated us very nicely."

Makudi is a businessman who had his own club, a college team and moved into administration in Thai football: "many people think that I have the capability." He continued: "FIFA always gives us … FIFA is ready to help if they know what you require, what you want, this is what I understand from FIFA. They are very, they are ready, they are ready. FIFA help and FIFA treat us the same as the other continents, and whatever FIFA give we all receive and that's normal."

Businessman, football administrator, FIFA top committee member: in all this giving and receiving I asked whether any conflicts of interest arose in Makudi's duties and activities: "I don't get the meaning of your question." As the 2000 vote was approaching for the 2006 World Cup,

Makudi's business interests included car dealerships in his native Thailand with a major German company. Makudi remains as a member of the ExCo, but in May 2013 lost the contest for the Asian Football Confederation's presidency to Sheikh Salman Bin Ibrahim Al Khalifa of Bahrain, getting only seven of the 46 votes available, one more than the candidate from the United Arab Emirates: Al Khalifa received 33 votes. Makudi, within weeks, was also facing legal challenges from within his own national association, and disruption of the electoral process for his presidential position.

The house that Jack built: Carnival time in Trinidad[22]

For more than 20 years, Trinidadian Jack Warner exerted influence over football business in Central and North America and the Caribbean, resigning in June 2011 after sight of a damning report into bribery allegations, and so avoiding personal investigation by FIFA. Warner was elected to the CONCACAF presidency on a reforming agenda in 1990; his ten-point manifesto stressed grassroots development and provision of support for more effective national associations. But the more precise objectives targeted expanded competition, sponsorship deals and tributes – point ten was "to establish the Dr João Havelange Centre of Excellence." He immediately relocated the CONCACAF headquarters from Guatemala City to Port of Spain. Within a decade, 72 of Warner's confederation men were on one or other of FIFA's 21 standing committees, a period claimed by CONCACAF as an *éclatement* – a bursting out – of regional football interests. It was certainly a flowering of the Warner family fortunes.

Warner was a history teacher by training and vocation, but became involved in football administration in the 1970s and 1980s, as secretary of the Trinidad and Tobago Football Federation from 1974 to 1990. He was known in the country's football world as autocratic and hostile to modernizing change. Progressive football initiatives by others, seeking to remedy low playing standards and the opaqueness and inaccessibility of Warner's decision-making processes, were blocked and thwarted by this ambitious man. Once in power he posed as progressive, but his manifesto and victory created a platform for self-interest and self-aggrandizement, manipulating the facts, riding roughshod over normal considerations of conflict of interest, shamelessly promoting his own image and interests, and encouraging ingrained deception and fraudulent practice in football matters.

Manipulation Facts could count for nothing in Warner's world; he could push the Trinidad and Tobago Football Federation president Oliver Camps out of the limelight in a pre-World Cup friendly between Trinidad and Tobago against Iceland in London in February 2006, allowing himself to be portrayed as the supremo of Trinidad and Tobago football.[23] In their warm-up schedule for the 2006 World Cup finals, Trinidad and Tobago played a friendly international fixture against Iceland. This took place in West London, at Loftus Road, the ground of Queens Park Rangers. Iceland's Football Association president, Eggert Magnússon – a biscuit magnate soon to become the owner of struggling English Premier League club West Ham United, on the other side of London – penned a message. TTFF President Oliver Camps had no such opportunity. Instead, fans were offered, as the first textual content of the match magazine, a "warm welcome from the FIFA Vice President, Mr. Austin Jack Warner." On a freezing English February night, Warner reminded England-based Trinidadians and other football enthusiasts of the popular cultural legacy in which the footballing success of the twin-island nation was anchored:

> Today, the people of Trinidad and Tobago are dancing in the streets, for it is Carnival Time at home, and the sounds of steel bands playing our infectious Soca music are ringing through the islands. A small piece of that Carnival spirit is here at Loftus Road tonight, as English-based steel bands provide the rhythm for our players.

Warner then trotted out his national side's support slogan: "Small Country – Big Passion." And the passion on this bitter midwinter evening was palpable.

Warner's appeal to his country's cultural traditions was made, though, from no official position within the TTFF. Magnússon nevertheless picked out Warner in his programme notes: "A special greeting goes to my friend Jack Warner, the president of the T&T Football Association. In my mind, a lot of the aforementioned success [qualification for Germany 2006] can be put down to his good work within the FA and the world of football." Experienced Dutch football coach Leo Beenhakker also knew who was in charge: "We will have a lot of meetings with Mr. Warner and the management team of the federation to arrange everything perfectly over the months of May and June." Oliver Camps was president of the federation according to FIFA's 1996 directory and still president according to CONCACAF's website on 28 March 2007; administrative and managerial continuity was indicated in the loyal vice-presidential tenure of Raymond Kim Tee across the same period. But Warner is a man who could fix FIFA elections, substituting yes-men for genuine delegates. Camps and Kim Tee were unlikely to undermine one of the FIFA vice-president's moments of glory: Warner's continuing involvement in the (now high-profile) affairs of the national side was an indicator of his abusive manipulation of institutional authority. He was not tempted to correct the side's current coach, or the Icelandic businessman, for there was hard work to be done soon, money to be made. The association with the national side, the Soca Warriors, was looking very lucrative for Warner.

Conflicts of interest never crossed his mind when lucrative business was secured by Simpaul Travel – co-owned by Warner, his wife and two of his sons. FIFA general secretary Michel Zen-Ruffinen's confidential paper to the FIFA ExCo in May 2002 revealed, in a section on "The Warner Family," that FIFA's Finance Committee accepted a budget from Warner of US$4.5 million for the Under-21 World Cup in Trinidad in 2001, but when the final cost for FIFA amounted to US $8.21 million, no questions were pursued.[24] Wrists slapped, Warner nevertheless survived the scrutiny of FIFA's tame disciplinary committee in 2006, not least because some of his dealings were said to predate revised committee criteria, and the committee was deemed to be dealing only with new cases. FIFA nevertheless fined Warner's son Daryan a million dollars in relation to the illegal reselling of 2006 World Cup tickets, and banned the Warner family travel company from dealing in tickets.[25]

Self-promotion has always been a big driver for Warner. Gaining FIFA monies for CONCACAF for the Havelange Centre in Trinidad, Warner never organized the US$16 million repayment, and the centre became a Warner resource, even charging for FIFA-based events, managed by one of Warner's sons. Opened in May 1998 by outgoing FIFA president Havelange – whose tatty-looking ornamental bust adorns the cage-like structure that dominates the entrance to the site – the centre soon served Warner business purposes, staging a Miss Universe pageant in 1999 and one crowning Miss Trinidad and Tobago in 2003. The organizer, Caribbean Communications Network Limited, clearly benefited from Warner's broadening of the centre's mission.

Deception runs deep in aspects of confederational and global football politics. It has been ingrained, embedded, accepted as an everyday aspect of life. At Trinidad and Tobago versus St Kitts in November 2002, the man on the gate at the Hasely Crawford Stadium handed me a ticket for a match against Panama (15 November 2000) and, when I asked whether this was a mistake, he said that it was the right ticket for the match. This occurred again at a Gold Cup match at the Havelange Centre. Such scams are second nature in Warnerland, and it is scarcely a surprise that practices like this have served Warner well in his wider FIFA career.

Zen-Ruffinen claimed: "The President has constantly taken decisions which are favourable to the economical interests of Jack Warner and some of his family members, and thus are contrary to the financial interests of FIFA."[26] These included TV deals for the region, travel deals for the family and lucrative consultancies and executive positions for kinfolk.

Warner has now gone. On 14 June 2011 the FIFA Ethics Committee faxed its verdict to Warner – a provisional ban from any national or international football-related activity while the investigation further pursued its preliminary verdict of guilty of bribery/corruption; the report noted that Warner defended himself only by "self-serving declarations" that the US$40,000 cash gifts from Qatar/AFC's Mohamed Bin Hammam to Caribbean associations were for grassroots programmes: "Financial means for the promotion of grassroots sports programs are usually not provided in the form of cash money, in particular during the course of extraordinary meetings nor are they distributed in the context of election campaigns of candidates for the post of FIFA president."[27]

Warner was jammed, in a corner, and resigned all his positions, which meant a deal with FIFA to terminate proceedings against him. Almost two years later, the new post-Warner, post-Blazer Integrity Committee of CONCACAF presented a "Report of Investigation," 144 pages long, to its Executive Committee. The Integrity Committee was chaired by Sir David Simmons, former Chief Justice of Barbados, and included Ernesto Hempe, a retired PricewaterhouseCoopers partner, and Ricardo M. Urbina, a former US District Judge.[28] The report concluded that Warner and his general secretary, US citizen Chuck Blazer, in relation to CONCACAF's financial statements and audits, committed fraud against the confederation. This involved misrepresentations, material omissions, breach of fiduciary duties, and violation of CONCACAF statutes "through the same fraudulent conduct."[29] Blazer was also said to have violated US federal tax laws, and misappropriated CONCACAF funds. It is worth quoting the Simmons report at some length:

> The Committee concluded that Chuck Blazer misappropriated CONCACAF funds in two ways. First, after his contract with CONCACAF expired on July 17, 1998, Blazer caused CON-CACAF to make over $15 million in payments to Blazer in the form of commissions, fees, and rent expenses without obtaining proper authorization. Second, Blazer misappropriated CONCACAF funds to finance his personal lifestyle by causing CONCACAF to, among other things: subsidize rent on his residence in the Trump Tower in New York; purchase apartments at the Mondrian, a luxury hotel and residence in Miami; sign purchase agreements and pay down

payments on apartments at the Atlantis resort in the Bahamas; and obtain insurance coverage for his personal residence and automobile and employee health insurance for himself and his girlfriend.

The Committee further concluded that Blazer breached his fiduciary duties to CONCACAF through such self-dealing and that he violated the CONCACAF Statutes by not properly managing CON-CACAF's financial affairs. The Committee also concluded that, beginning in 2006, Blazer violated the FIFA Ethics Code by paying himself in the form of commissions without obtaining express authorization from the CONCACAF Executive Committee or the Congress. The Committee concluded that Jack Warner breached his fiduciary duties to CONCACAF in connection with Blazer's compensation because Warner was aware that, after July 17, 1998, Blazer had no employment contract but continued to pay himself without authorization for 13 years, and Warner did not raise the matter with the CONCACAF Executive Committee.[30]

Warner left his ministerial post in the government of Trinidad and Tobago in the wake of the Simmons Committee's findings; Blazer had refused to meet the Committee, and was still making legal claims against CONCACAF. The two CONCACAF and FIFA veterans had lost their power base. But for more than two decades many close to Warner were fully aware of his abuse of his position, and did nothing; the same pertains to Blazer. Warner survived by combining a threatening and bullying personal style with the inbuilt immunity from scrutiny within the FIFA and CONCACAF institutional structures and procedures. His departure from the world scene was sparked by revelations by Blazer himself, whose own financial indiscretions and windfalls were the subject of concurrent investigation, both by journalists and researchers, and through US legal channels.[31] In early October 2011, Blazer himself announced that he would be stepping down from his CONCACAF position, and possibly his FIFA positions.[32]

That the house that Jack built has crumbled is a sign of potential change to FIFA practice, but as in political and other comparable spheres, there is always likely to be another Jack in the box, ready to spring up and undertake house repairs to gain the status and benefits that continue to accrue to those in the top positions at FIFA House, or the Home of FIFA. Announcing his impending departure, Blazer pointed to the occupancy of key FIFA positions by Swiss – including the chairs of the Ethics and Disciplinary Committees as well as Blatter himself – and stated that the structure of FIFA, revolving around the national associations, should be changed, with broader representation of clubs, leagues and women, none of whom have ever had representation in the ExCo. "Won't come close," he noted, though, when asked whether the ExCo was likely to look towards broader forms of representation.

Mission impossible

Authenticity, unity, performance and integrity – these principles, presented at the beginning of this chapter, constitute FIFA's core values and goals. "Develop the game, touch the world, build a better future" is the brand expression that heads up the organization's mission statement. FIFA's organizational structures and processes are in theory dedicated to the defence and cultivation of these values. But dealmaking within its inner circles, its regional federations, international associations and corporate sponsors shows where FIFA ambitions and loyalties really lie, and personal aggrandizement, as well as sporting and international ideals, have shaped FIFA policy; at the same time, though, FIFA's finances have boomed, and the organization can claim to be developing the game and touching the world on the basis of unprecedented levels of economic resource. Its KPG-audited accounts for 2006 (the men's World Cup year marking the end of a FIFA four-year economic cycle) declared an income of US$749 million against expenses of US$500 million – at that point FIFA's richest ever year. Yet four years later this income was dwarfed, with the 2010 financial report indicating income of US$1291 million against expenses of US$1089 million. Reserves – "a solid level of reserves" noted the financial report – stood at US$1280 million. Overall in the 2007–2010 four-year cycle, revenue amounted to US $4189 million with expenditure of US$3558 million. That's US$631 million – and no doubt some loose change – left to play with in the interests of building the better future.[33]

This is a story of spectacular recovery from a financial crisis in 2001, when the agency and long-term FIFA partner International Sport and Leisure (ISL) went bankrupt. In April 2003, Blatter and FIFA secured a £329 million loan, offset against projected media and sponsorship rights for World Cup competitions, described by British journalist Nick Harris as "the deftest of juggles from a veteran schemer." For the cycle 1999–2002, FIFA could report that it was £55 million in the black, though in May 2002 FIFA's then-Finance Director Urs Linsi had been predicting a £100 million deficit for the period. Blatter pushed firmly on the rhetorical buttons:

> FIFA has proved that it can weather the stormiest circumstances ... .
> Aside from the two world wars in the last century, FIFA has just

endured the most difficult years in its history ... . We took immediate precautions entirely on our initiative to counteract the consequences. Now, FIFA is financially more stable than ever.[34]

And yet, particularly since the autumn of 2010, the higher echelons of the FIFA establishment have been under unprecedented levels of global scrutiny. As Blatter invoked more meteorological metaphors, of fading sunlight (football "cannot always have sunny days") and stormy seas, and talked of stabilizing the rocking ship,[35] the world, to which FIFA had been relatively unknown, looked on aghast. Blatter announced the setting up of a Solutions Committee, made up of veteran world fixer Dr Henry Kissinger, football legend Johann Cruyff and – FIFA frequently betters fiction – Spanish opera star Placido Domingo. "Make 'em laugh, make 'em laugh, make 'em laugh" was a showbiz phrase that came to mind as FIFA blundered on, with Blatter claiming his fourth presidential spell unopposed, hailing the biggest affirmative vote in the history of the organization's presidential election.

The FIFA mission is delivered and monitored from the Home of FIFA, opened in May 2006 and officially inaugurated a year later. It is a vast building, 134 meters in length, 41 metres in width and 12 metres high. Built at a cost of 240 million Swiss francs (US$256 million, £166 million), it lies at the heart of park-like grounds, with a ground level and two upper floors visible to the eye. The visitor is welcomed into the "head" of the building, with an extensive foyer offering seating for groups, and water pools reflecting the interplay of light with the grey or black Brazilian granite used throughout. Above the foyer is an auditorium holding more than 200 for press and media events, such as announcements or appearances by partners and sponsors; the building might be at the heart of a high-security operation for days, to ensure the safety of the McDonald's CEO as he makes his ten-minute pitch on the qualities of FIFA to a waiting world.

The president's and other management offices and ample and elegant lower-level conference rooms complete this part of the building. But there is more to the Home of FIFA than meets the eye: "2/3 of the Home of FIFA are below the surface," FIFA's celebratory brochure tells us.[36] The grounds around the building are themed, with plants from all of the continental federations represented in the park: "a mix of indigenous and exotic vegetation, mirroring the activities of FIFA as the world governing body and organiser of global sports events."[37]

In the underground level where the FIFA president presides over the ExCo a crystal chandelier shaped like a football stadium perimeter illuminates a *lapis lazuli* floor, at the centre of which is the foundation stone of the building; an oversized football within a concrete cube contains bags of earth from all of the countries of the member associations of FIFA. A meditation room next to this council chamber is constructed from shining onyx shell. The FIFA president and his executive and the standing committees conduct their business in an environment that would not be out of place in a Bond movie. At the Home of FIFA there is no doubt that "build a better future," that third pillar of the organization's mission, has been taken to heart as a guiding principle.

At FIFA's 63rd Congress in Mauritius in May 2013, Blatter reflected on his 15 years in power: "It has been my goal and my duty to improve what FIFA does and how we do it, making FIFA more transparent, more stable and more accountable."[38] He then claimed six achievements since 1998, when he won the presidency: FIFA World Cup rotation; annual financial auditing for FIFA and member associations; strict budgeting and payment control; an ethics committee, a Code of Ethics and robust Statutes; heavy and sustained investment for the development plans of all member associations; and an economic turnaround guaranteeing good financial health. Blatter presented this as if it were the materialization of a manifesto, a product of his prescient leadership, rather than a survivalist strategy forced upon a beleaguered and exposed regime. But no one in the Congress disputed the claims; and back in the Home of FIFA, in the deep-hewn underground levels, there would be plenty of opportunity and space to deal with the suppressed secrets and to continue to monitor, sift and classify documents and information. FIFA continues to be, despite Blatter's claims, widely unaccountable, and shaped and directed by the nature of its leadership. We return in more detail to the figure of Blatter, the nature of his presidential style and the sources of his sustained power base, in Chapter 4. First, we review in the next chapter the contribution, influence and impact of Blatter's predecessors.

Notes

1 David Hills, "Said & Done: FIFA: strict cost control," *Guardian*, 31 March 2012, http://www.theguardian.com/football/2012/mar/31/said-and-done-fifas-week, consulted 22 November 2013. This author's more recent estimate suggests an average salary of approximately US$136,000 for 510 staff.

2 *All About FIFA: Develop the Game, Touch the World, Build a Better Future* (Zurich: FIFA, January 2012), 7. This remained unchanged in 2014.

3 FIFA.com, "The Organisation: Mission and Statutes: FIFA Brand – Our commitment," http://www.fifa.com/aboutfifa/organisation/mission.html, consulted 14 January 2014.

4 Ibid.

5 FIFA, *FIFA Statutes: July 2013 Edition* (Zurich: FIFA, 2013), http://www.fifa. com/mm/document/AFFederation/Generic/02/14/97/88/FIFAStatuten2013_ E_Neutral.pdf, consulted 6 December 2013, s. 1, para. 1.

6 *Swiss Civil Code of 10 December 1907 (Status as of 1 January 2013)* (Berne: Federal Assembly of the Swiss Confederation), English translation, 18, http://www. admin.ch/ch/e/rs/2/210.en.pdf, consulted 23 June 2013.

7 FIFA, "FIFA Financial Report 2010: 61st FIFA Congress, Zurich, 31 May and 1 June 2011" (Zurich: FIFA, 2011), 65.

8 FIFA, "FIFA Financial Report 2012: 63rd FIFA Congress, Mauritius, 30 and 31 May 2013" (Zurich: FIFA, 2013), 85.

9 Personal communication with author, fax, 1 July 1997.

10 FIFA, "FIFA Financial Report 2010."

11 International Football Association Board, *125th Anniversary of the IFAB: 125th Annual General Meeting: International Football Association Board, FIFA/IFAB, 3 March 2012*, 16.

12 Ibid., 19.

13 International Football Association Board, *Minutes of the Annual Meeting Held at 22, Rue de Londres, Paris, on Saturday, 13th June 1925*. Consulted in the Minutes of the Football Association of Wales, Cardiff, Wales.

14 International Football Association Board, *Minutes of the Annual Meeting Held at Grand Hotel, St. Andrews, 12th June, 1926*. Consulted in the Minutes of the Football Association of Wales, Cardiff, Wales.

15 This detail on ExCo's membership is compiled from http://www.fifa.com/ aboutfifa/organisation/bodies/excoandemergency/index.html, consulted 22 June 2013.

16 American Samoa became affiliated to FIFA in 1998, enfranchised for the FIFA Congress at which Blatter was elected president. The United States protectorate lost a match to Australia 31–0 in 2001, a record score for an international football game. In late 2011, American Samoa achieved its first ever international victory, beating Tonga, also drawing with Cook Islands before losing 1–0 to Samoa in an Oceania tournament. A feature documentary about the record defeat, *Next Goal Wins* (2012), celebrated this underdog narrative, which forms part of the central dynamic of FIFA's operations. See Rob Bagchi, "Wonders of the island winners," *Observer (Sport)*, 27 November 2011, 8; and on the team's breakthrough run, see http://www.washingtonpost.com/sports/dcunited/samoa-wins-to-advance-in-world-cup-qualifying-ending-american-samoas-dream-run/ 2011/11/27/gIQAJrLg0N_story.html, consulted 30 November 2011.

17 For a profile of Chung, see OFC, "About OFC: President," http://www.ocean iafootball.com/ofc/AboutOFC/tabid/182/PageContentType/PRESIDENT/ language/en-US/Default.aspx, consulted 13 November 2011.

18 See FIFA, "Papua New Guinea," http://www.fifa.com/mm/goalproject/png_ eng.pdf, consulted 13 November 2011.

19 The *FIFA Code of Ethics: 2009 Edition* is quoted in this section. It is available at http://www.fifa.com/mm/document/affederation/administration/50/02/82/ efsdcodeofethics_web.pdf, consulted 26 November 2011.

20 This vignette is based on an interview with the author in Paris, 11 June 1998, and the BBC *Panorama* TV programme, "Fifa and Coe" (2007).

21 This vignette is based on an interview with the author in Abu Dhabi, 20 December 1996, and the BBC *Panorama* TV programme, "Fifa and Coe" (2007).

22 This section on Jack Warner is a summation of Alan Tomlinson, "Lord, don't stop the carnival: Trinidad and Tobago at the 2006 FIFA World Cup," *Journal of Sport & Social Issues*, 31/3, 2007: 259–282. See also Alan Tomlinson and John Sugden, "Once upon a time in Fifaland," *M People Trinidad*, 2, June 2011: 62–63.

23 Camps himself no doubt benefited from many of Warner's initiatives, and resigned his position in October 2011, so avoiding any investigation by FIFA in the wake of the bribery scandal preceding the FIFA presidential election earlier in the year. Staying loyal to Warner, he stated: "In him, I see a true leader, a true champion, a Caribbean man, one who was prepared to do whatever was required to keep the Caribbean flag flying with dignity and pride. ... To the very end, my friend and I remain committed to his inspired leadership." See "T&T FF president resigns in scandal row," *The Gleaner*, 30 October 2011, http://jamaica-gleaner.com/gleaner/20111030/sports/sports5.html, consulted 26 November 2011.

24 Michel Zen-Ruffinen, "STRICTLY CONFIDENTIAL – Presentation by the General Secretary (GS), Michel Zen-Ruffinen, FIFA EXCO – Meeting May 3, 2002, Zurich," 1121:Englpres.doc/2.5.02, 17.

25 By the spring and summer of 2013 an emboldened Trinidadian press was reporting Daryan Warner's arrest in Miami, USA, by the FBI, in relation to money-laundering offences and confederation business connected to FIFA events. It was claimed, though not established, that Daryan would give evidence against his father and others in order to reduce any potential jail sentence. The story was fuelled by a Reuters report; see Mark Hosenball, "Exclusive – FBI has cooperating witness for football fraud probe: sources," *Reuters*, 27 March 2013, http://uk.reuters.com/article/2013/03/27/uk-usa-fbi-soccer-idUKBRE92Q116 20130327, consulted 21 July 2013: "The New York-based FBI squad which is conducting the football investigation is a squad that specializes in 'Eurasian Organized Crime.' It is unclear why this particular squad is involved in the probe," the Reuters report observed. For the broader context see Andrew Jennings, "What I told the FBI about the FIFA crooks," *Transparency in Sport*, 27 March 2013, http://transparencyinsportblog.wordpress.com/2013/03/27/what-i-told-the-fbi-about-the-fifa-crooks, consulted 21 July 2013.

26 Zen-Ruffinen, "STRICTLY CONFIDENTIAL," 17.

27 FIFA, *Decision Ethics*, 110155 PRV TRI ZH, 29 May 2011.

28 Integrity Committee, "Report of Investigation," 18 April 2013, presented to Executive Committee of CONCACAF.

29 Ibid., viii.

30 Ibid., vii.

31 See Andrew Jennings, "Chuck's world of offshore bank accounts," 14 August 2011, http://www.transparencyinsport.org/Chucks_world_of_offshore_bank_accounts/chucks_world_of_ offshore_bank_accounts(page1).html, consulted 26 November 2011. Blazer had routinely channelled large sums from CONCACAF revenues into personal bank accounts in Grand Cayman and the Bahamas.

32 See Richard Conway, "Whistle-blower Chuck Blazer says Fifa must become more representative," BBC News, 7 October 2011, http://news.bbc.co.uk/sport1/hi/football/15222586.stm, consulted 26 November 2011.

33 FIFA, "FIFA Financial Report 2006: 57th FIFA Congress, Zurich, 30 and 31 May 2007" (Zurich: FIFA, 2007); FIFA, "FIFA Financial Report 2010: 61st FIFA Congress, Zurich, 31 May and 1 June 2011" (Zurich: FIFA, 2011).

34 Nick Harris, "Blatter secures Fifa's survival with £329m loan," *The Independent*, 9 April 2003, 24.
35 Blatter was speaking in Zurich, after his re-election to the presidency in June 2011.
36 FIFA, "Home of FIFA" (Zurich: FIFA, February 2010), 11.
37 Ibid., 15.
38 FIFA, "The President's address to Congress: 63rd FIFA Congress 2013, 30 and 31 May, Mauritius," http://www.fifa.com/mm/document/affederation/bodies/02/08/92/56/presidentaddresstofifacongress2013_neutral.pdf.

3   Leaders

Visiting FIFA in the Zurich suburb of Sonnenberg in mid-1996, I was shown around the "modern and functional FIFA House,"[1] opened in 1979 in Hitzigweg, just by Aurorostrasse (in English, "Street of the Sunrise"). Modern and functional it may have seemed a third of a century after its construction, but it is prime real estate and quite magnificent for its day. The building was inaugurated on the occasion of FIFA's 75th anniversary, also celebrating Dr João Havelange's first half-decade as president. It is set in an idyllic position, with a panoramic view of the city and the lake below, justifying its location on a street named after the rhythm of daily renewal. FIFA had moved up the hill to this exclusive residential and discreetly commercial neighbourhood in 1954, the year when Belgium's Rodolfe Seeldrayers succeeded Jules Rimet as president; for almost a quarter of a century, under the stewardship of Seeldrayers then Englishmen Arthur Drewry and Stanley Rous, FIFA had operated from a picturesque base there, in the Villa Derwald. There had been just eight employees at the Villa at the end of Rous's tenure. From 1974 onwards, though, an expanding employee base, to service the implementation of Havelange's manifesto commitments, prompted and justified the construction of FIFA House. Exponential growth in the FIFA administration, as FIFA expanded its projects and brought functions such as marketing in-house, necessitated a later move to a more expansive site at the edge of the city. Land was acquired from Credit Suisse in 2003; in the following year the long-established Adolf-Jöhr-Weg was renamed FIFA-Strasse, and excavation was begun for the 44,000 square metres of the property's surface area; the Home of FIFA was occupied two years later, in 2006.[2]

FIFA, nestling in two modest offices in Bahnhofstrasse in central Zurich for 20 years from 1932, grew to produce one of the city's iconic buildings; now, visitors follow the road or tramway to FIFA, well sign-posted along with the zoo, to find its grandiose HQ at the end of the line.[3] FIFA infrastructure has expanded to support the professional administration – in mid-2013, 380 in the Home of FIFA and 130 in FIFA House – for a globalizing organizational brief, and this has reflected the aspirations and the styles of the men who have led FIFA. It could be said that the move from the Bahnhofstrasse to the estate on the edge of the city have been vanity projects for particular styles of leader.

To trace the growth of FIFA is also to map seismic shifts in an increasingly global consumer economy, and within and across the constituencies of international sport, spanning the worldwide geopolitical landscape. Its transformation can be seen in the changing profile and projects of those who have led the organization. Following the historical overview of the birth and growth of the organization in the opening chapter, it is these men and the values that they have stood for that are the focus of this chapter. The first seven presidents of FIFA are portrayed, with a focus upon the three most influential: Jules Rimet, Stanley Rous and João Havelange.

The men who have dominated FIFA, its eight presidents, include three Englishmen who between them presided over the organization for 30 years, while the French president, Jules Rimet, held the position for 33 years. In the most expansive phase of the game and the organization, though, it was not a European who led FIFA, but the Brazilian Havelange. The presidents are:

Robert Guérin	France	1904–1906
Daniel Woolfall	England	1906–1918
Jules Rimet	France	1921–1954
Rodolphe Seeldrayers	Belgium	1954–1955
Arthur Drewry	England	1956–1961
Stanley Rous	England	1961–1974
João Havelange	Brazil	1974–1998
Joseph Blatter	Switzerland	1998–2015 (projected)

For the first 70 years of its life, then, FIFA was controlled by northern European administrators. Robert Guérin, the French inaugural president, resigned when his efforts to organize an international competition came to nothing, with no entries coming in by the deadline. Englishman Daniel (D.B.) Woolfall took over, with a clear mandate from the FA to uphold the values of the English game "as a pure sport" if it were to spread to the continent and beyond.[4] Woolfall was a civil servant from the northern English town of Blackburn, and had been a committee-based contributor to Blackburn Rovers's domination of the English FA Cup competition in the 1880s.[5] He led FIFA through a period of steady growth up until the end of World War I, but the disputes over sporting relations between "former enemy nations" led to ostracisms, resignations, the temporary dissolution of FIFA and the setting up (by Denmark, Finland, Norway, Sweden and Italy) of a new Federation of National Football Associations. Woolfall died in 1918, and FIFA emerged from the aftermath of the Great War with French lawyer Jules Rimet taking the position of provisional head in 1920, officially becoming president in 1921; his name was given to the World Cup trophy after the first World Cup tournament of 1930, and during his presidency the number of member associations grew from 20 or so to 85, and five World Cup tournaments took place.

This dramatic growth was consolidated during the presidencies of the Belgian Rodolphe Seeldrayers and the Englishmen Arthur Drewry and Sir Stanley Rous. The men who ran FIFA symbolized their eras, but they also impacted on and influenced, not merely reflected, their societies and their times. They warrant attention not based on any "great man" theory of history, but rather due to the recognition that "men make their own history, but they do not make it just as they please; they do not make it under circumstances chosen by themselves, but under circumstances directly encountered, given and transmitted from the past."[6] Rimet, Rous, Havelange and Blatter and the social and political relationships in which they have been embedded are indicative of the globalizing forces that have driven the world game, from the mid-twentieth century onwards.

FIFA's first two presidents established the foundations for the French and English domination of FIFA in its first 70 years. Guérin was an engineer and newspaper editor who did all he could to bring the English and the British into FIFA at the beginning, but with little success in the face of English arrogance and obduracy, as shown in Chapter 1. Woolfall, championing football excellence but rooted in amateur values, led FIFA's growth from seven members to 24 by the eve of World War I. These pioneers laid the foundation for the first of FIFA's patrician leaders, Jules Rimet.

The first patrician: Rimet spreads the word[7]

Rimet's great achievement was to truly internationalize FIFA, not least through the creation of the World Cup. Rimet was a self-made professional and religiously motivated social interventionist who dominated the growth of the international game. Trained in law, as an older man the bearded, bowler-hatted and thoroughly bourgeois-looking Rimet was an established figure among Parisian polite society. But he came from humble origins, born in 1873 into a modest family in rural France, and from an early age helped his father in the family's grocer's shop. A conscientious and able schoolboy, from the age of 11 he was raised in Paris, where his father had moved in search of work. He lived in the heart of the city, learning to survive and play football on the street and working ambitiously at school and in church. The young Rimet worked his way towards a full legal qualification, and was active in encouraging football among the poorer children of the city. He was a philanthropist for whom sport was a means of building good character.

Christian and patriotic, Rimet's love of God and nation came together in his passion for football. He believed in the universality of the church and saw in football the chance to create a worldwide "football family" welded to Christian principles. Like his countryman and founder of the modern Olympics Baron Pierre de Coubertin, Rimet believed that sport could be a force for national and international good. Sport and football could bring people and nations together in healthy competitiveness; sport could be a powerful means of both physical and moral progress, providing healthy pleasure and fun, and promoting friendship between races. His philosophy of sport was more egalitarian than de Coubertin's, though, and he promoted full-time professionalism as a form of meritocracy. In World War II his principles marginalized him in Vichy France, when he resigned from his position in charge of French football, opposed to the nationalization of the game implemented by the regime.

Despite his idealist commitment to internationalism, Rimet resisted the development of continental confederations and the empowerment of football confederations in Africa and Asia, being reluctant to loosen Europe's control of the world game. He did not believe that the administration of world football should be based on geographical or regional groupings. His consistent goal was to preserve FIFA as a family unit, and he argued that "decentralisation will destroy FIFA, only direct membership will retain FIFA as one family." He was traditional and conservative, but clever. As Rous recalled, elderly and inert committee members were useful to Rimet, who saw such "dead" committee men as preventing unnecessary change. The Rimet philosophy was reaffirmed in his opening address to the FIFA Congress in Rio in 1950, in which he listed four "finest human qualities" which football should impart. These were discipline, with the aim of achieving a common goal; loyalty to the spirit of the game; moderation in competition and sporting rivalry; and solidarity in clubs and games. He proposed that such ideal qualities be transferred from the game to everyday life. With one heart and one will, he preached, the world football family showed a "perfect unity that holds us together, the spiritual community to which we all adhere."[8] The speech expresses Rimet's vision:

World unity of football, the essential goal of FIFA, has been an accomplished fact: unity both moral and material ... . These results are not a matter of chance; they are the pursuit of voluntary action resolutely pursued, the consequence of the magnificent enthusiasm displayed by an elite of directing minds in all the national Associations, of the work, often obscure but always persistent, of the devoted moving spirits of large and small clubs, of the referees who put up with abuse because they have faith, and finally of the patient plodding of all, apostles and disciples, towards a common ideal that fully deserves to be held aloft.[9]

This is the language of the messianic visionary, linked to a sense of voluntarism as a form of vocation. The Rimet model of administrative leadership of the worldwide game would not be shared by newly independent nations, nor by his successors as president.

An Englishman abroad: Rous at the helm

Sir Stanley Rous was preceded as FIFA president by Belgian Rodolphe Seeldrayers and fellow Englishman Arthur Drewry. Belgian Seeldrayers was a veteran football diplomat who held the post for less than two years. He was, like Rimet, a lawyer, but he was also a classic all-round sportsman of the old school: a founder member of a prominent football club, a hockey international and a national champion in the 110-metre hurdles, and he had been president of both the Belgian Olympic Committee and the Belgian Football Association. Throughout his life he espoused the values of British athleticism.[10] Seeldrayers was very much a figure in the Rimet mould.

Arthur Drewry's tenure lasted five years. He was close to Rous, who at the time was secretary at the English FA and very much the power behind Drewry in international football administration. Drewry, a fish-processing businessman from Grimsby in Lincolnshire, was a faithful football administrator, president of the (English) Football League from 1949 to 1954[11] and, before that, chairman of the FA's International Selection Committee from 1944. In November 1945 he was, as chair of the FA's International Committee, with Rous in Switzerland, negotiating Britain's re-entry into FIFA, and was appointed vice-president of FIFA.

His background was in local football politics and administration. After service in the Middle East during World War I, Drewry had returned to Grimsby and married the daughter of Grimsby Town Football Club's chairman, beginning work in his father-in-law's fishing business. He became chairman of the Grimsby club in turn, and was increasingly involved in the administration of the English game and its international dimensions, through both the League and the FA. By now in his mid-sixties, Drewry left the League to become chairman of the FA in 1955, with Rous as secretary, and was soon moving on to succeed Seeldrayers as FIFA president. The Englishman defeated France's M. Lafarge by 38 votes to 16 for the position; Dutch, Italian and Chilean nominations withdrew in his favour, indicating the post-war alliances that England was able to make in FIFA.[12] He died, after a year-long illness, in March 1961.

Rous, although he did not assume the FIFA presidency until 1961, was already influential in the world game by the 1940s. He was secretary of the English Football Association from 1934 to 1961, and even though England was not a member of FIFA he retained relations with the world body.[13] Taking over at FIFA in his mid-sixties, he grasped the new challenge with typical energy and commitment. Walter Winterbottom, England's first manager, observed that "in our own country he took us out of being an insular Association Football League and got us back into world football and this was tremendous." Winterbottom also praised Rous's exceptional charm and diplomatic skills.[14]

A son of the lower middle classes (his father was a shopkeeper and merchant in the tiny village of Mutford, Suffolk, then in Norwich, Norfolk), Rous played football at school and while serving in the army during the Great War. He went on to study physical education and became a teacher. Hence he was not born into the establishment but through football became an establishment figure. For him, teaching and football were sources of personal pleasure, but also acts of public service. However distinguished Rous might look in his national and international activities later in life, he was a product of the opening up of education as potential source of social mobility.

Rous's commitment to education and to amateur ideals led him to a distinguished international refereeing career, and this is where he made his first impact on world football. His rewriting of the rules of the game in 1936/7 was immensely influential. In administration, he went on to modernize the English game, establishing a more efficient bureaucratic base, introducing teaching schemes for all levels of the game – coaching, playing, refereeing. But this mission was about more than just football. Britain was in crisis after World War II, losing an Empire and looking for a role. Educating football players as coaches, practitioners as educators, was one way of restoring British prominence in the world as well as in the world's most popular sport.

The FA had left FIFA in 1928 and Rous believed that it should be reintegrated into the world football family. In a paper presented to the

Football Association, first drafted in May 1943, he claimed that the activities of the FA's War Emergency Committee had boosted football's international profile by fostering relations with government departments and by establishing links with influential people through cooperation with the armed forces. "The unparallelled opportunities which the war years have given the Association of being of service to countries other than our own," he wrote, "have laid an excellent foundation for post-war international development."[15] Recognizing that Britain's formal political empire was about to shrink dramatically, Rous saw in football a chance to retain some influence over world culture.

Coming from the old world of the English lower middle class, but going on to negotiate a volatile world of post-colonialism, Rous's life and philosophy were a bundle of contradictions. He could be innovative and traditional, adventurous and cautious, modern and steeped in established values. These contradictions, and controversies over China, South Africa and Chile and Russia in particular were to be cleverly exploited by Havelange.[16] With World Cup finals looking increasingly lucrative, and emerging third-world nations wanting more representation in the world game and increased participation in the World Cup finals, Rous was to appear more and more old-world next to the visionary Brazilian. Even within Europe, Rous was viewed as too English: his home country strolled to its home-based World Cup victory in 1966, and an English FIFA president, Drewry, had been in place when Rous secured the 1966 World Cup finals.

One Swiss commentator saw this, and the culminating clinching of the cup, as far too cosy and collusive. In a fascinating document called "Thoughts on the 1966 World Championship" within FIFA's technical study of the event, the coach of the Swiss national team, Dr A. Foni, argued that top Latin American and European teams were favoured in their respective continents, meeting the weakest teams in opening games and having more rest between matches. In Chile in 1962, for instance, European teams had only 48 hours of rest between games, the Latin Americans recovering and preparing for a day more. Foni had some genuine complaints:

> Four years later the story was repeated in England, naturally with the necessary changes being made and, let me add, with a subtlety that worked still more … in favour of the host country.
>
> I mean simply that England won its victory with the last two games, but also that the premises for this victory were created well in advance: selection of a definite ground, longer breaks between games, decisions by referees that were slightly but very clearly favourable. It is very likely that English football, no doubt one of

the best in the world, did not need these little "nudges," but it is a fact that they were given, they were not refused.[17]

To raise the "moral and the athletic level of the World Cup," Foni proposed a more representative participation. The 1966 finals had offered just one place for a team from Africa and Asia, promoting a boycott by those confederations and a wildcard entry from North Korea. "The Jules Rimet Cup will have attained its aim only when the five continents are effectively represented – football probably being the most universal of all sports," prophesied Foni. Rous's response, in immaculate longhand, was "disappointed – unfair, shows himself partisan, attacks referees officials organisers, is *bitter* ... inaccurate, uninformed." But there was an objectivity to Foni's analysis – after all, England played all its games at the London stadium, Wembley – and it reflected widespread concern about presidential bias throughout the membership of FIFA, a concern that Rous was unwilling to recognize. The resentments of the football world would simmer throughout the years that followed.

When he stood for re-election as FIFA president in 1974, claiming that he wanted "just a couple of years to push through some important schemes," Rous had conceded too much ground to his young rival from Brazil. He stood on the basis of a misplaced confidence, having miscalculated the institutional politics of FIFA. Ten years on Rous put his defeat down to the limitless ambitions of his rival: "I know what activity was being practised by my successor, the appeals that he'd made to countries."[18] Rous, parvenu member of the fraternity of the MCC (Marylebone Cricket Club), of Wimbledon's All-England Club (tennis), and of the Hurlingham Club (polo), makes "appeals ... to countries" sound like a nasty disease.

Rous's recollections have some truth in them, as Havelange did run a ruthless and aggressive – even corrupt – campaign. But football administrators in the third world believed that Rous viewed them and their problems through the eyes of a British imperialist. Rous ran the world game with the concerned air of the reforming patrician schoolmaster, though paradoxically with a perceptive and realistic grasp of the need to modernize. In the years leading up to the 1974 election Rous could have sought to challenge and change the perceptions of him as out of touch and out of time, but he chose not to do so. Rous played what he saw as a fair match in the election campaign, but in the conclusion to his last-minute campaign brochure, in April 1974, he made it quite clear that he would not stoop to vulgar electioneering, emphasizing his belief in the "President's role as world ambassador for football," and playing up his honourable motives and style:

I can offer no special inducements to obtain support in my re-election nor have I canvassed for votes except through this communication. I prefer to let the record speak for itself. I have always played by the rules and respected the laws: I have administered them fearlessly and without favour on the field and off.[19]

Unfortunately for Rous, the needle was stuck on this particular postcolonial record, and the sounds were coming through too softly and too late. There were 122 votes available, and 37 of these were African. Many Asian friends of Rous's also sensed the tide turning. For all his respect for Sir Stanley's accomplishments, the young Peter Velappan, then secretary of the Malaysian football association, was one of those to take Rous by surprise. Velappan recalls that Rous's football credentials were beyond doubt, but "I think Sir Stanley did not take the election too seriously. He didn't believe in campaigning. But Dr Havelange and his people did a lot of groundwork, and specially promising Asia and Africa many benefits."[20]

It was a close-run contest, but Havelange edged over the required mark by 68 votes to 52 in a second ballot, put in place above all by the expectant Africans (who had pledged 37 votes) and Asians. Rous was shattered by this outcome. His secretary, Rose-Marie Breitenstein, recalled his response as "certainly one of deep upset, and in some senses as a betrayal."[21] The outcome also stunned his European colleagues. Letters of condolence poured in from figures in world sport administration, such as Lord Killanin of the International Olympic Committee, some referring to the "dark forces" underlying Havelange's electoral triumph. Also referred to was the £500,000 said to have been spent by Havelange on his campaign (equivalent to around £4 million in 2010 using the retail price index, or £6.5 million using average earnings).

Havelange had warned Rous of what was to come. He claims that he did not want at first to contest the presidency, but that those requesting that he do so "were very insistent." So Havelange then visited England to dine with Sir Stanley: "I told him that of the two of us there would be only one winner, and as I was originally a swimmer I told him there would be only one medal. Either I would win the medal, or he would win the medal. He put his arms around me, as a grandfather would a grandson, and I think he didn't believe it."[22] Rous, and he was far from alone in this, did not realize that in this historic moment the Grandfather was on the way out, the Godfather on the way in. The Havelange victory signalled a sea change in the affairs of FIFA as, largely through the intervention of African, in alliance with South American and some Asian countries, the balance of power in world football shifted from the northern to the southern hemisphere.

Havelange and the FIFA business model

In FIFA House in 1997 I was handed, hot from Rio de Janeiro, a glossy hagiography of the FIFA president Dr João Havelange. Entitled *Young Havelange*,[23] it was particularly revealing of the way in which Havelange generated deference. On the back cover of the book there are two portraits of the man: in one he stands, straight-backed and muscular, attired in single-piece, dark swimsuit, by a poolside in Rio de Janeiro, the matinee-idol athlete who competed at the Berlin Olympics; in the other, he hails the crowd and hosts inside a football stadium in Dublin in 1993, hands raised in Papal gesture, robed in a black Gestapo-style greatcoat. The text summarizes Havelange's charisma, charm and business acumen in wooing the bankers and burghers of Zurich on his accession to the presidency, gaining capital and planning permission to build FIFA House in the residential setting of Sonnenberg.

In the FIFA HQ, Havelange was talked of in hushed tones – always as "the President" – when talked about at all. I was told of how, when the phone goes in FIFA House and it's Havelange on the line, the backs of the FIFA apparatchiks straighten and stiffen. People stood erect and to attention. The man is in South America; the FIFA secretariat is in Europe. But when he's on the line, it's like a Royal visit. "Oui, Monsieur le Président," was the reported general response to any such call. No discussion, just the affirmative, and the reaffirming. FIFA House in Havelange's time became like a court of the Ancien Régime, though Havelange dispensed with the collective royal "we," and asserted the individualistic, autocratic and charismatic "I": "'I' give the World Cup to … ."

How did FIFA fall into the hands of this ambitious and sometimes ruthless man? The network of alliances that sustained his power base for almost a quarter of a century brought the interests of world football and global sport closer than ever to business and professional motives and outcomes. In this sense, Havelange can with good reason lay claim to having done most to shape the destiny of the world's most popular sport. He had the aura of the despot, and a physical presence and power that he was never slow to use in his presidential role. "Havelange had such an aura about him," commented vice-president David Will, a Scot: "people were actually physically scared of him, were frightened of him, in a one-to-one situation. He's devastating. His control of himself is amazing."[24] In 2006, during the men's World Cup, he ventured outside FIFA's luxury base in the Adlon Kempinski hotel by Berlin's Brandenburg Gate, walking with a companion. It was a cautious adventure, more focused on the luxury goods and jewellery in the hotel store windows than the fan culture in the streets or the upcoming football action, but the hauteur was intact, the confident swagger sustained in his ninety-first year.

Havelange recalls with relish and self-congratulation how he made his way in the world.[25] Son of a Belgian industrialist and arms trader, Jean-Marie Faustin Godefroid de Havelange was born on 8 May 1916 in Rio de Janeiro. He went to his father's arms company as a youngster and learned the rudiments of business administration. When João was 18 his father died, and he began working and studied part-time: "I wasn't earning very much, but I was learning something for life." He went on to build a business empire in the transport and financial industries of a modernizing Brazil. This involved, *Playboy* reported, dealing in the sale of "80,000 grenades to the government of Bolivia, under the command of the dictator Hugo Banza" in 1973 – the same year in which Havelange was charged with fraud as the head of the company Orewc.[26] He worked for an iron and steel company which had a Belgian link, before serving as a lawyer for a couple of years and then going on to become managing director of his own transport company. Early in life he decided that he could not work for anyone else; after working as an employee for six years, he went to the company boss and told him that he was resigning and never wanted to work for another boss in his life: "I have never had another boss in my life, except maybe my wife." In 1997 Havelange boasted that 20 million people a year were transported by his company, which he'd been with for 57 years (53 as chairman). He had also been the director of the biggest insurance company in Brazil: "When I became president of FIFA," he said, "I had to take a step down in that company."

The young Havelange was an athlete of some distinction. He had played junior football with Fluminense, the amateur sporting club for Brazil's elite. To belong to this club, it was necessary to belong to a family of means – which meant being white. Professionalism would later bring more opportunities for non-whites and also herald the end for mediocre upper-class footballers like Havelange. Not good enough to play alongside the talented professionals, he redirected his energies into swimming. From the mid-1930s to the early 1950s Havelange competed at the top, elite levels of his two chosen disciplines, representing Brazil in the Olympics in Berlin in 1936 in swimming and in Helsinki in 1952 in water polo. He said that "water polo served to discharge my aggressiveness and all my occasional ill humour" – it became a common boast of his that he swims every morning of his life.

Havelange's memories of the Hitler Olympics are extraordinary. "The first thing I remember is that the organisation of the transport was perfect, and the equipment and the facilities for 25,000 people were very well arranged." He remembers the convivial hospitality provided by the Nazis and the seven visits some athlete guests made to hear the 700 musicians playing in the Berlin Philharmonic. "From the start it was a pleasure to be in Berlin," Havelange recalled, and like many others he received the travel privileges that Hitler's and Goebbels's friends in the Olympic movement laid on. Trains could be booked at a 75 per cent discount, and the 20-year-old Havelange saw 25 different cities.

Returned from 1930s Germany, Havelange built up business and social contacts in Brazil's capital, São Paulo. Brazil declared war against Germany and Italy on 22 August 1942, but had a relatively quiet war. It joined the defence of the South Atlantic against Axis submarines and also sent an expeditionary force to Italy in 1944, which conducted itself courageously in several bloody engagements. Back home, the young entrepreneur sensed some real business openings in the transport industry. The state had taken over public transport and this would be re-privatized after the war. Brazil nuzzled up to the US during the war, giving it use of naval and air bases. In exchange, the two countries signed a number of agreements for economic development and for the production of Brazilian raw materials. With the state in temporary control of the economy and a black market thriving, it was a busy and productive war for a young businessman. The city government requisitioned the transport system, creating a municipal company. This was not to Havelange's liking, nor in line with his individualist market philosophy, but he was not slow to spot a business opportunity. In his own words, the post-war years were for him ones of opportunity for fighting government interference in the market: "Since I did not want to be a public servant, I and some friends founded the Viação Cometa in 1947." Highway construction was top of Brazil's post-war agenda of modernization, and from this foundation Havelange established a power base in national business networks. The sport world provided big-business contacts too. During his São Paulo years, Havelange had swum and played water polo at the Espéria rowing club, cultivating and consolidating friendships with some of the country's leading industrialists. From his mid-twenties onwards, he was displaying the qualities of the wheeler-dealer fixer that would serve him well for the following half-century, when he would combine sports and business networking and interests on an international scale.

In Havelange's view, a Brazilian pedigree made him an ideal candidate for FIFA's top job. "It was an advantage for me when I became president of FIFA," he says, "that since a small child I have lived together with all the different races and understood their mentalities. It is nothing new for me to be in FIFA's multi-racial environment ... . In São Paulo and Rio there are streets with Arabs living on one side and Jews on the other side and they live in the same street in perfect harmony." He points out that Brazil is the eighth industrial power in the world and that São Paulo is a city just like industrial Germany, yet Northern Brazil is less developed, a little like Africa. Havelange claims that Brazil is both a midpoint and microcosm of the world: a leader of the non-aligned nations with first-, second- and third-world features. With this self-image Havelange cleverly positions himself as representative of the advanced world as much as of the third world, and with an empathy for the whole world.

Trading on his achievements in the swimming pool and associated networks and contacts, in the late 1950s Havelange brought his business and administrative skills into Brazilian sport. His base in the Brazilian Sports Federation (the CBD), gave him authority over all the country's major sports, as well as football. "I brought with me the entrepreneurial skills, the business skills from my own company to the federation," he says, adding that he was the man behind Brazil's triple World Cup success: "There were just [sports] coaches, but I brought in specialist doctors, administrators for the federation to give it a wider basis. This is what made the difference and why we won the World Cup in 1958, 1962 and 1970." When he seized the reins of power in FIFA from Rous, he used his experience of restructuring football in Brazil, with an expanded national and regional league and cup set-up underpinned by commercial involvement, as a model for the expansion of the world game. He also went on to establish a long-term power base, via his son-in-law, in the Brazilian football federation.[27]

Once in the FIFA presidency, though, Havelange set about taking control of world football from its established northern European, Anglo-Saxon stronghold. To do this he would have to fulfil the commitments he had made to the developing world – especially Africa and Asia – during his election campaign. There were eight of these: an increase in the number of World Cup final teams from 16 to 24; the creation of a junior, under-20 World Championship; the construction of a new FIFA headquarters; the provision of materials to needy national associations; help in stadium development and improvement; more courses for professionals; medical and technical help; and the introduction of an intercontinental club championship.[28] Rous was no match for this manifesto, as Havelange's presidential victory confirmed.

When Havelange took over at FIFA, it was a modest operation with few personnel and negligible finances, fewer than a hundred member national associations, and a single tournament, in the form of the 16-nation World Cup finals. A quarter of a century later, when Havelange stepped down in Paris in 1998 on the eve of the first ever 32-nation senior competition, according to his own estimates FIFA had more than US$4 billion on its way into the coffers, and he reckoned football to be worth in the region of $250 billion annually as a global industry – way in excess of General Motors' $170 billion, as he liked to add. This huge expansion, including the addition of a series of world championships for youths and women, was achieved in partnership with transnational media partners and global business interests, including the giants Coca-Cola, Adidas and McDonald's – a revolution in the financing of world sport considered in Chapter 5. Towards the end of his time in power, Havelange listed the competitions that FIFA was by then staging, and summarized his achievements:

> For all of these 11 competitions, FIFA bears the cost of travelling, board, accommodation and local transport.
>
> Allow me to inform you that the principle for the evolution of industry lies in improvement and this also applies to football. Since I have been President of FIFA, which is now 22 years, we have organised courses for technical matters, refereeing courses, sports medicine courses as well as administration courses in every continent on a permanent basis, for the benefit of approximately 40,000 people. This is the reason for the global expansion of the game ... .
>
> Apart from that, the FIFA administration service may be considered perfect. The economic and financial situation due to the development which has taken place has been envied. Under the economic aspect, I would mention the buildings which have been constructed and acquired in favour of the continuity of football development. On the financial side we are, together with our sponsors, attaining such conditions which will permit us to reach all our aims.[29]

Five years later, as the collapse of partner ISL prompted a fiscal crisis for FIFA, the Havelange business model did not look quite so perfect. But when at the end of 1997 Havelange announced that he would not stand again as president, so fuelling endless speculation on his succession and giving Sepp Blatter plenty of time in which to plan his strategy, Havelange could bow out from the presidency with a sense of mission accomplished. With the help of his close ally and confidant, the late Horst Dassler of Adidas, Havelange had been the first in football to recognize fully the commercial potential of sport in the global market, and to open the game to the influences of new media and new markets.[30] He was also elected to the IOC in 1963, three years before Juan Antonio Samaranch, and along with Horst Dassler was influential in winning the IOC presidency for the Spaniard in 1980. In Guatemala City in 2007, an hour before the announcement of the host city for the 2014 Winter Olympics, Havelange was predicting that the winner would be Sochi, not the favourite Salzburg.[31] As David Miller carefully observes, "there are private agreements in these matters" trumping issues of the quality of bids, and involving powerbrokers such as Vladimir Putin, who could guarantee monumental budgets. These are the circles of power in which Havelange moved, a consummate political operator both within and beyond FIFA, acting in his own domain in autocratic style. Henry Kissinger, spokesman for the US's failed bid to host the 1986 World Cup, experienced Havelange's managerial style. "It made me feel nostalgic for the Middle East," he said. British sports minister Tony Banks declared in 1998 that compared with Westminster, the politics of FIFA in the Havelange era were "positively Byzantine."[32]

Former FIFA media director Guido Tognoni said that on a clear and sunny day "Havelange could make you believe that the sky was red when it was really blue."[33] People wondered at Havelange's almost supernatural powers of strength and concentration. "Havelange was a master of managing meetings," Tognoni recalled, "He was also a master of giving people the feeling that they are important without giving power away. He was just a master of power." There is a physically competitive side to Havelange's use of power. "He was always the toughest guy and even when he was tired he didn't want to stop the meetings," said Tognoni. "He was always fully informed about everything, whereas the members, they were not professionals, they had to eat what was served." After a reflective pause, Tognoni concluded that Havelange "had the power to do everything that he wanted." This power could be widely and profitably distributed; Havelange's football family included business and media magnates who stood to profit dramatically from football's commercial growth.

Havelange in his prime dispensed patronage and pledges of support to countries scrambling for the World Cup finals. Morocco and the USA were rival candidates to stage the event in 1994. Both countries fought to outdo each other's hospitality. Havelange enjoyed an audience with President Reagan in the White House and received the Grand Cordon Alaouite from King Hassan of Morocco. The FIFA president did not mark France out as a favourite in his early pronouncements on the race to host the 1998 finals. In late 1988 – within five months of receiving his Nobel Peace Prize nomination from the Swiss Football Association[34] – he praised Switzerland for its good transport network, telecommunications systems, hotel provision and stable currency. Havelange told the Swiss what they wanted to hear, that their country was "able to organise an outstanding World Cup as in 1954, but brought up to date." The stadia would require extensions and renovation, but "given the financial strength of the country," Havelange could see no problem there. But it was France that gained the finals, and Havelange himself a Légion d'honneur along the way.

One of Havelange's final ambitions was to organize an international "friendly" between Israel and the fledgling Palestinian state in New York, the seat of the United Nations, to show, in his words, "that football can succeed where politicians cannot." This was initiated by US Vice President Al Gore, who approached Havelange during the 1994 World Cup finals. Havelange recalls that Gore was "very upset" when the suggestion was not received with great enthusiasm, the FIFA boss initially saying, "No, we are a sport, we are not politics in that sense." Magnanimously, in his own telling, Havelange reconsidered, and through Prince Faisal of Saudi communicated with the Saudi King, Fahd, who "offered to give the Palestine Football Federation 100 million dollars to get them going. Now things have moved on and Palestine is a more clearly defined political entity."

Havelange, within a year, was seeking to arrange this game for the end of 1997. Palestine was accepted as a full FIFA member at the June 1998 Congress. It was a defining moment when a delegate carried Palestine's flag around the Equinox stadium, and it was welcomed along with a few other nations as one of the newest members of the FIFA family. There were few doubts as to where Palestine's vote would go in the election for the FIFA presidency later in the day.

FIFA claims to be non-commercial as well as democratic, an association based on ideals and not profits, with, as we have seen, non-commercial, almost charitable status under Swiss law. A FIFA document in 1984 claimed that Havelange was a "football magnate who combined the qualities of far-sightedness and openness, an entrepreneur in body and soul" who "in no time transformed an administration-oriented institution into a dynamic enterprise brimming with new ideas and the will to see them through, so that now the administration is managed in the form of a modern firm."[35] Guido Tognoni, though, said that "people say that he was leading FIFA like an industry – but he was leading FIFA like a private enterprise, like a proprietor." "As if he owned it?" I asked. "Yes, exactly," Tognoni replied.

Throughout Havelange's presidency, deals on the scale of the television rights for the World Cup finals of 2006 were completed without reference to FIFA's Executive Committee. David Will recalled, "It's depressing. I think we just have to keep chipping away at this. The first task is to have the committees properly chosen, and not to have committees packed with pay-offs. We don't know how the [2006 television] deal was made. We know the money and we know everything else." He sighed, "Per Omdal and I have seen the contracts, but we asked that the contracts be laid before the Executive Committee for final approval, and instead we were told at the Executive Committee that the contracts were signed that day."

So Havelange's self-proclaimed "perfection" has come at a price, exposing the world game to the pervasive intrusion of market forces, and handing power and influence to people who view football primarily as a source of profit and personal glory. Havelange has ridden a torrent of allegations concerning missing funds in the accounts of the Brazilian sports federation, bribes routinely paid to him and others during and beyond the years of his presidency, while seeking to keep his football empire together on the basis of the concept of the worldwide football family. Even as he planned for his retirement in 1998, he worked ceaselessly behind the scenes to ensure that the regime which he had installed at FIFA House would continue through the election of his hand-picked protégé, Joseph "Sepp" Blatter. The ambitious Havelange had moved quickly, noted the body's official history, giving

> FIFA truly international and universal dimensions. His first concern was a comprehensive, world-wide football development programme, which was pursued with the International Academies. As FIFA did not have the necessary financial means, the FIFA President implemented his vast experience and fantasy [the FIFA translation is in all likelihood a misrepresentation of "imagination"] as a businessman, in order to materialize these ambitious plans. With their great involvement in sports and their world-wide business interests, the Coca-Cola Company were very positive towards this idea and assumed the sponsorship of these projects.[36]

Havelange, with Blatter as his aide and ally, accomplished much of his agenda, but at a high ethical and moral price. In Chapter 7, the fraudulent economic practices of Havelange's presidency, which led to his withdrawal from both FIFA and IOC life membership, are covered in more detail.

But Havelange always believed that he did no wrong. Responding to criticism of his visit to Nigeria as dissident Ken Saro Wiwa was about to be executed, Havelange gave a comment stunningly revealing of his personal philosophy: "I don't want to make any comparisons with the Pope, but he is also criticised from time to time, and his reply is silence. I too am sometimes criticised, so explanations about such matters are superfluous."[37]

In the earlier days of FIFA, figures such as Rimet and Rous led world football as volunteers, as idealist missionaries. They both had modest backgrounds as grocers' children from rural settings, making their way in life through education and public service. Their successors were from far different backgrounds, in business, economics and marketing. The motives of the men who ran and made FIFA changed as the power base was transformed. In the last quarter of the twentieth century FIFA was developed into one of the most high-profile and lucrative businesses in the global consumer and cultural industry. The story of FIFA's expanded football family is a story of the values, ideals, goals and ambitions of its leaders; latterly, one of alliances between emerging cultural and political interests in the developing world and entrenched economic interests in the developed capitalist world. Credit for the making of the modern FIFA must go to Havelange, inheriting the visionary internationalism of Rous, and accomplishing most of his stated objectives. But a key question remains as to the acceptability of the means whereby those objectives were attained. Havelange's accomplishments were in part achieved with his on-the-whole faithful follower Blatter, and it is to the figure of Blatter that we now turn, to consider whether and how in his elevation from general secretary to president FIFA's objectives and the organizational *modus operandi* have been sustained.

Notes

1 FIFA Communications & Public Affairs Division, *All about FIFA: Develop the Game, Touch the World, Build a Better Future* (Zurich: FIFA, January 2012), 21.

2 Dr Adolf Jöhr (1878–1953) was a patron of the arts and chairman of Credit Suisse. Local architect Tilla Theus was commissioned to design the new building.

3 My observations on FIFA sites were updated in April 2013, when I spent several days within and around the two neighbourhoods, and in both the Home of FIFA and FIFA House, as a participant at the FIFA-supported conference "The Relevance and Impact of FIFA World Cups, 1930–2010, 24–27 April 2013." I am grateful to the organizers of the conference for their invitation and hospitality.

4 See Chapter 1.

5 See his obituary in the *Blackburn Times* (26 October 1918), http://www.cotton-town.org/page.cfm?pageid=4377&language=eng, consulted 29 November 2011.

6 Karl Marx, "The Eighteenth Brumaire of Louis Bonaparte" [1852], in Karl Marx and Frederick Engels, *Collected Works Volume II, 1851–1853* (London: Lawrence and Wishart, 1979), 103.

7 This discussion of Rimet draws on two main sources: J.-Y. Guillain, *La Coupe du Monde de football – L'oevre de Jules Rimet* (Paris: Editions Amphora, 1998); and Sir Stanley Rous's memoir, *Football Worlds: A Lifetime in Sport* (London: Faber and Faber, 1978). It also uses material reported in John Sugden and Alan Tomlinson,

Great Balls of Fire: How Big Money is Hijacking World Football (Edinburgh: Mainstream, 1999), Chapter 2. See also Alan Tomlinson, "FIFA and the men who made it," *Soccer and Society*, 1/1, 1999: 53–71.

8 Rous, *Football Worlds*, 131.

9 Ibid., 131.

10 See H. Guldemont and B. Deps, *100 ans de Football en Belgique* (Brussels: Union Royale Belge des Sociétés de Football Association, 1995), 19.

11 See Simon Inglis, *League Football and the Men who Made it* (London: Willow Books/Collins, 1988).

12 The outcome of this election is covered in "An interim report of the F.I.F.A. Congress held in Lisbon on 9 June, 1956," Reference Minute 13 of The Football Association Minutes of Council Meeting of 4 July, 1956, held at the Imperial Hotel, Blackpool.

13 See Peter J. Beck, *Scoring for Britain: International Football and International Politics 1900–1939* (London: Frank Cass, 1999), 244–246; and Peter J. Beck, "British football and FIFA, 1928–46: Going to war or peaceful co-existence?" paper presented at the British Society of Sports History Annual Conference, University of Brighton, Eastbourne campus, 31 March to 1 April, 1999, published as "Going to war, peaceful co-existence or virtual membership? British football and FIFA, 1928–46," *The International Journal of the History of Sport*, 17/1, 2000: 113–134.

14 Winterbottom was talking in a BBC radio tribute to Rous (see note 18 below), and in a personal interview with the author, 24 November 1996. This synopsis of Rous's background is based on Tomlinson, "FIFA and the men who made it" (see note 7 above). See also A. Pawson, "Rous, Sir Stanley Ford (1895–1986)," rev., *Oxford Dictionary of National Biography* (Oxford: Oxford University Press, 2004), http://www.oxforddnb.com/view/article/40150, consulted 29 November 2011, 23 April 2010; and for a full biography of Winterbottom, see Graham Morse, *Sir Walter Winterbottom: The Father of Modern English Football* (London: John Blake Publishing, 2013).

15 S. Rous, "Post-war development – a memorandum prepared by the War Emergency Committee for the Consideration of the Council," May 1943, and "Post-war development – an interim report," October 1944. Both these papers are in the minute books of the Football Association's Council.

16 See John Sugden and Alan Tomlinson, "Global power struggles in world football – FIFA and UEFA 1954–74, and their legacy," *The International Journal of the History of Sport*, 14/2, 1997: 1–25, and *FIFA and the Contest for World Football: Who Rules the Peoples' Game?* (Cambridge: Polity Press, 1998). Also, on Rous's South African struggles, Paul Darby, "Stanley Rous's 'own goal': Football politics, South Africa and the contest for the FIFA presidency in 1974," *Soccer and Society*, 9/2, 2008: 259–72.

17 This annotated document is in the Sir Stanley Rous papers, in the author's private collection.

18 BBC, *Sir Stanley Rous*, radio broadcast, BBC Radio 4, 23 April 1985 (a 90th birthday tribute).

19 "A Message from Sir Stanley Rous C.B.E. President of F.I.F.A." (London, April 1974), 10.

20 Interview with the author, Abu Dhabi, UAE, 17 December 1996.

21 Interview with the author, London, 22 October 1996; confirmed in discussions in 2005–2013.

22 David Mellor, *The Moguls*, radio broadcast, BBC Radio Five Live, 11 June 1996 (feature on Havelange).

23 E.J. Farah, ed., *Young Havelange: FIFA in the Third Millennium* (São Paulo: J.S. Propaganda, 1996).

24 Interview with the author, Brechin, Scotland, 9 October 1996.

25 This discussion of Havelange draws on: Sugden and Tomlinson, *FIFA and the Contest for World Football* and *Great Balls of Fire*; David Yallop, *How They Stole the Game* (London: Poetic Publishing, 1999); Farah, *Young Havelange*; and an interview with Havelange by the author and his co-researcher John Sugden in Cairo, Egypt, September 1997 (quotes in the section which are not otherwise referenced are from this interview).

26 Roberto Pereira de Souza, "O Poderoso Chefão" ("The Powerful Chief"), *Playboy* (Brazil), May 1994: 126–127.

27 Veteran Brazilian sports writer and journalist Juca Kfouri, referring to Havelange's son-in-law Ricardo Teixeira's presidency of the Brazilian football federation from 1989 to 2012, calls the federation "a fruit of engineering created by ... João Havelange, who ... has always socialized with dictators. He reproduces in FIFA what he does here ... . [H]e took his son-in-law, an unsuccessful and broken businessman, and put him in the presidency of the CBF, the national squad, and transforms it into the Brazilian football brand." Kfouri was talking to Oliver Kawase Seitz; see Seitz, "Made in Brasil: Placing the Football Industry in the Brazilian Environment," PhD thesis, University of Liverpool, UK, 2012, 173–174.

28 Havelange manifesto, author's private collection.

29 Letter to the author, dated 29 October 1996, from FIFA, Zurich.

30 See John Sugden and Alan Tomlinson, "FIFA and the marketing of world football," in *The Production and Consumption of Sport Cultures: Leisure, Culture and Commerce*, eds. Gill Lines, Ian McDonald and Udo Merkel (Eastbourne: Leisure Studies Association Publications, 1998).

31 See Alan Tomlinson, "The making – and unmaking? – of the Olympic corporate class," in *The Palgrave Handbook of Olympic Studies*, eds. Helen Lenskyj and Stephen Wagg (Basingstoke: Palgrave Macmillan, 2012); David Miller, *The Official History of the Olympic Games and the IOC, Athens to Beijing, 1894–2008* (Edinburgh: Mainstream Publishing, 2008), 411.

32 The late Tony Banks was speaking to a parliamentary select committee. See also his comment "Sports politics presents a Byzantine complexity that would have made Machiavelli take up macramé" (HC Debate 5 June 1998, c. 678, http://www.publications.parliament.uk/pa/cm199798/cmhansrd/vo980605/debtext/80605–18.htm, consulted 29 November 2011).

33 Interview with the author, Zurich, Switzerland, 21 May 1996.

34 *Sport Intern*, 9/19, 12 September 1988, 4, quoting a *Sunday Times* report.

35 FIFA, *History of FIFA: Fédération Internationale de Football Association Official History* (Zurich: FIFA, 1984), 26. This encomium was reiterated in Andreas Herren, ed., *90 Years of FIFA: 20 years of FIFA Presidency – João Havelange, Brazil, Elected 11 June 1974* (Zurich: FIFA Souvenir Edition, 1994), 4–6.

36 FIFA, *History of FIFA*.

37 Mellor, *The Moguls*.

4   The Supreme Leader

"As the supreme leader of FIFA, the President and his rights and duties are extensively dealt with in the FIFA Statutes."[1]

Groomed for power

Sepp Blatter has mastered the protocols of power in FIFA over a third of a century. When he emerged victorious in the battle for the FIFA presidency in June 1998,[2] he had persuaded enough African and European countries to vote for him to fracture the Europe–Africa alliance upon which UEFA president Lennart Johansson's candidature depended. Blatter's run–in to the election was masterfully organized, with the support of a Swiss commercial partner and a private jet provided by Qatar. Blatter prospered on the back of his longstanding working partnership with his boss at FIFA, João Havelange, and all of the infrastructure of FIFA that had aided his bid, long before he formally declared himself just a few months before the vote. The circumstances in which so many nations supported Blatter are shrouded in controversy,[3] but his campaigning strategy was so effective that he came out of the first ballot with 111 votes to Johansson's 80. The devastated Swede soon realized that there was little point in proceeding to a second ballot.

Havelange, with heavy irony allied to consummate diplomatic skill, praised the UEFA president as "sportsman, gentleman, leader and friend," whose "qualities and values" would help the football family enter the next century. Blatter hailed his defeated rival as "a great personality, fair and realistic" and pledged "to unite football" and establish "continuity in the good sense." "I am a servant of football," beamed Blatter. "I shall play, live and breathe football," he said, "I am deeply, deeply touched, deeply, and offer a message of friendship, openness, understanding, a message of solidarity." Blatter had learned well under Havelange's tutelage, and he understood football politics in Africa.

While Johansson busied himself working on the hierarchy of the African confederation, Blatter, often accompanied by Havelange, had visited Africa in a private jet, meeting with the representatives of some of the continent's remotest and poorest countries, making personal contact with the men in the national associations who would be marking the ballot cards in Paris in June. The strategy had worked for Havelange in 1974 and it worked again for Blatter in 1998.

Blatter was steeped in the world of international sports politics. He had business and administration experience as an organizer of the 1972 and 1976 Olympic Games. He had headed public relations for a Swiss tourist board in the 1960s, and had been general secretary of the Swiss ice hockey federation. As Director of Sports Timing and Public Relations at Longines, he was noticed by Adidas boss Horst Dassler. Dassler alerted Havelange to Blatter's qualities, and Havelange brought him into FIFA, where he worked on the implementation of Havelange's programme, attracting the funding needed from early commercial partners such as Coca-Cola and Adidas itself. Blatter rose quickly through FIFA's hierarchy, becoming general secretary in 1981, even marrying the former general secretary's daughter *en route* to his promotion to the top job in the FIFA administration.

It is critical for any informed and adequate understanding of Blatter's career to appreciate the scale of his commitment to Horst Dassler. Talking to BBC's *Newsnight* in 2002, Blatter insisted that the long-term ISL–FIFA relationship was good for the financial development of world football in the 1980s and into the 1990s, but conceded that "at the end it is not a sweetheart, definitely not, but at the time when they also came in, in television, it was a wonderful partnership for everybody and for the benefit of football, for the benefit of the associations."[4] He worked closely with Dassler himself, and not just Dassler's company ISL and its associates.

When speaking of Dassler, Blatter sounds in awe of his career mentor: "He was an extraordinary man, a man of courage, of initiative, a visionary, the father of sport sponsoring; a great salesman but also a great diplomat. He always knew how to fix things when there were differences."[5] Blatter was groomed at Adidas's Landersheim headquarters from August to December 1975, and then joined FIFA as technical director. Dassler and Adidas paid Blatter's salary in those early days, and provided office space for FIFA's new technical director. Guido Tognoni, FIFA press officer in the 1990s, confirms: "Blatter was partly paid by Adidas in the early days because FIFA did not have any money. Blatter says that he only had his office in the Adidas office, this was while FIFA was building a new one ... it was doubtful, strange, you can also hire your own office."[6] Not so strange to Blatter: "If we hadn't had Adidas, and Coca-Cola … we would never have entered the world of football with such a fantastic programme of development. I will never forget Adidas … without Adidas I think that FIFA would not be where she is today."[7]

At the launch of his presidential campaign Blatter claimed that football stands for basic education, shapes character and combative spirit, and fosters respect and discipline. It can make a valuable contribution to health, he added. And it's theatre, entertainment, art. "But, first and foremost," he told his audience, "it is an endless source of passion and excitement. It stirs the emotions and can move its enthusiasts to tears of joy or frustration like no other game and it is for everybody." Let football keep its human touch, its spirited play and its constant challenge, pleaded Blatter, "but above all its universality." The key word here is "universality," a piece of routinely reiterated humanitarian rhetoric in the Blatter armoury but also a veiled reference to the European base of Johansson's campaign. Blatter was nominated for the FIFA presidency by several national associations, initially by Jamaica and the USA. Others backing FIFA's insider candidate included countries from the Gulf and South America. He came out of early skirmishes in the 1998 election battle looking smarter and quicker on his political feet than his opponent Johansson. By the time his formal declaration was scheduled he had disarmed his critics by getting Havelange to announce that the Swiss was to stand and that "the General Secretary asked for dispensation from certain duties so as to avoid any possible conflict of interest – a request which complies with a wish expressed by the Executive Committee."

As the date of FIFA's first contested presidential election for a mite under a quarter of a century drew closer, the Euro–African alliance was looking increasingly fragile. Johansson had even offered to keep Blatter on as general secretary should he win, but Blatter, Johansson reported, turned him down point blank. Here was serious evidence of the Swiss's confidence. In his last presidential address Havelange said that he took his leave with indelible memories of "Sepp Blatter at my side for twenty-three years. I leave, with a clear conscience, the governing body of the world's, the planet's most popular sport." With his protégé in charge, Havelange would be close to the action for the foreseeable future, not leaving the governing body until April 2013, forced into resignation from his position as life president when a report confirmed his fraudulent financial practices when president. Until then, though, he was welcomed across his old empire, ensconced in the rhythm of FIFA events; he was in Berlin's elite, luxurious Adlon Kempinski hotel in June 2006, window-shopping on a careful perambulation of the building during a quiet spell in World Cup action. In the lobby, people still stood back from him in awe, his charismatic hold on FIFA personnel and officials scarcely diminished in his ninety-first year. For his troubles, he had still been receiving welcome chunks of monies from FIFA: US $55,000 in September 2001 for instance. There were no "apparent objective reasons for these transfers ... . It would rather appear that an attempt was made with these payments to buy or retain Mr Havelange's good will in order that he should provide the Accused (FIFA president Blatter) with as many votes as possible from South America for his re-election in 2002."[8]

In the Equinox hall in 1998, in the post-mortem on the result, questions were still being posed as to the nature of Blatter's victory. Mihir Bose of the *Daily Telegraph* asked Blatter: "Was your campaign corrupt? Is FIFA not clean?" Blatter's face tightened, his smile subsided. "The accounts were cleared in Congress," he snarled, "no questions were asked then." Where are my accusers, Blatter then asked: "It might become uncomfortable for anyone whose name you mention." The day after Blatter's election, Kenya's *Daily Nation* reported how grateful the Kenyan football federation was to former president Havelange for promising to pay team travel costs to an obscure regional tournament in Rwanda. Chairman of the federation, Peter Kenneth, said in Paris, "It has been a gruelling battle but in the final analysis we are proud to have been associated with the winning candidate."

"You've got the FIFA you want, you want this FIFA of corruption, that's what you've got. Get on with it," said one Executive Committee member to another, CONCACAF general secretary Chuck Blazer. The latter responded: "Sure it's all about money. Your side didn't spend enough money." The disillusioned Johansson, still in charge at UEFA, raised in the context of Swedish principles of democracy, transparency and solidarity, confirmed: "I have had enough. I would never again go for the FIFA presidency. I will never engage myself in such dirty business," though he recognized that "we must be prepared to fight against corruption and bribery and dishonest people. We must fight for fair play."[9]

Holding power

Once in power, new president Blatter moved swiftly to neutralize his opponents and enemies. Chairing his first ExCo meeting he dropped a controversial proposal to create a special bureau or board – an inner circle empowered to take decisions outside of the Executive Committee "to cope with FIFA's increasing volume of work." Johansson and his supporters would never have stood for this. Dr Josef Mifsud of Malta, a

UEFA-elected ExCo member, was at the meeting, and recalled that the idea of a permanent executive board was a proposed way of dealing more swiftly with issues: "nowadays things are going so fast that you have to react immediately and with promptness to certain problems that arise."[10] Mifsud recognized this need, but favoured the expansion of the role and activities of the ExCo. Cleverly, Blatter withdrew his proposal at the last minute, proposing instead to double the number of full ExCo meetings: Mifsud confirmed that there was no serious argument on this issue – members would have to jet in to world capitals twice as often now, for the continuing "good of the game" (FIFA's motto at the time); and accept double the expenses.

Blatter soon reshuffled the FIFA committees, too, giving his supporters key positions but also making sure that potential opponents were kept inside the FIFA family. Scot David Will, vice-president representing the British associations, was punished for his open commitment to Johansson by being removed as chair of the prestigious Referees and Legal Committees, and handed the grand-sounding but lower-profile Associations Committee. Blatter also proposed that for the first time ExCo members should be paid, in addition to receiving already generous expenses. He suggested US$50,000 a year; no committee members objected. Blatter formed no executive board, but nevertheless soon put in place his inner circle of special advisers, known as the F-Crew (according to the then-general secretary, this *Führensgruppe*, or leadership group, comprised marketing, legal, communications and personnel heads, with PA support), with whom he could conduct FIFA business without reference to the hundreds of elected officials on FIFA committees and in Congress, and also choose, whenever convenient, to bypass the general secretary.[11]

England had turned its back on the European alliance and publicly backed Blatter for the presidency, and had also tried to mobilize Wales and Northern Ireland in an attempt to discredit David Will, and so get the FA president, Keith Wiseman, onto the FIFA committee that would be voting for the World Cup finals 2006. This had involved a projected gift to the Welsh FA of more than £3 million. Trying to get into the corridors of power of world football, the English looked simultaneously naive and arrogant. Their attempts backfired, as the FA forced Wiseman and long-term chief executive Graham Kelly to resign. FIFA pursued no formal inquiry into the English initiatives, the new FIFA president asking no questions of any of his supporters in his triumphant campaign.

Blatter provided FIFA with continuity, but within his first year in power showed that he lacked the presidential gravitas of his Brazilian mentor. His suggestions that the World Cup be held every two years and his vigorous promotion of a World Club championship would be controversial issues. He accepted the invitation to become the International Olympic Committee's (IOC's) 108th member, in the wake of its expulsion of exposed corrupt members and its drive to clean up its act following bribery and voting scandals; Blatter was in one sense asked onto the IOC as a symbol of new levels of transparency. But most revealing was his lack of authority over the FIFA Congress. In Los Angeles in June 1999, the Asian delegation walked out in protest at not getting an extra place in the 2002 finals, to be co-hosted by South Korea and Japan. In July 2000, his favoured candidate for the staging of the 2006 World Cup, South Africa, lost his Executive Committee's vote to Germany, a triumph for a Johansson-backed Euro–Asian alliance. Despite this air of vulnerability, though, and the lack of his predecessor's charismatic authority, when it came to the re-elections of 2002, 2007 and 2011, Blatter displayed masterly control of his Congress, if not his ExCo.

After the media blitz that greeted FIFA's decision in December 2010 to award the 2018 and 2022 World Cups to Russia and Qatar respectively, amidst allegations of bribery and corruption and the expulsion of two ExCo members, the presidential election of 2011 was headline news across the world. Qatar's Mohamed Bin Hammam, president of the Asian federation, planned to challenge Blatter, but was suspended, along with CONCACAF president Jack Warner, when evidence emerged of his buying Caribbean votes for his planned challenge. Bin Hammam withdrew from the election, and Blatter got 186 votes with 17 abstentions. As the allegations multiplied and the suspensions, expulsions and resignations mounted, Blatter sidelined his opponents, went to his Congress, and received the highest number of votes ever cast for a FIFA presidential candidate.

Power at any price

In the surroundings of one of Rome's smartest hotels, on the morning of the 2009 UEFA Champions League Final between Barcelona and Manchester United, I asked veteran football marketing man Jürgen Lenz how, in the annals of football history and the pantheon of sport leaders and inspirational figures, he thought Blatter would be remembered.[12] Lenz had said before our meeting that he would not talk about FIFA; we had discussed fully the story of the remarkable growth of the UEFA Champions League, the marketing template for which he has been jointly responsible, and I did not ask him about FIFA the organizational body, but instead prompted him to give an evaluation of the time in power of his long-term colleague and acquaintance, Sepp Blatter. What was the FIFA president's primary achievement? There was a long pause, and then a little chuckle:

> I just had a somewhat devious thought … Blatter's achievement is that he has managed to stay in power despite, erm, quite a few tests of getting out. His first achievement is to get in. And his second achievement is to stay in. And he has figured it out – and it really is very simple – he has figured out how to get in and how to stay. Let me backtrack a little.

What, then, was the secret of the FIFA top man's success? "You're both, you and Blatter, products of Horst Dassler," I reminded him. Lenz responded:

> Yeh yeh, but completely different. I joined the company [ISL, International Sport and Leisure] as international marketing manager. Blatter was basically pushed onto Horst Dassler by Havelange, he's a technical guy. … FIFA basically didn't have any money. Horst offered to take him on and introduce him to the world of football, the world of sport but football in particular. So the background was completely different. I was hired, Sepp was hired from FIFA. I've known him for a long time, I've known that he was, he is, he's clever, he's one of the cleverest, not only in FIFA, but in the sports federation world. He smells an opportunity and he takes it. You must know – I was there but I wasn't involved – he offered to the UEFA executive if they supported him he would unseat Havelange, he basically asked the UEFA executive to help him in stabbing his own boss in the back. You have to take your hat off to someone who tried it.

Blatter pulled back from this ambitious and treacherous strategy at the 1994 World Cup in the USA, and then worked with Havelange to make himself a credible candidate for the 1998 election, once Havelange stated explicitly that he would not stand for a seventh presidential term. Lenz warmed to his theme:

> Now, this is my analysis. He then realized that if I have enough money and I can go out to the small, the smaller and insignificant members of FIFA, then I can consolidate my power, because they all have one vote. He realized that about 148 members are financially dependent on handouts.

Following the strategy that his mentor Havelange had used to beat Stanley Rous, Blatter saw that he needed to make these 148 member associations – or single individuals who represented them – dependent on him:

> Realizing that, then you are in power, and you stay in power. As long as you've got, he's got, Jack Warner with all those little Caribbean members in his bag; as long as he's got enough in Africa.

"Can you ever see Blatter retiring or withdrawing?" I asked. "Only in the horizontal," Lenz said wryly, but added, presciently, that "Blatter has used the most pragmatic approach ... and the next time is always more than that." In other words, it costs more and more to stay, for the dictator to buy his subjects' silence. This in part explains the role played by CONCACAF president Jack Warner in Mohamed Bin Hammam's foiled and failed challenge to Blatter for the presidency. Keeping your 148 dependents happy all of the time becomes an increasingly expensive business. They may turn to a higher bidder.

Blatter's cleverness, as Lenz calls it, is allied to a deep-rooted cunning, and an awareness of the power of the well-established political and organizational strategy of divide-and-rule. This is confirmed by former UEFA General Secretary Gerhard Aigner, at the helm of the European body's administration from 1989 to 2003.[13] Aigner watched closely as his long-term colleague, friend and UEFA president Lennart Johansson was defeated by Blatter in the vote to succeed Havelange in Paris in 1998. Johansson stayed at UEFA after this crushing blow to his "Vision" manifesto (reproduced in the Appendix to this book), leaving only when challenged and defeated by 27 votes to 23 in 2007 by Michel Platini, Blatter's running mate at the launch of his campaign to succeed Havelange. Aigner agreed, albeit with the wisdom of hindsight, that the 77-year-old Johansson should have retired years earlier, as the 1998 defeat hurt him, hit him hard: "From that moment on" Aigner says, "Blatter was dividing UEFA," exploiting the "double membership of the associations":

> They are members in UEFA, they are members in FIFA. So, who is constantly working in our garden? You can't control. He [Blatter] is telling them stories about UEFA, saying "UEFA's against you," to somebody who's no longer a member of a committee, "I know that they are against you." He created all the time problems.

Blatter, in Aigner's understandably Johansson-sympathetic view, planted Platini in UEFA:

Blatter had already arranged that Platini was elected in the UEFA ... committee – already done, from the FIFA. And Lennart could not get it under control ... . Lennart is someone who looks you in the eye and says let's agree on that, and for him the matter is settled. He wouldn't say I give you this, or that, if you do this. He doesn't do that.

From the depth of his experience, and on the basis of a lifetime's career watching Blatter's ascent and survival, Aigner implies that Blatter does do that.

Aigner's successor as chief executive officer (CEO) of UEFA, from 2004 to 2007, Lars-Christer Olsson, elaborates on the Blatter style.[14] I asked him how he would characterize FIFA–UEFA relations. He smiled, laughing a little: "You only need one word. Complicated." Communication and "exchange of views" between Blatter and the newly elected UEFA president Platini were now better than before, he emphasized, so his own observations were about the time of Johansson's presidential tenure at UEFA, when the organization was modelled on "a Swedish way of working ... always to invite others who even have different opinions to find a consensus, which is totally clashing with some of the Mediterranean ways of doing things." Johansson "was always trying to keep the door open to find common solutions, and he was cheated all the time":

> For example, there was an agreement that UEFA and FIFA should always act together when it comes to European Commission matters, and then you find out that the FIFA president has organised his own meetings behind the back of UEFA, and he never has informed anybody. And also the concrete example was in the year 2000 when we found out FIFA was on its way to sign an agreement with the Players' Union without having informed UEFA at all ... a lot of things like that happened behind our back.

The Swedish model, Olsson stressed, identified areas of responsibility, and promoted the principle of "proper delegation," particularly in relation to the work and interests of the continental confederations and their constituent national associations. He was emphatic about the crucial nature of this type of delegation and of taking appropriate action at the different levels of football administration across the world; the FIFA Club World Cup, which began in 2000, is "not really a competition. It has never worked and it never will."[15]

It might be argued that this is a Eurocentric view, which denies emerging leagues and national associations in less developed confederations the opportunity of contact with the world's best. But there is a compelling logic to Olsson's position, in that FIFA's domain is really that of global, international football, staging the competitions at world level for international teams, and, with the IFAB, overseeing the rules of the game; perhaps, too, regulating player transfer procedures, and the education of referees. I asked whether such a clear delegation of responsibilities has ever been achieved in the governance of the game: "No not really, because it's not in the interests of FIFA. It should have been in the interests of FIFA, because the organization would then be more efficient, or I would say effective … . [I]t was always the aim of Lennart [Johansson] to come to that kind of solution, but he never managed to get there."

Olsson made his own attempt to establish more transparent exchanges and practices between FIFA and UEFA, working with Urs Linsi, FIFA general secretary from 2002 to 2007:

> We really tried to do things together, tried to find common solutions, to support each other rather than compete. We would have found solutions, also accepted by the other confederations. But it was not in line with some people's views. There was a clash between the administration levels and the political levels.

This might be the cautious language of a quintessential administrative professional; what it really amounts to, though, is an illumination of Blatter's dictatorial style. Speaking with a cool analytical precision, Olsson expanded on this:

> He [Blatter] is an executive president. He has never had any ambition to be anything else. I had a lot of discussions with him and he said he wanted to talk to me because I was the CEO of UEFA and he was the CEO of FIFA, even when he was president. So he never saw himself as something else other than executive president.

"Do you think FIFA's lacked administrative stability?" I asked:

> Yes, because those on the top never allowed stability because, and this is where I think Sepp Blatter is a mastermind, I've never seen anybody who is as good as he is to manage individuals … . I don't like his charm, but a lot of women do, and plenty of men too. We are coming from totally different schools. He is more Machiavellian, Napoleon-orientated than I am. I am not saying that one is right and one is wrong, there are different ways of getting from A to B.

But I would never work in that kind of organization. You cannot have a president walking in one direction and a CEO walking 90 degrees. It will not work.

And in "that kind of organization" Blatter has dispensed with the services of administrators in ruthless fashion and charmed people into positions of vulnerability, mobilizing a rhetoric of inclusivity – the good of the football family – with close ally and rival alike. After I'd asked whether, for Olsson, Platini was too close to Blatter and FIFA for Olsson to have worked with him, Olsson describes the role of Blatter in crowbarring Platini into the UEFA presidency:

> If it wouldn't have been for Sepp Blatter, Platini would not have been elected UEFA president. He was installed in the Executive Committee on support from Sepp Blatter. The president of the French FA who was on the UEFA executive at the time was forced to leave and I'm sure that FIFA had an important role in that game, and he would not have been elected even if he was a member of the Executive Committee unless he'd had the full support of FIFA, not only the FIFA president but some of the FIFA administration. There were FIFA administration people travelling around Europe making the campaign for Platini. There were individual employees of FIFA travelling around together with Platini in European countries, and also moving on behalf of Platini to make his campaign tours, and promising associations rewards like getting a FIFA committee position. Blatter has been teaching him, but when it comes to the essence of things Platini has got his own views, a genuine belief in his own morals.

I asked whether Platini has a vision:

> I doubt it. He's got one kind of vision but it's based on a very limited sense of facts. He's absolutely no administration in any management whatsoever, never had any significant position in any boards, so this is where Sepp Blatter has had a lot of influence and I think that the FIFA president will always ask to be rewarded and that is the problem, because he put the UEFA president in place.

An unaccountable, dictatorial president stacking up favours and obligations in a gift and graft culture: this is a consistent picture of the Swiss model, as personified by Blatter. His charm can soften up opponents as he works his disingenuous ways, and Olsson, with a note of begrudging respect for Blatter, told of how Johansson was given the Blatter treatment in the build-up to the UEFA presidential election:

> We have had two meetings where Lennart has been talking to Blatter, when I was present, and asking him if he thought it was a good idea, for Lennart, to stand again. And Blatter said "Of course, I will support you, it's an excellent idea." And that was done twice, because I said to Lennart, "You should ask once more because I'm not so sure you will get the support," and he was actually asked by Blatter to stand. And that is of course because Blatter is clever because it would probably be better to have Lennart as an opponent to Platini than to have somebody else. When Blatter had made this promise to Lennart twice and then came out in Swiss newspapers saying "I'm supporting Platini" ... I thought, even if it's a political game where lots of things are happening, that's not decent. I don't agree to that kind of behaviour.

The former UEFA CEO's views are obviously framed by his UEFA experience and Swedish idealism, and he announced, after Blatter's betrayal of Johansson, that he would leave his post immediately should Johansson lose, a pledge that he honoured. He sees Platini's influence at UEFA as a reversion to the FIFA model, the CEO replaced by the old general secretary model, "moving the organization back to what it was in the early 1990s, which is the biggest risk for the future":

> Everybody knows you can't bribe UEFA. When you introduce an executive president and you start mixing the political set-up, committees and administration, you are also creating the first foundation for ... what you've had in FIFA all the time: it's always been the president or the general secretary making all the decisions, then you go to the committees to get the confirmation of what is already decided, things like that. So when you don't have a clear separation between the administrative part and the political part you lose the stability and you opt up for all kinds of things happening.

As Blatter's unopposed nomination for his fourth term produced a vote of acclamation at his re-election in June 2011, it was clear that his tactics were still, for the moment, working in his favour. The Supreme Leader can reign in Congress, but if his subjects disperse worldwide, they are open and vulnerable to even better offers. Supremacy is contingent and fragile, as even the arch survivor Blatter began to learn, when his hold on FIFA's executive, if not its Congress, began to unravel in the face of increasing media scrutiny and worldwide opprobrium, following mounting crises and allegations against prominent figures in the international football world. At its peak, Blatter's exercise of power has been masterful: his acolytes have been minions worthy of a place at the court of the Borgias.[16] He is surrounded by flatterers and hypocrites, supported by many who praise and some who would supplant him. A veteran of FIFA administration in the 1990s, in position at the time when Blatter gained power, but brutally dropped as the new FIFA supremo reshuffled the top positions on his re-election in 2002, confirms that Blatter is a workaholic obsessive, sometimes working and drinking alone in a deserted FIFA House at the weekend.[17]

FIFA employees report that they walk in fear of the communications control room at FIFA House or the Home of FIFA, and tell the story of Blatter entering the room for a meeting, saying "Do not worry, we are not bugged," then grinning: no one laughed. A former FIFA administrator recalls how his emails had been scrutinized and a couple of innocuous ones to his son and friends (in which he'd expressed some support for the English FA and commented on Zen-Ruffinen's dignified departure from FIFA), quoted back at him by Blatter, were given as the reason for his dismissal:

> Blatter sacked me on the spot. Friends and relatives were packing cases in my office until 10 at night. I had to be out, not let back in the next morning. I was left high and dry. I'd known this man for 30 years. Blatter changed. I told him that he couldn't be both a manager and a president, and he said nobody had ever said that to him before, and thanked me and hugged me. But he lost all sense of what honesty is. His definition of honesty became whatever he wanted, whatever worked for him. Blatter doesn't forgive. He's surrounded by sycophants who tell him just what he wants to hear. He doesn't listen to anybody unless they say what he wants. And he never forgives. It's a dreadful situation, and everyone's scared of Blatter. It's all so Machiavellian.[18]

In power, the despot or the Prince continues to be courted, but there was an air of desperation in Blatter's public image at the end of 2011. In November, as part of a charm offensive before the end-of-year ExCo meeting, his new PR and media adviser Walter de Gregorio arranged some interviews, and Blatter provoked a massive reaction, from Britain in particular, after stating that racism on the football pitch could be resolved by a handshake at the end of the game.[19] When David Bond of the BBC secured an exclusive interview with Blatter at FIFA HQ,[20] the

FIFA president appeared contrite, shaken by the torrent of critique that his comments had provoked. There was little of the manipulative charmer in the Supreme Leader's manner as Bond built up to the climax of his questioning. No smiles, no jokes, no temper, no threat; but a bout of impatience at the very end, when he reiterated that he still had the energy to deal with the unfinished business of his life's work: "I have got the power now and I will do it." Bond put it to Blatter that his comments on the racism question – Manchester United's Rio Ferdinand, Bond told Blatter, had in a tweet called Blatter an "out-of-touch buffoon" – had prompted widespread calls for his resignation: "I cannot, I cannot resign ... it would not be fair play and would not be compatible with my fighting spirit." Bond also pointed out that, though Blatter was seeking to present himself as "the great reformer," just a few days earlier FIFA had confirmed a lucrative commission for a company in which his nephew was employed. Blatter was visibly riled, asking why one should "penalise a company working with us for more than 10 years ... if they are better than the others ... . [I]t is against the interests of FIFA, there should be a little bit of fair play and understanding."

Blatter had politely corrected Bond on the remaining length of his tenure, but looked anxious for most of the interview, his hands coiled together and his brow tight. He spluttered a sort of apology, using the words "sorry" in relation to the impact and reception of "my very very unfortunate words" which "I deeply deeply regret." He nevertheless continued to play his Statute cards cleverly and accurately, though disingenuously, reminding Bond that "I am accountable to the Congress of FIFA," but that in relation to ExCo votes on World Cup hosting decisions for instance, even though collusion in voting blocs and strategies might become apparent, "I have no influence on members of the Executive Committee [who] are elected by nations."

Blatter regularly punctuated his apologies and proposals for reform and greater transparency with reassertions of his humanitarian mission: "I started my FIFA career in Africa 36 years ago. I will not stop until we have stamped out racism in football. My life is linked to football, my life is football. I'm still a development officer," working for the good of "the human race." Blatter has claimed this humanitarian mission for himself on numerous occasions. In 2002, he explained his personal gift of US $25,000 to African referee Bouchardeau, for information relating to allegations concerning vote-rigging at the 1998 election, as "money ... of my own pocket":

> I felt sorry for him because he said he had to leave his country. I have paid more for other people, they are in need. I am a generous

man, definitely I am … much money I spent on humanitarian works, personally. I live alone, I am alone, I have no family, so therefore I give a lot of money to humanitarian community. I have committed some errors. If you work a lot you commit some errors. But I am not in corruption and I am not what you say, mismanagement.[21]

Blatter's desperate tone in his one-to-one with the BBC's Bond almost a decade later was tinged with an air of melancholy, which surrounded the beleaguered Blatter in the early phase of his fourth term. I suggested this to Lars-Christer Olsson: "You're absolutely right. I think he's quite lonely. The day the lights go out, he won't have many friends."

Notes

1 FIFA, "FACT Sheet: The eight Presidents," FS-110_01E_Presidency.DOC 09/ 07, 1, http://www.fifa.com/mm/document/fifafacts/organisation/52/00/03/fs-110_01e_presidency.pdf, consulted 27 November 2011.
2 Discussion of Blatter's initial presidential triumph is based upon my personal observation of and notes on his launch event for his candidature at the head-quarters of the French Olympic Committee, his presentations and responses during the FIFA Congress in Paris on 8 June 1998, and his networking and presidential style at various hotels, stadia and functions throughout the 1998 World Cup finals tournament. The chapter is also informed by my continued monitoring of his style and impact from this first year of presidential office through to the FIFA congress in Mauritius, in May 2013. I am grateful, too, to Andrew Jennings, Clare Sambrook and John Sugden for responses that have been incorporated into some of the material in this chapter, elements of which were first published in John Sugden and Alan Tomlinson, *Great Balls of Fire: How Big Money is Hijacking World Football* (Edinburgh: Mainstream Publishing, 1999); John Sugden and Alan Tomlinson, *Badfellas: FIFA Family at War* (Edinburgh: Mainstream Publishing, 2003).
3 See David Yallop, *How They Stole the Game* (London: Poetic Publishing, 1999); and John Sugden and Alan Tomlinson, *Great Balls of Fire*.
4 BBC, *Newsnight*, TV broadcast, 22 and 29 May 2002.
5 ITV (Independent Television) rushes of interview with Blatter, in the Adidas Club in Paris during World Cup 1998.
6 Interview with author, Zurich, Switzerland, 21 May 1996.
7 ITV rushes (see note 5).
8 See paragrah 48 of papers delivered by hand to the Public Prosecutor's Office, Zurich, 10 May 2002, based on evidence accumulated by FIFA general secretary Michel Zen-Ruffinen.
9 Alan Bairner and Paul Darby, "The Swedish model and international sport: Lennart Johansson and the governance of world football," *International Review for the Sociology of Sport*, 36/3, 2001: 337–359, 355.
10 Interview with author, Paris, France, 11 June 1998.
11 The composition of this group was divulged in Michel Zen-Ruffinen's documentation prepared for the FIFA ExCo meeting of 3 May 2002. See also

Sugden and Tomlinson, *Badfellas*, 29–31. Later the same month, Blatter stated that the F-Crew, or group, comprised himself, the general secretary (Zen-Ruffinen himself), the director of finance and a PA support staff member (BBC *Newsnight*; see note 4).

12 Interview with the author, Rome, Italy, 27 May 2009.

13 Interview with the author, Nyon, Switzerland, 6 November 2008.

14 Interview with the author, Nyon, Switzerland, 24 April 2008.

15 The internecine politics of such developments was highlighted in the controversy surrounding the inaugural event in Brazil, when Manchester United, as champion club of Europe, was all but ordered to represent England, and so had to withdraw from the FA Cup. The (English) FA was insistent about this, as part of its sycophantic strategy in bidding to FIFA for the 2006 World Cup. Manchester United manager Alex Ferguson confirmed that the trip to Brazil was undertaken under considerable pressure from the FA, the 2006 England World Cup bid team, and the UK government. Later that year, England's bid was brushed aside in the first round of voting. See Sugden and Tomlinson, *Badfellas*, Chapter 13, "Bidding Wars."

16 Rodrigo Borgia came to power as Pope Alexander VI in 1492, and his family name became a byword for European Renaissance power and ruthlessness: "the name of Borgia is symbolic of all that is reckoned corrupt and criminal in the church of the fifteenth century" (from Geoffrey Parker's introduction in Johann Burchard, edited and translated by Geoffrey Parker, *At the Court of the Borgia, being an Account of the Reign of Pope Alexander VI written by his Master of Ceremonies Johann Burchard* (London: Folio Society, 1963), 7). Machiavelli, as a Florentine diplomat, was ambassador to Cesare Borgia in 1502 and 1503, and took him as a model for the ruthless leader, as portrayed in *The Prince*. Cesare "acted without moral compunction in using murder, conspiracy and treachery to achieve his own ends" (Burchard, *At the Court of the Borgia*, 27).

17 Interview with the author, Nyon, Switzerland, 24 September 2004. I asked my source whether Blatter appeared lonely in his post: "Lonely! Let me tell you, in the days just before email was really the big thing he used to have a weekend rota to check faxes, to sort out urgent ones and just keep an eye open for important things. Well one Sunday when it was my turn I went in and sorted the faxes and there was an urgent one so I thought I'd put it as usual on Sepp's desk. I went over to his office and out of habit I knocked and walked in, and there he was. It was a glorious Sunday sunny afternoon in Summer, and there was Blatter sipping a glass of whisky, office blinds down, watching a crappy French game show on television."

18 Interview with the author, Manchester, 28 May 2003.

19 Al Jazeera English, "Sepp Blatter interview in full," video, 16 November 2011, http://www.youtube.com/watch?v=SEWVQHW8UoY, consulted 17 November 2011.

20 BBC, "Blatter tells BBC he is sorry," video, 18 November 2011, http://www.bbc.co.uk/news/world-15791432, consulted 27 November 2011.

21 BBC, *Newsnight*, (see note 4).

5 Moneyspinners

Noting a "confusing breadth of ... interlocking interests" with reference to multinational commercial organizations and their relationships with national and international sport federations, the UK's 1983 Howell Report recommended that the "International Assembly of National Organisations of Sport, in cooperation with the General Association of International Sports Federations, should accept responsibility for monitoring and enforcing the application of high ethical standards in areas of international sports sponsorship."[1] Lord Howell's committee also noted the "spectacular success" of the recently formed sport marketing company ISL, one of whose clients was the sport product company Adidas.[2] These "interlocking interests" and financial involvements led Howell's committee to recommend consideration (by which it really meant investigative scrutiny) of the financial dynamics of the sport–sponsor relation, "in order to ensure that such involvement is compatible with the interests of international sport."[3] There are two premises underlying these recommendations, which are made in the chapter entitled "Ethical Considerations": first, that the emerging political economy of international high-performance sport should operate with some sense if not code of ethics; and second, that there are "interests of international sport" that may be in need of protection. Unfortunately for the traditionalists of the Howell committee, the FIFA of João Havelange and Sepp Blatter showed no interest in even a basic sense of ethical morality or conscience, nor in a traditional, implicit conception of international sport's "interests." Not until he was compelled to introduce some organizational reforms three decades later would Blatter accept the introduction of an ethics committee into the FIFA institutional structure. In this chapter we show how FIFA and it partners developed in the early Havelange and Blatter years, taking international football into the heart of the global media and consumer markets.

Football was becoming, from the middle of the twentieth century, an unprecedentedly valuable asset in expanding media markets. Within

FIFA's most prominent confederation partner, UEFA, relations with the press, broadcasting and television constituted an intensifying challenge, with "great public interest in international competitions" such as UEFA's Nations' Cup, Champion Clubs' Cup, and Cup Winners' Cup. In 1965 the UEFA general secretary, Hans Bangerter, asked how "these powerful media could best be employed to serve the game."[4] He argued that the expert correspondent or commentator should act as guide or instructor, "educating the public" on, for instance, interpretation of the laws of the game; that commentators should be sensitive to players, and had a responsibility to censure gamesmanship. The reporter was portrayed as a moral agent, a communicator with the capacity to convert the unconverted to the values of the game:

> The football correspondents and radio and television commentators have the possibility to keep older and younger generations away from pubs, bars, dancings, teddy-boy mobs and other unhealthy entertainments of modern life, and to engage them in active sports, which is certainly a most important and gratifying mission.[5]

Over the following 30 years such traditional concerns about the effects of consumer, youth and media culture were to give way to a much more realistic and profitable appraisal of the impact of television on the game. Bangerter had joined FIFA as Kurt Gassmann's assistant general secretary at the age of 29, while Rimet was still president, and went on to join and lead UEFA as general secretary in 1959, five years after the formation of the European football union.[6] Recalling the transformation of the sport, he said that when he left FIFA it had only four employees, and on his arrival UEFA had the same number. He conceded he had underestimated the power of television to bring benefits to sport, and recognized that the world must change, but he sustained a romantic's view: "Sport must remain sport, and it must not fall down into showbusiness; when I was in charge at UEFA it was 75 per cent football, and 25 per cent business, money, and now it's the opposite, a total change." As part of this total change, the football–television relationship was becoming much more the concern of the lawyers and the accountants, rather than the educationists or idealistic volunteer officials. Bangerter recognized this with a fatalistic smile, while reliving his own contribution to an earlier phase of modernization of world football.

Bangerter mourns the passing of a more innocent model. Planned with the precision of a military operation, the orchestration of the twenty-first-century sporting spectacle now aspires to structure the environment of the football game, and to control the cultural presentation of the event. It is a science of event management which goes way beyond the objective, technical transmission of the sporting occasion, and seeks also to control the most minute details in the wider context of the event and the interests of its partners. The construction and presentation of the game as a valuable and sought-after commodity has produced a colourful and glamorous, though standardized and ruthlessly mediated, spectacle: "The SPECTACLE is *capital* accumulated to the point where it becomes image."[7] Control of the image, by media organizations and corporate sponsors, has become a highly valued skill within the cultural industries. The genesis of this cultural–economic model lay in the recognition of the growing scale of the television market.

World Cup television rights

World Cup finals provide some of the largest television audiences of all time, and on Havelange's election to the presidency exploitation of the expanding broadcast market became central to FIFA's business plan. At the beginning of 1974, *FIFA News* reported that more than 2100 press reporters, 750 photographers and 1200 radio and television reporters had applied for accreditation to cover that year's finals in West Germany.[8] The press and photographer applications came from 66 countries across five continents. Of those approved, Germany and Brazil had the largest contingents. On the eve of the World Cup, Rous wrote a piece on FIFA and made no mention of television, its potential and its problems.[9] But this was his last World Cup as president and the broadcasting landscape was about to change dramatically. By the men's World Cup in Germany in 2006, numbers had more than quadrupled, and the hosts had to welcome and accommodate 18,850 media professionals.[10]

In July 1976 in Montreal, during the city's disastrous Olympic year, Havelange was securing an unanticipated deal for worldwide transmission of the finals; for Argentina 1978 the sum was DM25 million (German Deutschmarks), in a contract with the European Broadcasting Union (paying 31 per cent) the International Radio and Television Organisation (paying 16 per cent) and host regional broadcaster the Organization of Iberoamerican Television (paying 53 per cent).[11] Eleven years later, in 1987, Havelange dedicated his editorial in *FIFA News* to the issue of television, a statement of the recognition of its importance, and an announcement of FIFA's long-term partnership with the television industry.[12] The editorial opened with a nostalgic recollection of the first occasion on which World Cup football was seen on television, "when young Pelé was demonstrating his football skills," and contrasted those days of television as a luxury and an adventure with the technical advances which could relay "the virtuosity of a Diego Maradona" to viewers all over the world. Havelange expressed his view of the reciprocal benefits of the relationship, for FIFA and its "equally competent and loyal partners" in television:

> Last June, people in 160 different countries watched the final between Argentina and the Federal Republic of Germany: surveys have shown that an estimated 580 million viewers were watching.
> These figures reflect, on the one hand, the fascination of football and, on the other, the results of television's superlative contribution. The world's number 1 sport and the most prominent means of communication became partners during the so-called "television age." Each of these partners has contributed to the success of the other.[13]

FIFA's obligation in promoting world football, Havelange continued, is to provide the best possible television service, "from the qualitative and quantitative point of view." Though in 1986 FIFA had received very attractive bids for forthcoming rights from private television companies, it decided to continue working with the European Broadcasting Union for the following three World Cups, the first time such rights had been sold on such a long-term basis:

> In view of its positive experience, FIFA has decided to conclude contracts not only for the next World Cup Final Competition but also for the 1994 and 1998 competitions at the same time. FIFA is convinced that the best possible broadcasting coverage for the next World Cup Competitions has thus been assured, FIFA will receive a total of Sfr. 340 million from the consortium for the broadcasting rights of all three World Cup Final competitions.[14]

This cumulative figure was broken down by former FIFA media officer Guido Tognoni into 95 million Swiss francs for 1990, 115 million for 1994 and 130 million for 1998.[15] Critics of Havelange have said that it was unwise and poor business to grant the rights for such a long period, and Tognoni commented that the 1987 figure was very good for the 1990 event, but would have been much higher with separately negotiated deals for 1994 and 1998. Whatever the business sense or otherwise of the three-event deal, it undeniably ensured the stability of FIFA finances, as Havelange himself asserted. In his editorial for the December 1987 *FIFA News*, Havelange justified this strategy as "a policy of continuity and stability with our former partners," assuring "FIFA's financial existence into the 21st century."

Coca-Cola sponsorship monies had helped launch Havelange's 1974 development programme. Television money stabilized FIFA finances, based on the ever more attractive and money-spinning event of the World Cup Finals. Guido Tognoni described the critical importance of TV money to FIFA, and the simplicity of the money-making process, once the television industry had recognized the almost limitless potential of football's cross-cultural appeal and of its biggest international event:

FIFA has never a problem finance-wise, it's a monopoly enterprise, the money is always there. Maybe sometimes you put some money in a bad place but everything is under control, you had not to work for money you have to work for an idea. This is something beautiful ... in FIFA you have not to sell product, product is a self-seller.

FIFA is living from one event, which is the World Cup, and this event is living from marketing and television receipts, television money, and marketing money. Marketing money is only possible thanks to television, but it was not Havelange who invented television, it was not Blatter who invented television, it was not you and me who invented television, and made all this dream of money floating. It was the time, starting in the 70s, where television got important then somebody invented publicity on television, the Dassler boards you know ... .

Then in the 80s it started to explode, the money, and this is not the merit of Havelange and not the merit of Blatter, it is the merit of the circumstances of the time. In the monopoly sport like football [where] you have all the rights, then you can also praise yourself that you have done a lot of work for FIFA. I mean, Sir Stanley, he was president during a time when it was much more difficult to manage an international federation, and the people before they deserve a big respect. Havelange also deserves some respect, but he did not invent TV. He was just the right man at the right place in the right moment. And the moment was important, more than the players and the men, the moment was the moment when television grew and television made everything possible.[16]

Havelange was the ideal man for such a moment, though – for FIFA, football, partners and associates, and himself. His business links, personal networks and dictatorial leadership style meant that the moment was right for the man and vice versa. By the time of the 1994 World Cup in the USA, FIFA could report that more than 3 billion viewers had followed the event, across 188 different territories, with a global reach as follows: Europe, 51; Middle East, 16; Asia Pacific, 29; Africa, 44; North America, 2; South and Central America, 19; Caribbean, 18; Others, 9.[17]

By the mid-1990s, FIFA reported the football–television relationship as being more tempestuous, due to the presence of "new factors in an elusive equation."[18] The major new factor was the "boom in satellite television," transmitting games involving the top teams to all corners of the world, and making local or national coverage less attractive to broadcasters. Economically, too, the FIFA report notes, the television boom could have perverse effects: "while TV rights change hands for ever more colossal sums at the top of the football pyramid in Europe, the smaller countries, far from being able to capitalise on the knock-on effect of the sport's TV popularity, are often obliged to pay their national network to cover the local action to a neo-discerning public."[19] Perverse or not, this did not stimulate FIFA to downplay the auction for the 2002 and 2006 rights just a few months later.

Television rights, as for the Olympics and the IOC, have therefore become the biggest part of FIFA's income stream and regular revenue. The television rights worldwide, excepting the USA, for the 2002 and 2006 World Cups were awarded in 1996 after consideration of seven bids. These included Mark McCormack's IMG, and TEAM Marketing. Other offers were received from ABC Television (USA, owner of the cable network ESPN), Cable TV (Hong Kong) and CWL (Switzerland). The European Broadcasting Union also coordinated an international consortium which placed a bid of more than £1 billion: "This consortium holds the current contract for World Cup TV rights for the 1998 World Cup in France. The consortium's agreement with FIFA also covered the 1990 and 1994 World Cup finals and includes a provision for priority negotiations, which have been continuing since last December," FIFA stated in a media release of 15 May 1996. Priority negotiations recognize a preferred candidate, should the working relationship with an incumbent go smoothly and produce satisfaction on both sides; but such an arrangement can also weaken the negotiating position of the incumbent. The 1998 worldwide rights had been valued at 130 million Swiss francs; this figure was expected to be far exceeded in the new agreement for 2002 and 2006, and the EBU's "priority negotiations" were in practice a hindrance rather than a help, involving the early revelation of its thinking. FIFA's Blatter added, on the day bids closed: "It is clear that the rights for 2002, wherever the event is held, will show a substantial increase over the current contract. FIFA is very gratified by the interest shown in the World Cup by so many prominent companies." Rupert Murdoch's News Corporation/Sky Television was not one of these, reputedly due to "widespread scepticism about the bidding process."[20] The successful bid came from an alliance of FIFA's long-term marketing partner ISL, in Switzerland, and German entrepreneur Leo Kirch's media conglomerate.

Kirch could add World Cup football to his interests in film rights and pay-TV, his 35 per cent stake in the Axel Springer publishing group, including Germany's top tabloid *Bild*, his stakes in seven German radio stations, the Sat 1 private TV channel and four other television channels. His interests in digital development were shown by his partnership with Silvio Berlusconi in Italy.[21]

The ISL/Kirch bid was worth £1.45 billion, comprising £650 million for the 2002 finals and £800 million for 2006. This enabled ISL/Kirsch to auction World Cup coverage worldwide, but FIFA retained a power of veto, which General Secretary Sepp Blatter argued would be used to guarantee that the World Cup should "remain accessible to viewers who do not possess expensive satellite or cable systems."[22] This worthy sentiment was not likely to have been shared by the media moguls, to whom a deregulated and fragmented sports media market meant more pricing options:

> Their interest comes not just from the bucketfuls of cash from advertisers and subscribers, but from the stratospheric income potential of the next generation of TV technology, with its digital services, computer links and, in the not too distant future, the advent of virtual stadia.[23]

The trend was established for the full exploitation of the media football market, and led Keir Radnege to comment that: "The 1998 World Cup will be the last which European viewers can watch live, 'clear' of some form of encryption."[24] Within four years, Radnege predicted, football would be "dictating a twin-track approach to football coverage," with the top games accessible only by cable, satellite or pay-per-view, and state broadcasters providing networked coverage on a late-night highlights model only. Radnege was proved wrong in the medium term, though the digitalized transmission of the football product was to generate multiple modes for following and consuming the big event.

At the heart of FIFA's problem in negotiating television rights across the world is the tension between the resourced centre and the under-resourced periphery: the lived culture of the local gives way to the cultural prominence of the global. It is remarkable that in something so simple as the game of football, these disparate elements can be held together, as recognizably part of the same overall cultural phenomenon. Viewing figures for World Cup Final tournaments 1998–2010 have been reported as huge, Italy 1990 attracting "cumulative TV viewing audiences" close to 27 billion; France 1998, 24 billion plus; Korea/Japan 2002, almost 29 billion; Germany 2006, 26 billion plus; and for a single match, the final in South Africa 2010, 3.2 billion – 46.4 per cent of the global population.[25] These figures, certainly inflated and widely disputed, nevertheless provide FIFA with a source of celebratory hyperbole that its representatives can rarely resist:

> Almost half the world tuned in at home to watch 2010 FIFA World Cup South Africa
>
> The 2010 FIFA World Cup South Africa was shown in every single country and territory on Earth, including Antarctica and the Arctic Circle, generating record-breaking viewing figures in many TV markets. ... [T]he final between Spain and the Netherlands ... reached 909.6 million viewers based on watching over one minute and is likely to have surpassed one billion when out-of-home viewers are included. Indeed, all the figures cited do not include people watching out-of-home at the FIFA Fan Fests and other public viewing venues, as well as in pubs, bars, restaurants, clubs, hotels, or even online and via mobile handsets. ... "[W]ith an unprecedented level of TV production geared to serve screens of all shapes and sizes, it was also the first major sports event to be distributed globally across all platforms, namely TV, radio, mobile, broadband as well as in 3D" [said Jérôme Valcke, FIFA general secretary].[26]

Revealingly, sponsors did not respond to British journalist Nick Harris when his article in the *Independent*, in July 2007,[27] debunked such claims and overblown estimates; they were content to live with the reported figures collated by Infront Sports and Media, whose chief executive was Philippe Blatter, nephew of the FIFA president. Although a FIFA official conceded, in the 2007 article, that the reported figures were confusing and in many cases only estimates, four years later FIFA's General Secretary Valcke, as quoted, continued to make the most of such barely verifiable figures.

Undeniably, the broadcasting revolution and its digital dimension have made the peak moments of the peoples' game accessible on undreamt-of scales; sports marketing specialists saw the synergy that could be created with the burgeoning global communications and broadcasting business. As part of this boom business, corporate sponsors began to queue to bid their way into reaching these vast global audiences. FIFA's partnerships with commercial sponsors are the focus of the next section.

The marketeers

With the rising profile of the World Cups of 1950 (in Brazil), 1954 (Switzerland), 1958 (Sweden) and 1962 (Chile), it became increasingly clear that football, as a cultural product with worldwide appeal, could be exploited much more effectively for its business potential and financial profits. Sir Stanley Rous had shown awareness of this, but his own brand of internationalism was much more that of the missionary educator than the global businessman. On his succession to the presidency, Havelange was therefore faced with a serious problem. He had little chance of fulfilling his campaign commitments unless effective partnerships were established, but his commitments to the third-world allies who had helped him oust Rous had no economic basis. It was the German sports goods manufacturer Horst Dassler of Adidas, through the mediation of Patrick Nally, who secured Coca-Cola as a global partner for FIFA. This generated the expansion of the sports goods market, and accompanying forms of sport marketing, which became vital to FIFA's goals and achievements in the Havelange era. For the 1978 World Cup Finals, Coca-Cola paid FIFA US$8.33 million for exclusive rights to stadium advertising, "net, without FIFA having to pay any taxes."[28] It was clear where future monies – bonanza payments unimaginable to earlier administrations – would now come from.

Patrick Nally had been involved, with the sports commentator Peter West, in the early growth of sport sponsorship in Britain.[29] Through an advertising agency and then his own company West Nally, he had established sponsorship deals with brewery companies, Green Shield Stamps, Benson and Hedges, Kraft, Ford, Esso and Cornhill Insurance. According to Neil Wilson, "In those early days of sponsorship, when men like him were inventing the genre, he was the international cavalier for whom the British market was a base from which to conquer the world."[30] Nally's marketing initiatives paved the way for remarkable marketing deals, such as that achieved by ISL (International Sport and Leisure) for the IOC in initiating the inaugural TOP (The Olympic Programme) scheme for the 1988 Seoul Summer Olympics. There were difficulties, but ISL succeeded in buying back from each National Olympic Committee the right to market the Olympics (and the IOC rule on this was accordingly amended). It sold exclusive Olympic marketing rights to "nine companies: Coca-Cola, VISA, 3M, Brother, Philips, Federal Express, Kodak, Time Inc. and Panasonic, for a grand total of ... more than $100 million."[31] The marketing bonanza was such that the South Korean Organizing Committee itself signed up 97 Korean companies as smaller, national sponsors: "the income from sponsorship, supply and licensed deals already then [a year before the Games] exceeded $150 million, $15 million more than the hugely profitable Los Angeles Games made from marketing."[32] In the year of the Seoul Olympics, Wilson concluded that in the seven or eight years since Juan Antonio

Samaranch's succession to the IOC presidency "at least $2 billion [had] passed through" the IOC's "Swiss bank account."[33] ISL's negotiation of marketing rights, as much as the sale of television rights, was responsible for this. ISL was formed, Nally himself claims, as Dassler's own version of the partnership of the West Nally Company with the Monaco-based SMPI (Société Monégasque de Promotion Internationale) – this partnership was described by Wilson as "Dassler's money and contracts allied to Nally's ideas and marketing experience" and a joint beneficiary of the Argentina 1978 advertising deal with Coca-Cola.[34]

For Nally, the importance of getting a big name such as Coca-Cola into the soccer programme was twofold. First, it lent credibility and created the right image. Second, "if you're into Coke, you're into the biggest bluechip company on a global basis." Bringing Coca-Cola into the sponsorship of world soccer "became the blueprint for everyone who wanted to try and bring money into international federations through this source." The multi-million-dollar investment package put together for FIFA concentrated initially on the new youth World Cup, which could guarantee Asian and African participation on the world stage. In order to be a political player, with voting rights within FIFA, a nation had to participate in at least one FIFA competition, and so new competitions constituted an extension of FIFA's franchise.

Complementing the inward flow to Africa and Asia of coaching, administration and medical expertise, the competitive platform of the youth World Cup (first held in Tunisia in 1977) provided the opportunity to create an outward flow, from these regions, of teams that could compete at international level against European and South American nations. This was revolutionary, and though the champions of the first two youth (under-20) tournaments produced established winners, in the Soviet Union and Argentina (the young Maradona scoring the decisive goal in the 1979 final in Tokyo, against the Soviet Union), by the third tournament the value of the new initiative for developing football nations was becoming clear: Qatar, though losing 4–0 to West Germany in the final in Sydney in 1981, had beaten Brazil (3–2) and England (2–1) along the way; 30 years later Qatar would be celebrating the award of the 2022 World Cup finals.

African nations were soon to emerge on this stage: Nigeria won the third-place match, in and against the Soviet Union, in 1985, and in Saudi Arabia in 1989 lost the final 2–0 to Portugal. Ghana lost only 2–1 to Brazil in the 1993 final in Australia, having won the 1991 Under-17 title in Florence, Italy, beating Spain 1–0 in the final. The Under-17 World Cup was inaugurated in 1985, Nigeria beating West Germany 2–0 in the final in Beijing, having defeated Italy (1–0) and Hungary (3–1) *en route*. However sceptical the established football nations might have been about such events (some seeing them as peripheral, in comparison to their own apprenticeship systems and fully developed professional leagues), the FIFA initiatives clearly offered valuable international experience and competition, which were to stand Asian and African footballing nations in good stead on the larger world stages of the World Cup and the Olympic Games; they would also fire the ambitions of administrators from the Asian and African nations. These developmental initiatives would not have been possible without FIFA's Coca-Cola monies.

A worldwide skills programme was also created, to ensure widespread promotional activity for the sponsoring company. The base was established in the development programmes and the youth Cup, and a deal was then concluded whereby, at the cost of between US$8 million and US$12 million, Coca-Cola was brought in to the 1978 World Cup in Argentina, and "financed and funded the whole of the marketing programme." The external negotiations with Coca-Cola were conducted by Nally; the internal fixing was accomplished by Dassler and Havelange: "All the politics, he [Dassler] wanted handled through him and his team ... the selection of putting Sepp Blatter in as Gen Sec of FIFA – the selection of Sepp out of [Swiss watchmaker] Longines, the training of Sepp at Landersheim ... the convincing of Havelange to put Sepp in as the new development man as he then was – all that political selection of personnel was done by them." Landersheim was the French base from which Dassler controlled his sports marketing and merchandising empire.

By Argentina '78, the first World Cup of Havelange's presidency, Nally had contracted five further major sponsors to FIFA to line up alongside Coca-Cola, including Gillette and Seiko, though he was still juggling the advertising billboards of companies contracted with different national teams. This was soon to be streamlined, with FIFA creating a template for what became the TOP scheme for the Olympics. From then on the only option open to sponsors was the complete marketing package: "The sums were so vast that lots of companies couldn't touch it but it was a lot easier to work with the few who could," recalled Nally.[35]

Havelange had made major commitments to the development of African and Asian football. Dassler "would commit himself to help Havelange to get the money" – for example to "take an event that's been running at 16 teams and go to 24 teams – to get the Spanish [organizers of the 1982 World Cup] to agree to do it – politically it's important for the Africans and Asians." It was then Nally's task to "create a marketing programme to justify bringing big money into that sport to help Horst fulfil his obligations." The cost of the marketing rights for international football were therefore unprecedentedly high, because of the range and scale of deals needed to fuel this expansionist programme, as Nally alleged – because, for instance:

> Horst committed to give 36 million Swiss francs extra to Havelange to enable him to persuade the Spanish to take the World Cup up from 16 teams to 24 teams as part of his commitment to get more Asian and African teams in … . [I]n Spain, in the Palacio de Congresos, in the gentlemen's toilets, Horst said the going rate with the Spanish organizing committee wasn't going to be $4 million which I'd already negotiated and agreed, we had to pay an additional 36 million Swiss francs.

Nally saw the effects of such financial flexibility as "good," evidenced by improving African and Asian performances in the World Cup, following on from the developmental youth programmes, and pouring in such large amounts of money was made possible by the scale of the Coca-Cola investment:

> Coca-Cola if you like legitimized the industry, the amount of money that was going into soccer … but I don't think ever quite realized the importance of their association and how it being abused enabled this club, this whole mafia going on within sport, to be really supported by them because they gave it all credibility.

Dassler got Havelange to impress the Coca-Cola people, at the company's world headquarters in Atlanta, by flying in on his private plane to meet with them. Nally argued that the Coca-Cola connection gives sports organizations an aura of respectability, generated by the Coca-Cola global image of corporate cleanliness:

> [The federations] are in some ways, because of Coca-Cola, beyond reproach. There's no government checking on them. There's no auditors checking them. Nobody's trying to see where the payment goes or what the individuals get so somehow the IOC and the IAAF and FIFA is totally beyond reproach. They have the same aura of credibility and pristine cleanness and Coca-Cola helps that and yet they can get away with blue murder.
> … but if the can of worms ever really got open and people started challenging why these people have the ability to do what they do and why they are there and why do they get all these things – the

club – then I think Coca-Cola are going to get a lot of stick from it and Coca-Cola's image is going to suffer immensely … this pristine image of Coca-Cola is suddenly going to have a big dent.

One outcome of this new political economy of world sport was the elevation in status of positions in sports organizations, as noted by Nally:

It's suddenly becoming an extremely important and powerful position to be in, the president of an international federation that is rich because there is money flowing in from the Olympic Games and other things. Now, it means trips, it means travel, it means awards, air tickets, it certainly beats sweeping out the back of the garden at the weekend if you're flying first class everywhere to major international events.

How did Horst Dassler hold together an operation on this scale? Clearly he provided lavish hospitality: the "compulsory Adidas dinner" at every international sports federation meeting, at a time when the federations were relatively impoverished, and "Adidas was the only company that ever supported them"; his own residential and catering complex at Landersheim in Alsace; and, allegedly mostly for Africans and Asians in Paris, his sports shop and restaurant with other hospitality facilities in Montmartre. He retained useful individuals in bogus capacities – for instance Harry Cavan, Northern Irish football administrator and FIFA vice-president, in the capacity of, as Nally puts it, "shoe consultant." And he made commitments and kept promises that would catapult sport into a new phase of economically expanded and financially lucrative transnational practice. Former UK sports minister Lord Howell and his committee investigating sponsorship in sport were right to target Dassler as a pivotal figure in the evolving pattern of the global sports economy, as Howell recalled:

I started by asking a question such as "Can you give me any justification as to why a football boot manufacturer should wish to decide who should become the President of FIFA and control world football?" And his reply was that he had in his office a tremendous computer and records department which had every periodical and newsletter issued by every sports body round the world and these were all tabulated. Therefore it was very natural that if anyone wanted to pursue a career like Havelange … they would come to him to get the names and addresses of all the contacts. That is what he supplied and the same facilities, he said, were available to Sir Stanley Rous, except Sir Stanley Rous didn't ask for them – and I don't suppose could have afforded to have made all these contacts around Africa and Asia, which enabled Havelange to get himself elected as President of FIFA.[36]

Dassler had spoken with "commendable frankness" to Howell's committee: "We exist to sell boots and shirts and wherever the action is, we need to be there," he said.[37] This "simple philosophy," as the committee called it, operated in a range of settings: congresses determining events and fixtures; draws for tournament schedules or fixtures; any IOC meeting; and matches where players might be wearing Adidas products:

> We discussed with Mr Dassler the apparent involvement of his company in the election of officers of international sports organizations. He told us very frankly: "Our company receives all official publications of national Olympic committees, international federations and regional federations of all Olympic sports and many non-Olympic sports. We have a department which collects and files all information contained in these publications. This gives us, probably, a better overall view of the total situation in sport than it would be possible for any individual national or international federation or organization to gather alone. It is, therefore, natural that if people seek information on who holds which position in sporting bodies, they should turn to us. We are ready to make this information available to those who ask for it."[38]

This rang the alarm bells among the committee members: "We would find it unacceptable if such information was made available for use in any way in connection with the election of officers of international federations."[39] But the committee also noted Adidas's "close involvement" in the affairs of FIFA, citing the company's presence at a World Cup draw. Dassler did not hide things, stating that "Adidas has undertaken, in cooperation with FIFA and its President, João Havelange, an extensive programme of activity for the development of soccer in many countries in Africa."[40] The committee, with restrained understatement, expressed its surprise "that an organization as important and powerful as FIFA should need to use a commercial company for such development work."[41]

Dassler's openness prompted the Howell committee to offer a judgement: "We are concerned at the close association of Mr Dassler and Adidas with FIFA and the IOC and we consider that there should be a proper examination of the situation. ... [T]he best safeguard for sport, the international federations and commercial companies concerned, lies in the full disclosure of the financial interests of all companies and their subsidiaries or associates who have such business involvements in international sport."[42] In fact, the cautious language of the committee and its carefully worded recommendations could do little to halt the mounting momentum of sponsorship, commercialization, marketing and branding of the mediated sporting product.

What in 2005 became the FIFA U-20 World Cup had been founded, as outlined, in 1977 as the FIFA World Youth Championship; on Coca-Cola's headed notepaper in 1982, the 1983 tournament in Mexico was billed "La Copa FIFA/Coca-Cola." Here, a year before the publication of the Howell Report, Frank W. Bean was writing from Coca-Cola head office in Atlanta, Georgia, to a Peter Hunt at the Coca-Cola Export Corp. in London, advising on how tobacco companies could get in on, or make sure they stayed in on, the sponsorship game. US tobacco manufacturer R.J. Reynolds "has purchased signage at the World Cup (football), and Toyota Cup and similar internationally telecast sports events. Thus, trademark exposure is not viewed in the same light as direct sales message advertising."[43] Havelange, with his right-hand man Blatter and his Coca-Cola deals and Adidas alliance, had already established the framework that would launch football as a serious force in the globalization of culture.

A major step in consolidating FIFA's commercial base was the setting up of ISL (International Sport and Leisure). By mid-1983, within a matter of months of its creation, ISL was handling merchandising rights and rights for stadium advertising for FIFA, UEFA and, embryonically at least, the IOC. By October 1983 the company had also signed to handle any of the Seoul Olympic Games Organising Committee's merchandising, licensing, sponsorship and supplier contracts, and was publicizing, in a special supplement to *Time* magazine's European edition, its successes in attracting sponsors for its football marketing programme – not least via advertising in the supplement reserved exclusively for the company's own regular clients such as Canon, Camel, JVC, Seiko, Fuji and Air France.[44] Andrew Craig, marketing manager of ISL Marketing, expounded (presciently, and in advance of much globalization theory) the company philosophy on "Globalisation, the Real Opportunity in Sports Marketing." Craig argued that the multi-domestic system of management and control of international corporations, in which products are marketed locally by local management, was close to anachronistic in an age of accelerated communications, increased population mobility and the growth of mass audience communication. However appropriate this system may have been in the past, "the changing patterns of international business, the blending of market requirements and the resultant development of homogeneous world wide products suggest that global marketing philosophy will ultimately prevail." Craig then quoted his boss, Klaus Hempel, on how sport provides the ideal focus for companies seeking to have an impact in the global marketplace:

> the traditional media have been unable or unwilling to respond to the needs of global marketing companies. The result is that it is still extremely difficult for a major corporation to communicate a unified message on a world wide basis without first making a massive investment in both time and resources. It is up to sports marketing companies to fill this gap. ISL's Intersoccer 4 Programme for example makes use of soccer's world wide appeal to create an immediate and highly flexible universal communications language for its sponsors.[45]

Globally minded corporations, as Hempel put it – such as Coca-Cola, Bata and Cinzano – quickly saw the benefits of the sponsor programmes, and ISL put these in place for its contracted clients for the 1984 European Football Championships in France and then the 1986 World Cup. The main benefit was perimeter advertising in all of the stadia during the tournament, guaranteeing sponsors worldwide television exposure. Exclusive franchising rights were also included in the package, and further exposure in event-based media. Sponsors also provided services to the media – a harried press person could borrow photographic equipment from Canon and photocopy on a Canon machine, take a refreshing drink of Coca-Cola, admire the ball-boy kit and opening ceremony equipment provided by Bata, watch on television monitors provided by JVC, and check copy deadlines and match timings via the official timekeeper Seiko.

ISL, over-reaching itself in the world markets, went bankrupt in 2001 after a series of unsuccessful initiatives in international markets and failed partnerships with other sports beyond football, notably tennis.[46] Kirch too, ISL's partner, failed spectacularly, and FIFA brought control of future marketing and broadcasting rights into the organization itself. The ISL model of the lucrative "golden triangle" (sport–media–marketing) was, though, widely adopted, and dominated world football marketing in this formative phase, establishing a potent new force in the political economy of world sport. The media and marketing rights would launch, sustain and revive at a moment of crisis the economic fortunes of FIFA. In the period 2007 to 2010, FIFA's income was generated by

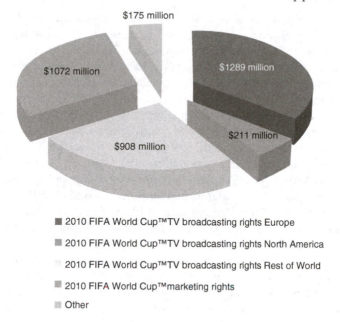

$175 million

$1072 million

$1289 million

$908 million

$211 million

■ 2010 FIFA World Cup™TV broadcasting rights Europe

■ 2010 FIFA World Cup™TV broadcasting rights North America

  2010 FIFA World Cup™TV broadcasting rights Rest of World

■ 2010 FIFA World Cup™marketing rights

■ Other

Figure 5.1 FIFA 2007–2010 revenue sources (millions of US dollars), FIFA Finance Report 2010, pp. 36 and 37

broadcasting rights (65.9 per cent), marketing rights (29.3 per cent), and unspecified other sources (4.8 per cent). Figure 5.1 shows the income from different sources, with that from broadcasting rights broken down by region.

Of these vast sums, totalling US$3655 million, Europe provided the most money, but an increasing global audience in North America, Asia and Africa would secure the long-term commitment of broadcasters and sponsors to the football product, primarily the men's World Cup, but increasingly also the Women's World Cup.[47]

From culture to commodity

Football is a cultural product, and its meanings and significance are not wholly determined by its political economy. People in pubs or domestic lounges, as well as at live games at various levels of performance, can chant, sing, shout, speak and respond in their own appropriate ways as, with varying degrees of freedom and choice, they negotiate the expression of a particular cultural identity through the public culture of the game. But at the top level, football represents more and more graphically the triumph of the universal market,[48] and wherever it is watched – live or in its transmitted forms – it is an increasingly commodified cultural product, in a structured environment operating highly effectively at all levels of football consumption, distributed in multiple ways within and by new as well as mainstream social media and digitalized platforms.

Watching FIFA's partners of the Havelange and Blatter eras police the fully commodified modern football stadium – checking every detail of their constructed world like bodyguards protecting an American president, from Korea to Germany, France to South Africa – is to catch a glimpse of the global political economy at work, at the heart of which are those who have controlled international football's golden triangle (sport–media–marketing) in an expansionist phase of the peoples' game. The growth of global forces in the contemporary world is fuelled by the influence of transnational bodies such as FIFA. Arguably, FIFA has been influential in what David Andrews and George Ritzer label the "grobalization" process, in which "global processes … overwhelm the local."[49] Football, preserving its essential common and accessible simplicity, can express local styles or hybrid conceptions of what it might be, how it might be played, what it represents of a local or regional culture or values; but it is increasingly framed by the needs and requirements – and profits – of those institutions that frame its global media reach. In 1996, News International's Rupert Murdoch called sport a "battering ram" for the expansion of his global pay-television network, noting: "Sport absolutely overpowers film and everything else in the entertainment genre."[50] In 2010, ESPN president George Bodenheimer reaffirmed the centrality of sports and big sporting moments in the changing global media landscape: "You can read about it in the business section, in the entertainment section, in the social section. It's all pervasive. It's no longer just the sport; it's a major part of the culture of the world."[51] Sport has been reshaped in its modern form by interconnected processes of globalization, marketization and more recently digitalization.[52] As owner of the exclusive product of the men's World Cup, FIFA has been a harbinger of a model of mediated sport consumed ever more voraciously at levels of individual and collective, public and private – and increasingly digitalized – experience.

The Howell Report warned of the vicissitudes of the market in the emerging sport sponsorship field: "Governing bodies should guard against an over-reliance upon sponsorship income and should maintain as wide a portfolio of sponsorship as is practical in order to minimize the dangers when sponsors end their involvement. They also should endeavour to avoid an over-dependence upon any one product."[53] The Howell Committee did not foresee the scale of the transformation of the marketplace for a sport with football's international reach. Its warnings might fit a local or regional sport with a limited market, but FIFA, along with the IOC – both federations working with and through ISL – was pioneering partnerships that would in their exclusivity guarantee the availability of top company sponsorship, revolving for the most part around the one lucrative event, in FIFA's case the men's World Cup. Toby Miller combined important elements of the cultural, the economic and the political in his adaptation of the theory of the new international division of labour (NIDL);[54] in what he labelled the NICL (new international division of cultural labour), we see the transnational cultural industries operating in international markets beyond national boundaries, and the sporting body (as individual performer or spectator/fan) trained and commodified for global consumption.[55] FIFA, speaking a language of modernization as spokesbody for the marginalized global South, could break the rules of the sporting establishment of traditional institutions and countries. In doing so it could also reshape its product and trigger a transformation of the economic and cultural profile of the sport, and of other sports that could see how the golden triangle might fuel a seemingly endless flow of money-spinning actions and initiatives. In the next chapter, we track in more detail the explosive growth of the FIFA World Cup and its contribution to an expansionist, globalizing, mediated consumer culture.

Notes

1 "Committee of Enquiry into Sports Sponsorship: The Howell Report" (London: The Central Council of Physical Recreation, November 1983), 89.
2 Ibid., 91.
3 Ibid., 90.
4 *UEFA Bulletin*, 32, October 1965: 329–330.
5 Ibid.
6 Interview with the author, Berne, Switzerland, 19 March 2009.
7 Guy Debord, *The Society of the Spectacle* (New York: Zone Books, 1995), 24.
8 *FIFA News*, 129, February 1974: 82–83.
9 Rous was writing in *FIFA News*, 131, April 1974.
10 2014 FIFA World Cup Brazil Local Organizing Committee, *2014 FIFA World Cup Brazil*, eg_br_054867.pdf, undated (approximately 2010).
11 FIFA TV contract, 1978, confidential, made 19 July 1976.
12 *FIFA News*, 3/87, 1987: 1.
13 Ibid.
14 Ibid.
15 Interview with the author, Zurich, Switzerland, 21 May 1996.
16 Interview with the author, Zurich, Switzerland, 21 May 1996.
17 FIFA, *Report – FIFA World Cup USA '94*, (FIFA, 1994) 197, ed. Jürg Neptor with the assistance of the members of the Technical Study Group USA '94.
18 Keith Cooper, FIFA, *Activities Report April 1994–March 1996*, 50th FIFA Congress, Zurich 1996, 50–51.

19 Ibid.

20 Jimmy Burns, "Murdoch Quits Race for World Cup TV," *Financial Times*, London edn. 1, 15 May 1996: 4.

21 L. Guest and P. Law, "The revolution will be televised," *World Soccer*, 37/4, January 1997: 15.

22 Keir Radnege, "Cashing in," *World Soccer*, 36/12, September 1996: 25.

23 Guest and Law, "The revolution will be televised," 15.

24 Radnege, "Cashing In," 24.

25 InfoPlus, *The FIFA World Cup TV Viewing Figures* (Zurich: FIFA, TV audiences ip-401_05a_tvstats-2659.pdf [SECURED], undated), http://www.fifa.com/ mm/document/fifafacts/ffprojects/ip-401_05a_tvstats_2659.pdf, consulted 30 June 2013; and Nick Harris, "Why FIFA's claim of one billion TV viewers was a quarter right," *The Independent*, 1 March 2007, http://www.independent.co.uk/ sport/football/news-and-comment/why-fifas-claim-of-one-billion-tv-viewers-was-a-quarter-right-438302.html, consulted 30 June 2013.

26 FIFA.com, "Almost half the world tuned in at home to watch 2010 FIFA World Cup South Africa," media release, Monday 11 July 2011, http://www.fifa.com/ worldcup/archive/southafrica2010/organisation/media/newsid=1473143/index. html, consulted 30 June 2013.

27 Harris, "Why FIFA's claim of one billion TV viewers was a quarter right."

28 FIFA, Stadium Advertising Contract, confidential, made 14 August 1977, between FIFA, the Coca-Cola Company, and Société Monégasque de Promotion Internationale West Nally S.A.

29 Nally was interviewed by Vyv Simson and Andrew Jennings in 1991. Unattributed quotes in the rest of this section are from the transcript of this interview.

30 Neil Wilson, *The Sports Business* (London: Mandarin, 1988), 176.

31 Ibid., 27.

32 Ibid., 28.

33 Ibid., 29.

34 Ibid., 179.

35 Ibid., 182.

36 Interview with the author, Birmingham, England, 8 October 1996.

37 Howell Report, 89.

38 Ibid.

39 Ibid.

40 Ibid.

41 Ibid.

42 Ibid., 90.

43 Letter from Frank W. Bean to Peter Hunt, 29 September 1982, in files of the Howell Committee, personal collection of the author.

44 *Sport Intern*, IV 20/21, 31 October 1983: 1–2.

45 Ibid., 6.

46 See Andrew Jennings, *Foul! The Secret World of FIFA: Bribes, Vote Rigging and Ticket Scandals* (London: HarperSport, 2006), Chapters 19 and 20.

47 The sums as presented in Figure 5.1 are based upon the FIFA financial report for the period 2007–2010, given in the report to the 61st FIFA Congress at Zurich, 31 May and 1 June 2011, and refer to the revenue generated in that period related directly to the 2010 FIFA World Cup, a total of US$3,655 million. With other sources of revenue in that period, FIFA could also report an accumulative

revenue of US$4,189, a figure used in later financial reports. In the report for 2010, Julio Grondona, chair of the financial committee, could also claim that the financial cycle closed "with a result of USD 631 million and also increased its reserves to USD 1,280 million" (p. 9). This enabled him to project a rise in FIFA's "investment in football development programmes"from US$691 million in 2007–2010, to US $800 million for 2011–2014. After the 2010 South Africa World Cup FIFA could also commit US$100 million for a legacy trust in South Africa, 80 per cent of which was directed towards social community projects. Blatter wrote, addressing his "Dear Members of the International Football Family", that the "conservative and careful financial policies that we followed in the 2007–2010 period" enabled FIFA to increase investment in its football development programmes so that "in 2010, we were able to give each member association a total extraordinary FAP [Football Assistance Programme] payment of USD 550,000 and each confederation USD 5 million" (p. 7). These extraordinary payments amounting to c.US$144 million were on top of the reported routine allocation of US$794 million (claimed as 22 per cent of overall expenditure) to development projects (p. 18). For commentary on the financial report presented at the FIFA Congress in 2013, see Andrew Jennings, "Davosman takes control at FIFA", *Transparency in Sport: Transparency in Sport News*, 8 April 2013, http://transparencyinsportblog.wordpress.com/2013/ 04/08/davosman-takes-control-at-fifa/, consulted 6 January 2014. Jennings points out that in the financial report for 2012 (p. 23) "money spent on football development *fell* from $183 million in 2011 to $177 million in 2012, just 15.2% of total revenue". It is not always easy to read sequential FIFA financial reports one in relation to the other, but this would represent a dramatic fall of almost 7 per cent in resources committed to the development of the game – this is in stark contrast to Grondona's commitment of 2011.

48 On the concept of the universal market, see Harry Braverman, *Labour and Monopoly Capital: The Degradation of Work in the Twentieth Century* (New York: Monthly Review Press, 1974); for discussion of the spread of the universal market into more and more spheres of everyday life and popular culture, see Deborah Philips and Alan Tomlinson, "Homeward Bound: Leisure, Popular Culture and Consumer Capitalism," in *Come on Down? Popular Media Culture in Post-War Britain*, eds. Dominic Strinati and Stephen Wagg (London: Routledge, 1992), 12–15.

49 David L. Andrews and George Ritzer, "The grobal in the sporting glocal," in *Globalization and Sport*, eds. Richard Giulianotti and Roland Robertson (Oxford: Blackwell Publishing, 2007), 29.

50 Quoted in R. Milliken, "Sport is Murdoch's 'battering ram' for pay TV," *Independent*, 16 October 1996, http://www.independent.co.uk/sport/sport-is-murdochs-battering-ram-for-pay-tv-1358686.html, consulted 21 January 2011.

51 Owen Gibson, "ESPN undaunted by the prospect of a challenging season on half rations," *Guardian*, 19 August 2010, http://www.guardian.co.uk/football/ 2010/aug/19/espn-premier-league-sports-rights, consulted 25 September 2010.

52 Raymond Boyle, *Sports Journalism: Contexts and Issues* (London: Sage, 2006).

53 Howell Report, 31.

54 Toby Miller, "*Mission Impossible* and the New International Division of Labour," *Metro*, 82, 1990: 21–28.

55 Toby Miller, Geoffrey Lawrence, Jim McKay and David Rowe, *Globalization and Sport: Playing the World* (London: Sage, 2001).

6   Cash Cow

Brazil "lost a great opportunity" to improve public services when it won the right to host the 2014 football World Cup, Rio de Janeiro's mayor Eduardo Paes said at the end of June 2013, a little over a year before the opening match. Mayor Paes conceded that the country should have seized the opportunity to invest in public services – healthcare, education, transport: "FIFA asked for stadiums and Brazil has only delivered stadiums. We should have used the opportunity to deliver good services too ... . We have almost no unemployment. The protests are much more connected to the quality of services in Brazil ... . People want more transparency, they want more openness and that is what we are going to do." Paes was speaking after close to 90 protesters were arrested, and the police used tear gas to disperse others, outside the stadium in the north-eastern city of Fortaleza, before the semi-final match in the Confederations Cup between Spain and Italy.[1]

The wave of protests had begun in São Paulo several weeks earlier, initially in response to a 10 per cent rise in bus fares. The rises were rescinded after two weeks, but the protest had by then embraced wider questions, and one focus, or target, was the high cost of the forthcoming World Cup, and the Summer Olympics scheduled for just two summers later in Rio. FIFA Secretary General Jérôme Valcke showed no sign of panic about the World Cup: "The first game will happen in São Paulo, the final will be in Rio. There is no plan B." His boss, President Blatter, claimed that football was being targeted unfairly: "I can understand that people are not happy, but they should not use football to make their demands heard," Blatter told Globo TV,[2] before scuttling off to the relative tranquility of the Under-20 World Cup in Turkey as the riots escalated. On his return to Brazil, he insisted that FIFA's reputation was enhanced by the Confederations Cup, and expressed his sympathies for the protesters, noting that their needs were the responsibility of the political authorities in the country, not an international football federation. The latter, he professed, was a force for good and hope:

> FIFA has come out of this stronger, with our image enhanced. Football has played a positive part here and given emotion. This [the unrest] is not our problem, it is a political problem, but we hope something will be changed so that by the time the World Cup begins next summer we can have a platform to deliver it.
>
> The World Cup provides practically 90% of the income of FIFA to ensure we can develop the game around the world. Hope is in football. We play football in all perturbed countries, not just where there are belligerent situations like Syria and Afghanistan.[3]

Brazil's most fêted footballer, Pelé, called for calm: "When the Brazilian football hero ... told fans to forget the protests and enjoy the football, he was greeted with derision."[4] But the estimated cost of the forthcoming World Cup and Olympics – US$27 billion – was not making sense to the population. Younger footballers backed the people, not the patriarchs:

> Brazilian soccer great Romario, now a member of Brazil's National Congress, took the analysis a step further, asserting that FIFA was "the real president of Brazil." Critiquing lavish spending on the World Cup, he said, "It's taking the piss with our money, with the public's money, it's a lack of respect, a lack of scruples."[5]

Blatter reminded his media interrogators that the FIFA monies from the World Cup were ploughed back into the member associations around the world, and pledged that FIFA would now find a further US $100 million to give to Brazil after the event, comparable to the social fund that had been received by South Africa after the 2010 World Cup.[6] It was a tactic to protect the image of FIFA's prime asset, and to show that FIFA had a conscience, though the risk to image and reputation in staging the event has not been so much FIFA's as the local organizers'. But the World Cup and its continuing value in the global marketplace is central to FIFA's profile and portfolio; it is an invaluable cash cow that can be milked indefinitely for riches. In this chapter, this equilibrium economics of cash cow and loss leader is demonstrated in an analysis of the growth trajectory of FIFA activity, and a consideration of the place of the World Cup in the calendar of global media events. As Table 6.1 illustrates, FIFA has sustained a strong spectator audience for an event that has become increasingly accessible through a multiplicity of media outlets and platforms.

Table 6.1 FIFA men's World Cup Finals tournaments 1930–2010

Year and host country	Winner	Number of teams	Total number of spectators and games	Average attendance at games	Number of FIFA member associations	Number of preliminary entries
1930 Uruguay	Uruguay	13	590,549 in 18 games	32,808	46	None: entry by invitation
1934 Italy	Italy	16	363,000 in 17 games	21,353	53	32
1938 France	Italy	15	375,700 in 18 games	20,872	57	37
1950 Brazil	Uruguay	13	1,042,246 in 22 games	47,375	70	34
1954 Switzerland	West Germany	16	768,607 in 26 games	29,562	80	45
1958 Sweden	Brazil	16	819,810 in 35 games	23,423	96	55
1962 Chile	Brazil	16	893,172 in 32 games	27,912	109	56
1966 England	England	16	1,563,135 in 32 games	48,848	126	74
1970 Mexico	Brazil	16	1,603,975 in 32 games	50,124	137	75
1974 West Germany	West Germany	16	1,865,753 in 38 games	49,099	141	99
1978 Argentina	Argentina	16	1,545,791 in 38 games	40,679	147	107
1982 Spain	Italy	24	2,109,723 in 52 games	40,572	150	109
1986 Mexico	Argentina	24	2,394,031 in 52 games	46,039	158	121
1990 Italy	West Germany	24	2,516,215 in 52 games	48,389	166	116
1994 USA	Brazil	24	3,587,538 in 52 games	68,991	191	147
1998 France	France	32	2,785,100 in 64 games	43,517	203	174
2002 Korea and Japan	Brazil	32	2,705,197 in 64 games	42,269	204	199
2006 Germany	Italy	32	3,359,439 in 64 games	52,491	207	198
2010 South Africa	Spain	32	3,178,856 in 64 games	49,670	208	206

Source: Data compiled from FIFA information sheets supplied to the author, April 2013

Previous chapters have highlighted TV and marketing rights as the major sources of World Cup Finals income for FIFA. But without the atmosphere and colour generated by spectators and fans at the live event the spectacle would be diluted and diminished; the US, in 1994, set its record for attendance by adapting facilities as much as creating new ones, and proudly filling the stadia as host to a world-leading event. Other potential host countries, though, have continued to invest in or project huge budgets for infrastructure and facilities to create conditions conducive to the carnivalesque dimensions of the international sporting encounter, though this will be severely tested in Russia in 2018 and Qatar in 2022. FIFA, though, can in the main continue to rely on a steady stream of willing hosts, and hence secure lucrative and long-term rights income and marketing partnerships.

Sponsors

The audiences for the world's biggest sport events have guaranteed continued and competitive interest in FIFA's main asset, and, as discussed in the previous chapter, Havelange and Blatter were pioneers in the transformation of the economic base of international sport. By the mid-1980s FIFA's network of partners was extending, attracting global and regional businesses in equal measure, constituting a formula for lucrative contracts and selective partnerships for the federation. At the World Cups from 1986 onwards the sponsors were as follows:[7]

Mexico, 1986 – 12 general sponsors with stadium advertising privileges: Anheuser-Busch, Bata, Canon, Coca-Cola, Cinzano, Fuji, Gillette, JVC, Opel, Philips, R.J. Reynolds (Camel), Seiko.

Two reserved sponsorship packages were granted to a selected group of Mexican firms to run local advertising; also to Arena Swimwear – as a result, it was claimed, of Anheuser-Busch not taking up an option of supporting promotion measures. These extra deals certainly made sense to the main players: the man running the World Cup was Havelange's long-term ally, Mexican FIFA vice-president Canedo; Arena was an Adidas subsidiary.

Italy, 1990 – 9 general sponsors with stadium advertising privileges: Anheuser-Busch, Canon, Coca-Cola, Fuji, Gillette, JVC, Mars, Philips, Vini Italia. The sum raised from these sponsors was reported to be 100 million Swiss francs, to be shared between FIFA, the Italian organizing committee and the participating teams.

Two further categories were sold: "Official Suppliers" were Alitalia, Fiat, Olivetti, the Italian post office, Italian railways, the RAI state TV

Company and the INA insurance company; the title "Official Product" was sold to a range of companies, including Adidas, Seiko, MasterCard, Barilla (pasta), Sagit (ice cream) and Grana Padano (cheese).

USA, 1994 – 11 general sponsors: Canon, Coca-Cola, Energizer, Fuji, General Motors, Gillette, JVC, MasterCard, McDonald's, Philips, Snickers.

France, 1998 – 11 general sponsors: Adidas, Canon, Coca-Cola, Fuji, Gillette, JVC, McDonald's, MasterCard, Opel, Philips, Snickers; 8 Official Suppliers: Crédit Agricole, Danone, EDF, France Telecom, Hewlett Packard, La Poste, Manpower, Sybase.

Korea and Japan, 2002 – 15 general sponsors: Adidas, Avaya, Budweiser, Coca-Cola, Fuji (2), Gillette, Hyundai, JVC, KTF (Korea Telecom Freetel), MasterCard, McDonald's, Philips, Toshiba, Yahoo.

Germany, 2006 – 15 general sponsors: Adidas, Avaya, Budweiser, Coca-Cola, Continental, Deutsche Telekom, Fly Emirates, Fujifilm, Gillette, Hyundai, McDonald's, MasterCard, Philips, Toshiba, Yahoo.

South Africa, 2010 – 6 FIFA Partners: Adidas, Coca-Cola, Emirates, Hyundai (Kia), Sony, Visa; 8 FIFA World Cup Sponsors: Budweiser, Continental, Castrol, McDonald's, Mahindra Satyam, MTN, Seara, Yingli Solar; 6 National Supporters: Ultimate, FNB, NeoAfrica, PRASA, Aggreko, Telkom.

Brazil, 2014 – 6 FIFA Partners: Adidas, Coca-Cola, Emirates, Hyundai (Kia), Sony, Visa; 8 FIFA World Cup Sponsors: Budweiser, Castrol, Continental, Johnson & Johnson, McDonald's, Oi, Moy Park, Yingli Solar; 8 National Supporters: ApexBrasil, Centauro, FIFA.com, Garoto, Itaú, Liberty Seguros, Wise Up, Football for Hope.

Russia, 2018 (as at January 2014) – FIFA Partners: Adidas, Coca-Cola, Hyundai (Kia), Visa; FIFA World Cup Sponsors: Budweiser, FIFA.com, Football for Hope.

Fast foods and snacks, soft and alcoholic drinks, airlines, cars and motoring essentials, batteries, photographic equipment and electronic media, credit sources – these are the items around which global sponsorship of football has been based, with their evocations of a predominantly masculinist realm of consumption: drinking, snacking, shaving, driving. The number of selected partners has reduced, as FIFA brands its events still more exclusively; more recently, some sponsors, rather than being primary partners, are part of the FIFA apparatus itself, in the field of public relations and promotion, and in sport development – an element that has expanded widely as a form of corporate social responsibility (CSR). But the consumerist nature of the marketing partners is noteworthy; the marketing of their commodities through the world game has clearly been effective. If it were not, companies of this stature would not have reinvested in the event, or sought mid- to long-term deals. The marketing partners of FIFA and other owners of sporting mega-events, such as the IOC, are buying not just into extensive consumer markets, but into a brand and a brand image. Celia Lury observes that a "brand is an example not only of a cultural form but also of a modality of economic power."[8] The FIFA brand generates cultural experiences through its events and development work, but it also, with the sponsors and media institutions selected as partners, constructs and constrains the financial parameters of the consuming experience.

Marketing specialists position brands, employing practices such as "product design, the promotion and positioning" of products in the media, and management of the brand's logo.[9] This, adds Lury, develops a brand image based on associations that a brand holds for the consumer. The FIFA brand works this very effectively by having evolved the visual representation of the brand into a minimalist form; the acronym of the French name of the organization has lent itself to this, so that *FIFA*, a pithy term flowingly easy to speak, recognize and reproduce, becomes the logo itself. Whereas previously FIFA's logo used interlocking circles a little too much like the Olympic rings, its corporate mark, as reworked in 2007 and 2009, accompanied by the revised motto "For the Game. For the World," communicates its message very simply; the eight syllables of the combined logo and motto associate the FIFA brand with (arguably) the most popular team sport in the world, and offer no exclusionary image, leaving the viewer to fill in whatever picture fits his or her understanding.

The FIFA brand is therefore potentially universal, and is very attractive to those paying to be associated with it; sponsors are willing to pay huge sums for this, and to gain access to worldwide markets to which this universal product is made available in the context of restricted consumer choices, both within and beyond the stadium. It is a brilliantly simple conception, luring the population of the world into the FIFA world, while simultaneously restricting their consumer choices and freedoms. And tacked onto the logo, to the right of the "A," is a warning that this is big business: "FIFA®" tells us that the name of the guardian of the peoples' game is private property; this registered trademark reminds us that the motto reaching out to us all, in the name of the game, for the world, marks out FIFA as a protector of its own and its partners' interests. In consumer culture, we make informed and not-so-informed choices, based on our backgrounds and a developing sense of individuality and selfhood. "A reflexive relation to self" generates a sense of belonging and self-identity; we assemble ourselves, put the self together – depending upon available resources – from a range of possibilities and choices.[10] In the world of FIFA®, our choices are constrained, limited, diluted. We have some choices; to boycott a brand, seek out another product. But FIFA operates a form of monopoly control too, on the elite events that it owns.

Brand guru Wally Olins asserts that we "have the power to shape brands to be what we want and to shape the society in which we live."[11] This underestimates the degree to which at particular consumer sites, such as the sporting mega-event, the mode of consumption of the brand can be tightly controlled, the brand itself celebrating the limited agency of the controlled consumer. FIFA and its partners operate in highly successful ways a branding of the football product that continues to deliver enraptured yet entrapped audiences, and undreamt-of income and turnover for the major players in the production of the sporting spectacle. While FIFA could celebrate its politically progressive decision to award the African continent its first ever World Cup Finals in 2010, the economic and commercial logic of the spectacle was as prominent as ever, ensuring the continued health of FIFA finances. We explore this in more detail in the next section.

South Africa 2010

South Africa felt stunned at the FIFA ExCo vote in 2000, when Germany was awarded the 2006 men's World Cup Finals (a story related in Chapter 7). What this allowed, though, within FIFA's commitment at that time to a rotation system, was a virtually uncontested candidature for South Africa for the 2010 event (and for Brazil, in an unopposed bid in October 2007 for the 2014 finals).[12] Although Morocco, Egypt and Libya also bid for 2010, after one round of voting of the FIFA ExCo, in May 2004 in Zurich, South Africa secured the decisive vote. Nelson Mandela, having given emotional backing to the bid the day before the decision, greeted the outcome by holding the World Cup trophy aloft, saying "I feel like a young man of 50."

It was an impressive delegation, including two other Nobel Peace Prize winners: F.W. de Klerk, the last president of the apartheid era, and

Archbishop Desmond Tutu. The bid's chief, Irvin Khoza, turned to this extraordinary trio and hailed the victory as a source for "African renewal," based on their "collective wisdom and support" that had not been "lost on FIFA." South Africa's president, Thabo Mbeki, described the World Cup as a "journey of hope," moving on from divisions, wars, conflict and poverty: "Soccer's World Cup in Africa will reaffirm our common humanity and prove we all belong to one family." It was a moment when the idealism of the sport and its potential for intercultural understanding and human cooperation transcended the grubby politicking of the football bureaucrats. The sports diplomacy employed by government personnel and football administrators as part of the bid had proposed four core ideals or values, in a pan-African vision: freedom, equality, solidarity and tolerance.[13] While still deputy president of the country, Mbeki had stressed foreign policy emphases on peace, democracy, respect for human rights and sustained development: these, he said, should be fundamental to the country's foreign policy, including initiatives in international sport.[14] Mandela knew the power of sport to symbolize social progress, express cultural transformations and reach for a better future: in the early years of the post-apartheid Rainbow Nation, his donning of the South African rugby team's shirt and cap for his country's victory in the final of the 1995 Rugby World Cup, celebrated in the movie *Invictus*, had confirmed his sincerity on this point.

Football has a deep-rooted place in the history of South African sport, despite the dominance of rugby and cricket in the (predominantly white) historical consciousness. At the end of the nineteenth and early in the twentieth century, football tours to and from South Africa contributed to the international growth of the game;[15] a black Orange Free State "Kaffir" side played English professional team Newcastle United, and other teams in Britain and France; the English side Corinthians toured South Africa; and a South African team played in several South American countries. The sport was popular across all social groups in pre-Union South Africa, with matches between black and white teams, though the racial divide and segregation were hardening. Chris Bolsmann provides an alliterative periodization of the white man's game – "development, domination and decline"[16] – up to the later 1970s, when football organizations in the country had to face up to their exclusion from the international arena. A single South African Football Association was not formed until 1991, after 16 years of expulsion from FIFA, and exclusion from Olympic status from 1970. The single integrated association was admitted to FIFA in 1992. Football in no small way contributed to a cultural politics contesting the apartheid system, as unity talks had been established in the mid-1980s between football associations that had for generations echoed and in effect perpetuated the apartheid system.[17] In the post-apartheid and democratized country, hosting and competing in the football World Cup would be a continuation of a long-term cultural and political project. The 2010 Finals, then, were great public relations for FIFA, bringing the event to the continent for the first time, and serious political idealism and progressive cultural politics for the host (rainbow) nation in the post-apartheid period. How, then, would the money-spinning side of FIFA events lie alongside this idealism? How could the cultural politics of integration and reconciliation be furthered by the World Cup circus coming to the country?

Germany 2006 had been a huge success, and some sponsors certainly had doubts about an African venue, compared to the more secure and lucrative consumer markets in Europe. But as long as the infrastructure – media, accommodation, transport, stadium safety – could be guaranteed, the exposure would justify the investment. If the events went smoothly, public order was maintained and the big teams got through to the later stages – generating massive global viewing figures – all would be well with the sponsors. Thomas Han, marketing executive at Hyundai, had no concerns about the image of FIFA and its main event, whatever the venue, as long as Hyundai could feature its banners, provide its fleet of vehicles and have its brand on prominent display throughout the tournament. He was more than satisfied with the market research on the Germany 2006 finals; and in a message to Hyundai colleagues, Jae-Wan Lee, Senior Executive Vice President in the company's Corporate Marketing Division, wrote about the 2006 event: "Now that it is over, we analyzed the results of our sponsorship of this global sporting festival, that is truly encouraging and magnificent. The importance of this encouraging sponsorship result ... for the Hyundai brand and our everyday efforts on PR and marketing activities as a whole is immense."[18]

Hyundai had implemented a "Goodwill Ball Roadshow" (covered by Eurosport and ESPN), sponsored football-themed TV programmes broadcast in 129 countries, and initiated "proactive use of the internet." For the latter, a website featured a Hyundai Fan Corner with Fan of the Match items, and a Virtual Showroom for the latest Hyundai models that were transporting the stars and the organizers across Germany. It hit 550 million page views. FIFA Fan Fests, the public viewing programmes that brought 18.5 million people out across the country, had four official partners, of which Hyundai was one. The company "implemented diverse on-site promotion and stage programs," and received the highest brand recognition of the four Fest partners, ahead of Coca-Cola and MasterCard. Hyundai's report summarized this marketing performance across the host cities of Germany as "astonishing." Its "unaided sponsorship awareness" rose by 78.5 per cent between September 2005 and July 2006, when the final was broadcast. In Russia, a country whose team did not even feature in the finals, brand awareness increased by a remarkable 253.3 per cent. Hyundai was eagerly anticipating a similar profile and level of exposure in South Africa 2010, and has ensured its status as a FIFA partner through to Brazil 2014 and Russia 2018. With a cumulative audience of 34 billion for 2006, the Korean company was not complaining about the cost of its long-term commitment, nor about any committee-room rivalries in the heart of the FIFA organization.

In South Africa 2010, Visa was at its first World Cup, having ousted MasterCard in an unethical behind-the-scenes process described in Chapter 7 of this book. In the stadia, fans could buy drinks (Coca-Cola of course) and snacks with cash, but not with any card other than Visa. Ticket sales demanded Visa transactions. Similarly, in the squares and malls of Johannesburg, Sony mounted impressive screen-based shows of the recent action; as you travelled down highways of host cities, Sony's logo and slogan – "make.believe" – were draped across the sky. Lest you'd flown in by another airline, Emirates reminded you of its privileged partner status on hoardings and billboards. Hyundai's air balloon hovered above FIFA's luxury hotels in Johannesburg's Sandton City. Adidas reported unprecedented sales of its Jabulani football, and installed out-door displays of its generations of high-selling World Cup balls in downtown Johannesburg. But in the townships and the poverty-stricken peripheral suburbs, there was little sign of football fiestas or cosmopolitan celebration. Few flags were flying on the dusty streets of the shanty towns, and many matches had far from capacity attendance. The FIFA-set prices included a special ticket category for South African residents, offering low-grade seats for US$18.15, but this far exceeded the reach of workers still paid in fruit and wine rather than cash, or of those with no work at all.[19] One of the greatest shows on earth, and in media history, was staged in large part for the metropolitan elites and the global con-sumer audience. Pitching to the affluent minority in the host country and the vast market worldwide, sponsors had no need to worry about the marginalized majority. The show would soon be over, and the sights of the marketing experts would be switched to Brazil.

South Africa prepared ten stadia for the tournament: Johannesburg's Soccer City and Ellis Park; Cape Town; Durban's Moses Mabhida; Port Elizabeth's Nelson Mandela Bay; Nelspruit's Mbombela; Pretoria's Loftus Versfeld; Rustenburg's Royal Bafokeng; Bloemfontein's Free State; and Polokwane's Peter Mokaba. Five of these ten were newly constructed, the others refurbished. Initial costs of 2 billion South African rand rose to 9 billion. Different pressures, not all from FIFA, affected outcomes. A 2004 FIFA inspection committee adjudged both Durban and Cape Town to have "suitable" stadia, yet both cities constructed new ones, the Cape Town one telegenically located between sea and mountains to please the eye of the global audience, and Durban's with a view to a future bid for the Olympics.[20]

I chose, during the 2010 event, to visit one of the newly constructed stadia, at Nelspruit, close to the border with Mozambique, for a match between Chile and Honduras; and one of the reconstructed stadia, at Rustenburg, for New Zealand versus Slovakia. It was easy to see how some argument might be made for the sustainability of the Rustenburg ground, being relatively accessible from urban centres such as Johannesburg and Pretoria. But the case for the Mbombela stadium was flimsy from the start, with administrative corruption within the local municipality well established, and little in the stadium's development linked to any sense of legacy planning.[21] The town boasted no established high-level sports team, and there was no available evidence of planned activity after the World Cup games. Local businesses might have benefited from a few bonanza days, in tea shops, gift shops or fast-food outlets close to the stadium on the edge of town, but most affluent fans and spectators got out of town as soon as the game was over, heading for the calm and comfort of a hunting lodge or boarding house in the high veldt, or the half-day drive back to Pretoria or Johannesburg. Chileans and Hondurans would hardly be swelling the coffers of the Nelspruit traders. The neutrals among us trailed away sadly, wondering how Mandela's dreams and aspirations might have worked out better for this small, essentially rural town.

There were nevertheless many positive dimensions to South Africa 2010. People of all backgrounds, ages and ethnicities flocked to each other's homes, and to screenings in malls, squares and public viewing spaces. Races and classes mixed to cheer on the South African team, *Bafana Bafana* (Boys Boys), for its three games; schoolchildren from Soweto were brought in to see Argentina play Nigeria in a carnival atmosphere in Johannesburg's Ellis Park. The opening and closing ceremonies were sources of great pride for people, and some spoke of this being the third time that sport had brought Nelson Mandela's post-apartheid Rainbow Nation together, after home victories in the Rugby World Cup in 1995 and the African Cup of Nations in Soweto in 1996.[22] These were passionately expressed feelings, transient though they may have been. They were the symbolic intangibles of the engagement of a public culture on a national level, with an event of international profile and impact.

The public is often more realistic than a disingenuous political class. More than half of 361 residents of Pretoria polled prior to the World

Cup recognized that problems such as crime, the economy, employment and racism could never be resolved by a one-off sports event.[23] Social scientists pointed out at an early point the realities of the business dynamics and commercial relationships underpinning the event: "FIFA's model has been a boost for old white capital and the new politically connected black elite who have joined hands in securing lucrative contracts."[24] Aspirations to stimulate business within South Africa were proved daydreams, as "for those aspects which are most central to the FIFA finals as globalized commercial enterprises – branding, promotion, mediatizing and the dissemination of match tickets – the agenda is firmly determined by transnational entities which are part of the FIFA corporate family."[25] A progressive development narrative that in part shaped the bid was also soon revealed to be an exploitative myth for the poor, the marginal and the homeless.[26]

Looking at the local context, the benefits to or betrayals of small communities and regional interests puts the rhetoric of the politicians and the myth-making of moneyspinners seriously into perspective. World Cup cycles are not just a cash cow for FIFA, in the generation of media and marketing rights; they are also close to risk-free for the federation. Only once in the modern period has a country had to renege on its World Cup hosting role and commitment: Colombia's political and economic volatility forced its withdrawal from the 1986 event, with Mexico stepping into the breach. England, with its hopeless and hapless bids for the 2006 and 2018 Finals, hoped and continues to hope to be the lucky substitute should Brazil fail to fulfil 2014 commitments, or should Qatar ever be deemed geographically, meteorologically or morally unfit to stage the 2022 event. In the end, the investment from the hosting country limits FIFA's financial inputs and costs. Financially, FIFA can hardly lose. It allocates the hosting role, demands close-to-unlimited standards of provision and infrastructure, and pockets the income from global media and marketing rights, for distribution according to its opaque financial procedures and organizational priorities and commitments.

This section ends with some consideration of the monies that have been spun in the financial cycle 2007–2010.[27] FIFA adjudged the 2010 World Cup "a major success from both an organisational and a financial perspective," with "a positive four-year result of USD 631 million. This result is based on total revenue of USD 4,189 million and total expenditure of USD 3,558 million." FIFA also noted, in the same overview, that it had survived unscathed the turbulence of the global financial crisis of 2008 onwards, with increased revenue compared to 2003–2006, so emerging in "a stronger position." This it attributed to increased income from marketing and television rights. Nevertheless, expenditure increased, on worldwide football development projects, higher prize money in 2010 and an increasing number of legal matters to fund. Systematic cost control is recognized to have matched costs to expenses, and "hedging foreign currencies" and a "conservative investment policy" protected the organization against losses, producing a "positive financial result of USD 77 million": "FIFA's reserves were further strengthened and stood at USD 1,280 million on 31 December 2010. FIFA has reached a solid level of reserves. Having sufficient reserves is of great importance to FIFA's financial independence and to its ability to react to unexpected events."[28]

The six FIFA Partners paid FIFA US$148.5 million in both 2009 and 2010. On a four-year cycle that would amount to US$594 million. If the six partners each pay the same, that's US$99 million dollars from each of them in a financial/World Cup cycle. Marketing rights are also bought by lower-order sponsors, with the World Cup Sponsors and National Supporters mentioned previously paying more than US$106 million in 2010, plus "value-in-kind transactions" of more than US$83 million, contributing to overall revenue from marketing rights for the World Cup of US$340,489,000; revenue from marketing rights for "other FIFA events" in the same year totalled a mere US$2,447,000.[29] Television broadcasting rights for the men's World Cup brought in US $715,144,000 in 2010,[30] more than double the marketing total.

From a position of near-bankruptcy in the early years of the century, following the collapse of ISL, FIFA, taking marketing into its own operation, has grown economically on an unprecedented scale. As its 2010 financial report acknowledges, despite the global recession, the commitment of sponsors has been sustained; the willingness of media outlets to pay higher prices than ever will not diminish as long as global audiences confirm the worldwide interest in the event. Sepp Blatter noted in his preface to the report that both existing and new multinational partners had already concluded long-term contracts.[31] The golden triangle of the sport, the media and the marketing agencies and sponsors has shown little sign of weakening, in FIFA's lucrative market. While Africa's first men's World Cup host country debated the ambiguities and sometimes dubious legacies of 2010, FIFA financiers and accountants smiled all the way home to their Swiss shores and shares; the financial report was introduced by chairman of the Finance Committee, Julio H. Grondona, of Argentina, and he emphasized the imminent reinvestment of "a significant propor-tion of FIFA's revenue" in football, anticipating therefore "lower annual results than in previous years."[32] A few months later, in November 2011, Grondona was answering queries as to how he, his family and his close associates had accumulated in excess of US$70 million in offshore accounts, much of it in the country of FIFA's headquarters, Switzerland.

Loss leaders

Competitions

FIFA's prime product and prize asset is, as focused upon in this chapter, the men's football World Cup, with its cycles of qualifying rounds and quadrennial World Cup Finals, featuring 32 teams in a month-long tournament that has become one of the most lucrative media events in broadcasting history. But FIFA also organizes other competitions for the national teams of its member associations and for top clubs. In 2015 Canada plans to welcome 24 teams for the FIFA Women's World Cup, in six cities spanning the world's second-largest country. The tournament was inaugurated in China in 1991; the first six Finals saw four winners, with Germany and the USA each gaining two titles, and Norway (1995) and Japan (2011) one. It is an event growing in popularity and profile. The final game in Germany in July 2011, between Japan and the USA, produced a new world record for tweets, peaking at 7,196 postings per second on the social networking site.[33] Yet the FIFA Women's World Cup is one of an extensive number of FIFA tournaments that are essentially bankrolled by the income derived from the men's World Cup. In late 2013 FIFA listed in its tournament timetable a cycle of ten men's events (excluding the Brazil 2014 World Cup), and five women's events.

In his 1974 manifesto, João Havelange had pledged to expand FIFA activities for the benefit of previously unsupported parts of the world. In the calendar of FIFA tournaments in Table 6.2[34] we see the dispersal of events beyond the powerhouses and centres of the world footballing elite. Early versions of these events were held in less traditional locations, as FIFA marketed the game in new territories. The first women's World Cup was in China, a huge and untapped market. In 1985, Nigeria won the first men's U-17 championship, in China. The men's U-20 tournament was inaugurated in 1977 in Tunisia, with Japan (1979) and Australia (1981) establishing the tournament's pedigree beyond the boundaries of the established football powers of Europe and Latin America. In 1989 Saudi Arabia showed its ambitions in the international football world by staging the event, followed by Qatar in 1995. This worldwide distribution of football events has been sustained by FIFA, keeping its long-term commitment to taking the game and some of its top events to smaller and less-developed countries and regions. In Sepp Blatter's administration, the needs of the small and the less well-off national associations have also been catered for in more direct, regular and financial ways, in the form of the *Goal* and Football for Hope initiatives.

Table 6.2 FIFA tournaments and venues, as listed in 2013

Men's tournaments	Women's tournaments
FIFA Interactive World Cup 2014	FIFA Women's World Cup, Canada 2015
FIFA U-20 World Cup, New Zealand 2015	Olympic Football Tournament, London 2012
FIFA U-17 World Cup, United Arab Emirates 2013	FIFA U-20 Women's World Cup, Canada 2014
FIFA Futsal World Cup, Thailand 2012	FIFA U-17 Women's World Cup, Costa Rica 2014
Blue Stars 2013/FIFA Youth Cup, Switzerland	Youth Olympic Football Tournament, Nanjing 2014
FIFA Confederations Cup, Brazil 2013	
FIFA Beach Soccer World Cup, Tahiti 2013	
FIFA Club World Cup, Morocco 2013	
Olympic Football Tournament, London 2012	
Youth Olympic Football Tournament, Nanjing 2014	

Source: FIFA website

Football development: the Goal project

Blatter came to power in 1998 promising the many small national associations whose votes he courted a form of "tailor-made" solution to their developmental problems. Under the letterhead "JSB for President" and with an address lent him by Michel Platini, joint chair of the France 1998 World Cup Organising Committee, he wrote to selected association presidents and general secretaries, addressing them as "dear friends" and saying that on election he would find resources to remedy their lack of money:

> After FIFA technical experts have taken stock of the individual situation for national associations on the spot, I want to make sure that these associations receive tailor-made assistance in establishing their technical, administrative and marketing programmes. For this purpose, every national association should have suitable possibilities for training and adequate resources for advancement at their disposal.[35]

"Suitable" and "adequate" could be defined case by case, and this is precisely what happened in the introduction and implementation of the *Goal* programme, FIFA's "special needs" model of aid to poorer, smaller national associations. *Goal* was launched in 1999, and by 2010 FIFA could report that it had "provided support for over 500 development projects across the world, with a total of USD 200 million having been invested in them."[36] Grass pitches, training academies, administrative headquarters; such football infrastructure mushroomed across the less privileged football world during Blatter's presidency. Futsal (the small-sided game, often played indoors) and beach football were also included in these developments:

> For the 2011–2014 cycle, and with the approval of the Congress, FIFA's Executive Committee has set funding for each *Goal* project at USD 500,000. In addition each project must be submitted to the *Goal* Bureau for its approval.[37]

Supplemented by the Financial Assistance Programme (FAP), the *Goal* initiative has kept Blatter's side of the bargain; in turn, 186 national associations backed his unopposed re-election in June 2011. Africa has had 143 projects, Asia 124, Europe 93, the Caribbean and North and Central America 79, Oceania 36 and South America 29. These have been shared by 193 countries, with 166 having had at least two projects.[38] While this has accomplished admirable and worthy objectives, it has also provided the FIFA president with a platform for constant campaigning and regular reminders about who's in charge.[39] The late Charles Dempsey of New Zealand, Oceania president, explained the simplicity of the *Goal* strategy:

> There are more have-nots than haves in FIFA. If the have-nots get anything, they'll stay faithful. Blatter's been very clever. *Goal* isn't delegated to the confederations, it's run from FIFA. We know he's done wrong, but he's got us this.[40]

Talking to the BBC, Blatter offered a robust defence of the programme: "This is so lovely, I have to tell you. In 1998, the one item of which I was proud, accepted by the Congress, I said I am launching the *Goal* project. I do it and now it is said it is for my promotion. No."[41] FIFA general secretary Michel Zen-Ruffinen, wholly informed from the inside, put the case for the prosecution, claiming that Blatter abused the *Goal* project by using visits as a means of "campaigning for the re-election":

> The prioritisation of the need analysis of countries was changed by the president in the presence of witnesses according to his travel schedules so that he could inform each visited country that it had been selected for the programme. For example, in the priority

orders Cameroon was replaced by Burkina Faso, Congo DR by Cape Verde, Angola by Botswana ... many associations are still persuaded that they will lose any financial support if they do not support the current regime.[42]

Goal could have been the flagship initiative that marked FIFA as a worldwide force for good. But conceived as a tailor-made solution by a power-hungry aspiring president, it is tainted by the politics of personal ambition and institutional survival. Nowhere has any evidence emerged of any remotely adequate form of monitoring of the monies that have gone to Blatter's "dear friends" in the most needy of the national associations.

Football development: Football for Hope

FIFA's programmes of intervention include its contribution to the "sport for development and peace" phenomenon.[43] In 2005, FIFA began integrating numerous community-based and non-governmental organizations in its Football for Hope initiative. Working with streetfootballworld, which was founded in 2002 by the German Youth Football Foundation, it aimed to provide direct support to organizations and raise their profiles. This, FIFA's website claims, created "a unique and global movement programme that uses the power of football to achieve sustainable social development." Children and young people are the target of these initiatives; tools are developed that make a difference to their lives, and FIFA reports that it is "contributing to positive social change on a global scale":

> Thanks to its many successes on the ground, its global reach and the strong commitment of its founders, the Football for Hope movement has become an attractive platform for public and private sectors, civil society and multilateral development institutions to invest sustainably and develop innovative partnerships for social development.
>
> Today, the Football for Hope movement provides access to programmes which serve hundreds of thousands of young people all over the world. The movement is a catalyst for innovation and social investment for various sectors of society and is increasingly gaining recognition and attracting new resources and expertise.[44]

Streetfootballworld reports working with 90 organizations in 60 countries, and in 2011 alone "empowering more than 600,000 young people."[45] This is an emotive sphere of work, and FIFA has gained the support of the UN Secretary-General Ban Ki-moon, who recognizes the "global reach" and "gender-transcendent" nature of football, and the game's capacity to "instil confidence, hope, and pride in the underdog, and promote teamwork and support."[46] Blatter confirms the "strategic importance to FIFA" of Football for Hope, linked to the sense of football as a "school for life." More than 200 programmes have been supported across all continents, with annual funding, exchange opportunities, material and infrastructure support and capacity-building. The scheme also "uses the promotional platform of the FIFA World Cup™ to raise awareness on social issues and develop legacy projects."[47] Europe has had 38 programmes, Asia 19, Oceania 8, North and Central America 15, South America 60 and Africa 93.

In 2010 a campaign, "20 Centres for 2010," was run (in fact was listed as an "Official Campaign" for the 2010 World Cup Finals[48]), to open Football for Hope centres on the African continent, six in South Africa, another 13 elsewhere on the continent and one in Cape Verde. Wilfried Lemke, Special Adviser to Ban Ki-moon on Sport for Development and Peace, observes: "The organisations which are part of Football for Hope are passionate about social change in their communities. With their commitment and experience, they contribute to the achievement of the UN Millennium Development Goals in Africa and worldwide."[49] This is powerful and positive publicity for FIFA, though much remains to be done in relation to consistent and reliable monitoring of the resources that are directed into the programmes. Sport in development contexts has been seen as a basis for both the generation of infrastructure to support the provision of sport, and for the cultivation of wider benefits that sport participation might stimulate in relation to social issues such as HIV and intercultural conflict.[50] FIFA has intervened to offer forms of support embracing both these emphases, and it remains to be seen whether any monitoring and evaluation materials will be used to gauge the degree to which this commitment and any associated idealism have led to the realization of tangible goals.

Balancing the books

Two economic ideas and their interrelationship therefore illuminate the finances of FIFA: the cash cow and the loss leader. They are both essentially simple ideas, and the trajectory of FIFA finances, once restored to credit, has been shaped by them.

A cash cow is an asset that, once bought and equipped to produce a desirable good or commodity, needs little upkeep or maintenance in order to keep creating a quality product and large profits.[51] The men's World Cup, and to a growing but still relatively peripheral extent the Women's World Cup, have rescued FIFA finances since the early years of the twenty-first century, when ISL's collapse showed how vulnerable

FIFA's budget was. Combining history, marketing, tradition, global expansion and local cultural nuances, the cyclical mega-event of the men's World Cup has become FIFA's cash cow. If the cow died, was stolen or malfunctioned, the consequences would be dire for the beneficiary of its prolific output. If FIFA lost the World Cup or the world audience turned to another sport, FIFA would have nothing, because FIFA's products beyond the men's World Cup are, in the main, loss leaders.

Loss leaders are products that are sold for very little because it is projected that these unprofitable sales stimulate sales of more desirable or profitable goods. It is in this sense that all the competitions listed in FIFA's event calendar, along with its redistributive initiatives and its CSR programmes, are loss leaders.

The advantages of such a balance, for FIFA, or at least for the FIFA administration and some leading figures in the organization, are that the loss leaders can stimulate interests and markets that feed into or overlap with the markets for the top product; and in fact, operating as a combination of a monopoly and a non-profit organization, FIFA can generate huge revenues, in particular from its sponsors, by selling the cash cow and loss leaders in the same package. Strategically, too, the main beneficiaries of many of the loss leaders will prove faithful followers of the funder and patron of their activities. The mission projected by Havelange in his 1974 manifesto can in many respects be said to have been accomplished; the economic equilibrium of FIFA is rooted in revenues from the advanced world and the continuing support of the majority of member organizations, which have consistently benefited from the Havelange vision and Blatter's inheritance and continuation of that agenda. In the next chapter, though, we consider crises that have threatened FIFA's stability and image, and begin to ask whether FIFA's achievements have been outweighed – or at least undermined – by some of the means by which they have been accomplished.

Notes

1 This account of the protests in Brazil draws on the BBC News report, "Protest-hit Brazil 'missed chance' to improve services," 28 June 2013, http://www.bbc.co.uk/news/world-latin-america-23093630, consulted 30 June 2013.

2 Jonathan Watts, "Sepp Blatter urges Brazil protesters not to link grievances to football," *Guardian*, 19 June 2013, http://www.guardian.co.uk/football/2013/jun/19/sepp-blatter-brazil-football-protests, consulted 30 June 2013.

3 Ben Smith, "Brazil protests have not harmed FIFA – Sepp Blatter," *BBC Sport*, 29 June 2013, http://www.bbc.co.uk/sport/0/football/23108001, consulted 30 June 2013.

4 Isabel Hilton, "Football, riches and protest," *New Statesman*, 28 June–4 July 2013: 27.

5 Jules Boykoff, "At Brazil's Confederations Cup, a dress rehearsal for dissent," *Dissent: A Quarterly of Politics and Culture*, 3 July 2013, http://www.dissent magazine.org/blog/at-brazils-confederations-cup-a-dress-rehearsal-for-dissent, consulted 20 July 2013.

6 *Fox Soccer*, "Blatter pledges $100 million to Brazil," 28 June 2013, http://msn. foxsports.com/foxsoccer/worldcup/story/sepp-blatter-pledges-100-million-dollars-to-brazil-after-unrest-062813, consulted 30 June 2013.

7 The detail presented here is compiled from *Sport Intern*, 7/9, 15 May 1986: 1; *Sport Intern*, 10/18 and 19, 15 October 1989: 5; FIFA, *Report – FIFA World Cup USA '94*, 202; and FIFA documents in the author's collection from the men's World Cups of 1998, 2002, 2006, 2010 and 2014.

8 Celia Lury, *Brands: The Logos of the Global Economy* (London: New York, 2004), 10.

9 Ibid., 12. See also FIFA, "The History of the FIFA Corporate Mark," Edition 2 – 09/02/2011 (fcm-history_090211.pdf [SECURED]), http://www.fifa.com/ mm/document/affedration/marketing/58/25/93/fcm-history_090211.pdf, consulted 20 January 2014.

10 Celia Lury, *Consumer Culture*, 2nd edition (Cambridge: Polity Press, 2011), 214–215.

11 Wally Olins, *On B®and* (London: Thames & Hudson, 2003), 249.

12 See CNN.com, "South Africa gets 2010 World Cup," 15 May 2004, http:// edition.cnn.com/2004/SPORT/football/05/15/worldcup.2010/, consulted 8 November 2011.

13 Sifiso Mxolisi Ndlovu, "Sports as cultural diplomacy: The 2010 FIFA World Cup in South Africa's foreign policy," *Soccer & Society*, 11/1 and 2, 2010: 144–153.

14 Ibid., 146.

15 Chris Bolsmann, "South African football tours at the turn of the twentieth century: Amateurs, pioneers, and profits," *African Historical Review*, 42/1, 2010: 91–112; and "The 1899 Orange Free State football team tour of Europe: 'Race,' imperial loyalty and sporting contest," *The International Journal of the History of Sport*, 28/1, 2011: 81–97.

16 Chris Bolsmann, "White football in South Africa: Empire, apartheid and change, 1892–1977," *Soccer & Society*, 11/1, 2010: 29–45.

17 Peter Alegi and Chris Bolsmann, "From apartheid to unity: White capital and Black power in the racial integration of South African football, 1976–92," *African Historical Review*, 42/1, 2010: 1–18. See also Paul Darby, *Africa, Football and FIFA: Politics, Colonialism and Resistance* (London: Frank Cass, 2002).

18 I was interviewing Thomas Han at the Hyundai headquarters, Seoul, South Korea, on 19 September 2007. The Lee quote and marketing results are from the *Hyundai 2006 FIFA World Cup*^TM *Sponsorship Report* (September 2006).

19 Alan Tomlinson, *The World Atlas of Sport: Who Plays What, Where, and Why* (Brighton and Oxford: Myriad Editions/New Internationalist, 2011), 20.

20 See Richard Tomlinson, Orli Bass and Udesh Pillay's introduction to their edited book *Development and Dreams: The Urban Legacy of the 2010 Football World Cup* (Cape Town: HSRC Press, 2009), 7; and André P. Czeglédy, "Urban dreams: The 2010 Football World Cup and expectations of benefit in Johannesburg," in *Development and Dreams*, eds. Tomlinson et al., 231.

21 Richard Tomlinson, "Anticipating 2011," in *Development and Dreams*, eds. Tomlinson et al., 107.

22 Hosting the continent's championship in early 2013 offered another opportunity for football to personify the Rainbow Nation in triumph, but South Africa lost to Mali in the quarter-finals.

23 Heather Gibson, Matt Walker, Kiki Kapalnidou, Brijesh Thapa, Sue Geldenhuys and Willie Coetzee, "The perceived social impacts of the 2010 FIFA World Cup: Resident perceptions from one host city," paper delivered at ISSA (International Sociology of Sport Association) conference, Havana, Cuba, July 2011.

24 Ashwin Desai and Goolam Vahed, "World Cup 2010: Africa's turn or the turn on Africa?" *Soccer & Society*, 11/1 and 2, 2010: 154–167, 163.

25 Scarlett Cornelissen, "Football's tsars: Proprietorship, corporatism, and politics in the 2010 FIFA Word Cup," *Soccer & Society*, 11/1and 2, 2010: 131–143, 140.

26 Percy Ngonyama, "The 2010 FIFA World Cup: Critical voices from below," *Soccer & Society*, 11/1 and 2, 2010: 168–180.

27 The financial detail is drawn from FIFA, "FIFA Financial Report 2010: 61st FIFA Congress, Zurich, 31 May and 1 June 2011" (Zurich: FIFA, 2011), http://www.fifa.com/mm/document/affederation/administration/01/39/20/45/web_-fifa_fr2010_eng[1].pdf, consulted 7 November 2011.

28 FIFA, "FIFA Financial Report 2010," 14.

29 FIFA, "FIFA Financial Report 2010," 73.

30 FIFA, "FIFA Financial Report 2010," 72.

31 FIFA, "FIFA Financial Report 2010," 7.

32 FIFA, "FIFA Financial Report 2010," 9.

33 Evan Fanning, "Women's World Cup Final between USA and Japan sets Twitter record," *Guardian*, 18 July 2011, http://www.theguardian.com/football/2011/jul/18/womens-world-cup-twitter-record, consulted 20 July 2011.

34 FIFA, "Tournaments," http://www.fifa.com/tournaments/index.html, consulted 12 December 2013.

35 Letter dated 22 May 1998, reproduced in John Sugden and Alan Tomlinson, *Great Balls of Fire: How Big Money is Hijacking World Football* (Edinburgh: Mainstream, 1999), 123.

36 FIFA, "Football Development: Goal: Presentation and status," http://www.fifa.com/aboutfifa/footballdevelopment/projects/goalprogramme/status.html, consulted 26 November 2011.

37 Ibid.

38 Ibid.

39 For an account of this less worthy side of the implementation of Blatter's tailor-made solutions, see John Sugden and Alan Tomlinson, *Badfellas: FIFA Family at War* (Edinburgh: Mainstream, 2003), 257–262.

40 Interview with the author, Auckland, New Zealand, 2002.

41 BBC, *Newsnight*, TV broadcast, 22 and 29 May 2002.

42 Zen-Ruffinen was presenting evidence to the FIFA ExCo. This is quoted in Sugden and Tomlinson, *Badfellas*, 261.

43 FIFA, "Football for Hope: Football's commitment to social development" (Zurich: FIFA), http://www.fifa.com/mm/document/afsocial/footballforhope/51/56/34/footballforhopebrochureen%5fneutral.pdf, consulted 21 July 2013.

44 FIFA, "Social Responsibility: Football for Hope," http://www.fifa.com/aboutfifa/socialresponsibility/footballforhope/mission.html, consulted 21 July 2013.

45 streetfootballworld, http://www.streetfootballworld.org/aboutus, consulted 21 July 2013.

46 FIFA, "Football for Hope," 3.
47 Ibid., 4.
48 FIFA, "2010 FIFA World Cup South Africa: Organisation," http://www.fifa. com/worldcup/archive/southafrica2010/organisation/partners/index.html, consulted 12 December 2013.
49 FIFA, "Football for Hope," 19.
50 Fred Coalter, "Sport in development. Accountability or development?" in *Sport and International Development*, eds. Roger Levermore and Aaron Beacom (Basingstoke: Palgrave Macmilllan, 2009).
51 Cash cows are defined in the "Boston matrix" business analysis tool as "mature businesses or products with a high market share but low growth rate" (entry for "Boston matrix" in Jonathan Law, ed., *A Dictionary of Business and Management*, 5th edition (Oxford: Oxford University Press, 2009), 77, http://www.oxfordreference.com/view/10.1093/acref/9780199234899.001.0001/acref-9780199234899-e-736?rskey=Y318UJ&result=761, consulted 8 December 2013). Typically for this type of product a business has already made its investment, but the product continues to generate substantial cash flow; the surplus can be used to support other products that need marketing or investment. FIFA's status as a non-commercial association does not prevent its exploitation of the men's World Cup as a classic cash cow product.

7   Crises

FIFA is no stranger to crisis and controversy, and the issues of democracy and accountability have frequently been at the forefront of its major crises. Any organization that claims to speak for every country in the world will encounter predictable and passionate challenges questioning its representativeness, and face predictable and recurrent calls to reform. As the profile of the sport has expanded, such challenges and calls have multiplied and intensified. Emerging countries have demanded more places at the table for the most lucrative events, continental confederations have sought to acquire more influence within FIFA positions, processes and decision-making, and countries have battled in increasingly bitter fashion to win the right to host the men's World Cup. All of these examples have produced high-profile crises, about organizational credibility, leadership styles and often abuse of power in the decision-making process. In this chapter I give an overview some of the major crises that FIFA has faced over the first decade of the twenty-first century, and then focus in more detail on two of these, showing how FIFA has responded to allegations and evidence concerning the nature of its organizational and business practices.

Crises

2000: Germany wins the right to host the 2006 World Cup finals, amid controversy over vote-rigging[1]

The German bid won by a single vote – 12 votes to South Africa's 11 – with New Zealand's Charles Dempsey, president of the Oceania confederation, abstaining. If Dempsey had voted for South Africa, the deciding vote would have gone to Sepp Blatter, ExCo chair, who in all likelihood would have felt compelled to award the event to South Africa, in part as a means of repaying the African confederation and continent for the votes that had helped him to gain the presidency two years earlier. Dempsey became a worldwide scapegoat for the lost South African cause. He had voted for England in the first round, and consistently stated that his voting actions were a personal responsibility, that he was not mandated by his confederation to support any specific candidate.

The English FA had been part of the campaign to stage the tournament, but was never close to winning the race. In March 1998, as the battle for the FIFA presidency was intensifying, outgoing president Havelange was welcomed to the official residence of Prime Minister Tony Blair, in Downing Street, London. It had become a commonplace by this time for FIFA and IOC leaders to talk up bids for their most exclusive events, and Havelange emerged from his half-hour meeting flattering and parroting the rhetoric of the English bid: England is the cradle of the game; its pedigree is outstanding, hosting and winning the 1966 World Cup and staging an exemplary Euro '96; the country would have, by 2006, the ultimate stage for the event, in the form of a rebuilt Wembley Stadium. "It's the personal wish of President Havelange," FIFA's interpreter and communications chief Keith Cooper announced, "that the FIFA Executive Committee will decide, in two years' time, that the World Cup of 2006 will indeed take place here."[2]

The FA, with little representation in the corridors of power of the international game at either European or world level, had a negligible base for its bid, and indeed alienated UEFA by going back on an agreement, albeit an informal one, with Germany. Former FA chairman, the late Bert Millichip, conceded that Germany had helped gain support for England's bid for Euro 1996, made at a time when the reputation of English football was at an all-time low in the wake of concerns about hooligan fans; in return, "Germany said that it would like to announce its interest to run at 2006 ... . I may well have indicated we will support you, at that time, but there was no agreement." UEFA president Lennart Johansson begged to differ and recalled: "We had a gentleman's agreement. All the big nations were present and they know we said 'let's go to England for Euro '96 and to Germany for World Cup 2006'."

Regardless of this, the FA ploughed on with the bid, and in May 1999 all 24 members of the FIFA ExCo, plus wives and partners, were flown to and from London, put up in the best hotels, offered circle seats at *Phantom of the Opera*, entertained at a royal party with Prince Charles at his Highgrove residence, and given VIP tickets for the FA Cup Final. The Foreign and Commonwealth Office helped gain access to key decision-makers; provided assessments of the attitudes of international sporting bodies; offered high-level hospitality within the UK to selected individuals and opinion-formers; facilitated visa applications; helped with dissemination of publicity; briefed journalists on positive image-making; organized special events at overseas missions and residences; and arranged formal and informal approaches to key personnel by heads of mission and senior diplomatic staff.

All this was to little avail, as the English bid was perceived as arrogant, disloyal, imperious, negative and doomed, by other British national associations as well as veteran football politicians across Europe, Asia, Africa and the Americas. This had nothing to do with the technical excellence of facilities – though the English bid was, provoking an incredulous response from the FA and its allies, ranked third behind Germany and South Africa by FIFA's inspection committee – and everything to do with networks, alliances and reciprocity. Germany, close to the date of the decision, was clinching business and trade deals worth millions of marks: 1200 bazookas to Saudi Arabia; aid to future FIFA partner Hyundai; purchase, by German FA sponsor Bayer, of Korean plastic manufacturer Sewon Enterprises; and further investment in Korea by chemical giant BASF. Bayer also invested in Thailand, home of ExCo member Worawi Makudi, in polycarbonate production in the Map Ta Phut plant.

England faded from the race early on. When Germany played an effective political game and pipped South Africa to the decision, Blatter was condemned as an incompetent leader. But he had New Zealander Dempsey as scapegoat, and stayed uninvolved in the vote itself, claiming the moral high ground as he could plot future World Cups for the African continent (2010), the romantic if not historic home of the game; Brazil (2014), the largest country in the world; Russia (2018); and the oil-rich Qatar (2022). He could also reassure his sponsors that the World Cup, following the shared Asian venues of Korea and Japan, would return to the heart of advanced consumer capitalism in Western Europe. There would be a place for idealism next time around, once the financial future of FIFA had been secured, for around the corner was the collapse of long-term partner ISL, precipitating one of FIFA's most serious financial crises.

2001: ISL bankruptcy, securitization and the ExCo fallout

Long-term FIFA partner ISL, the Dassler-inspired broker of so many FIFA, UEFA and IOC initiatives, collapsed in 2001 (as described in Chapter 5), leaving FIFA finances in a precarious state. Accounting practices covered the cracks, with FIFA reporting future income against World Cup rights – "securitization" – within its accounts, so minimizing the public profile of its financial crisis. But within the FIFA hierarchy, the increasingly autocratic style of the Blatter presidency stimulated a groundswell of opposition. The following May, 11 members of the FIFA ExCo and general secretary Michel Zen-Ruffinen mounted a challenge to Blatter just weeks before the FIFA presidential election in Seoul. Zen-Ruffinen presented a paper, marked "strictly confidential," to the ExCo meeting of 3 May 2002.[3] This makes for extraordinary reading. While CONCACAF's Chuck Blazer was claiming that "Blatter's administration [was] much more transparent" than the previous one,[4] Zen-Ruffinen produced a litany of charges questioning the integrity and competence of Blatter's presidential leadership. In his opening comment on Blatter's management practices, he wrote:

> The President, against the statutes, took over the management and administration of FIFA combining both, thereby working with a few persons of his trust only and manipulating the whole network through the material and administrative power he gained to the benefit of third persons and his personal interests. FIFA today is run like a dictatorship.[5]

The general secretary went on to catalogue cases of financial and legal mismanagement by the FIFA leadership. Versions of these charges were formulated in documentation dated 10 May in a "Criminal Complaint" against Blatter (the "Accused"), filed on behalf of the 11 ExCo members ("Complainants"). This document was delivered by hand to the public prosecutor's office in Zurich.[6] This was strong stuff indeed. The Complaint invoked Articles 138 and 158 of the Swiss Criminal Code, relating respectively to "misappropriation" or "unlawful use" of assets or property entrusted to an official, and to "criminal mismanagement" of another's resources. For each of these, an offender could receive a custodial sentence of up to five years. This was division on a scale never previously encountered in FIFA administration. Less than a month later, Blatter faced his electorate at the 2002 Congress.

2002: Blatter's re-election as president[7]

Defeating Cameroon's Issa Hayatou in Seoul at the end of May 2002, Blatter won his second presidential election. His rival was the incumbent president of the African confederation (CAF). With more than 50 national members, any concerted pan-African campaign, along with some strategic alliances with confederations or factions within confederations, could have threatened Blatter. The FIFA presidency rests on winning at least two-thirds of the available votes at the FIFA Congress.

But Hayatou gained only 56 votes, barely more than the total number of members in CAF. Blatter gained 139, a first-round winning majority of 83. Nine of FIFA's 204 members, for reasons of suspension and unavailability, did not vote. Four years on from 1998, following crisis after crisis in financial, institutional and ethical spheres, Blatter was granted a more than doubled winning majority.

Blatter had offered "tailor-made" solutions to small nations just days before his initial election to the presidency in 1998.[8] The Havelange administration (of which Blatter was of course the chief operating officer) had already apportioned every single national association a million dollars, payable over the next four years in annual instalments; the national associations would not want to see this jeopardized – particularly the smaller associations, to which this was big money. In a letter he now proposed that after "FIFA technical experts have taken stock of the individual situation for the national associations on the spot," some would receive "tailor-made assistance" in establishing administrative, technical and marketing programmes. The "less privileged" national associations, those without an "appropriate technical infrastructure," would stand to gain greatly from these tailor-made solutions. The outcome was the *Goal* programme.

As Blatter approached the 2002 election, in the aftermath of the revelations, accusations and court papers triggered by his general secretary, the *Goal* programme offered Blatter himself tailor-made solutions, at the Congress ballot box; recipients and beneficiaries of the *Goal* programme would have little interest in arcane legal proceedings in Zurich, while accepting the largesse of Blatter's redistributive strategy. By the time of the presidential election, seven member associations of the smallest confederation, Oceania, for instance, had received US $4,200,106, and FIFA had committed US$80 million to development around the world, with three development offices for the AFC (Asia), four for CAF (Africa), three for South, Central and North America and the Caribbean (CONMEBOL and CONCACAF) and one for Oceania. Just weeks after the presidential election, the Vanuatu Football Federation's share, US$424,827, had made possible the construction of four playing areas and a technical centre. In my researches, I had been looking for Johnny Tinsley-Lulu, president of the Vanuatu association, to discuss the detail of these developments, and saw the neglect of Port Vila's main football stadium, clearly untouched by FIFA's transforming generosity. But faxes and phone calls went unanswered, and Tinsley-Lulu turned up in Seoul no doubt unfaltering in his loyalty to the FIFA administration that could process such funds to his generally unmonitored administration. When FIFA had visited for the laying of the foundation stone of the Vanuatu development, Tinsley-Lulu had been there, presiding over the pig-killing part of an adapted traditional ceremony.

In Tonga, FIFA Congress delegate Ahongalu Fusimaholi welcomed Blatter to "shovel the first mound of soil to officially launch" his country's *Goal* project. Blatter was in Tonga for the Oceania congress the week before the 2002 World Cup kickoff, and the election contest with Issa Hayatou, but was happy to double up on duties. His lounge suit and grey silk tie were complemented by a garland of orange blooms around his neck, as he forced a smile while digging into the earth for the ceremony. Hayatou was in town too, but had no *Goal* gifts to promote in his run-up to the election.

Zen-Ruffinen's presentation to the ExCo did not mince words:

> The President has used and abused "GOAL" for his personal interests as a vehicle to retain the services of various personal advisers to the President and for campaigning ... . The President is taking advantage of GOAL and FAP [the Financial Assistance Programme] by using them as vehicles to influence the occurrences in and around FIFA. This is particularly evident in the CONCACAF region where many associations are still persuaded that they will lose any financial support if they do not support the current regime.[9]

The CONCACAF region was Chuck Blazer (general secretary) and Jack Warner (president) territory, and Blazer confirmed on the eve of Blatter's re-election that his confederation:

> can continue to deliver block votes where ... common interest is concerned. This is certainly the case in the Presidency and there are other issues as well, but this is one of the few which is voted on by the membership in full.[10]

CONCACAF had recently benefited from a US$1 million payment, accounted for under the *Goal* project, though "contrary to procedural rules for this project."[11]

In 2004, Blatter announced:

> Let the women play in more feminine clothes like they do in volleyball ... . They could, for example, have tighter shorts. Female players are pretty, if you excuse me for saying so, and they already have some different rules to men – such as playing with a lighter ball. That decision was taken to create a more female aesthetic, so why not do it in fashion?[12]

He retained the capacity to shock and entertain, and to be ridiculed by the wider world at the same time as being feared and respected in FIFA's inner world.

In 2006, FIFA replaced MasterCard with Visa as World Cup partner. This took FIFA into the judicial system of the United States, and is considered in more detail later. But scrutiny and condemnation in court cases on the other side of the Atlantic could be relatively easily brushed aside, with the grand project of the House of FIFA underway and close to completion. In May 2007, Blatter won a third presidential term after a fifth year in his second term, as elections had been switched to the year following men's World Cup Finals. He was nominated by 66 of the national associations and elected unopposed at the 57th Congress in Zurich. Two years later he was celebrating ten years in power. On 16 June 2008, he wrote to AFC president, Qatar's Mohamed Bin Hammam, recollecting the "very special moment in my life" when he was elected to the presidency: "Everyone knows that in football, very few matches are ever won by one player alone. Therefore I would like to thank you for your support and above all for your tireless work back then. Without you, dear Mohamed, none of this would ever have been possible." Let us "stay on the ball," Blatter continued, "with drive and commitment ... to work together in our duty to put football on the right path for years to come." Blatter signed himself "en profonde amitié," to the man who had provided jet transport and appropriate campaigning aid for that "very special moment" back in 1998.[13] Challenging for the FIFA presidency itself less than three years after Blatter's fulsome praise and thanks, Bin Hammam was near the end of his high-profile career, exposed then suspended for offering bribes to Caribbean nations for votes for the presidency.

In December 2010, FIFA's ExCo awarded the 2018 men's World Cup to Russia and the 2022 tournament to Qatar. The resulting furore, stirred up by Western commentators in particular but also by many football neutrals to whom the Qatar decision made little sense, generated an *annus horribilis* for FIFA, lasting through May and June 2011, when Blatter was re-elected unopposed as president following the suspension of Bin Hammam,[14] and into November 2011, completing the year of crisis and farce, when Blatter told the world that racism in a football match can be settled at the end of a game by "a handshake." If there has been any single issue that has rankled Blatter during his tenure of the presidency, it is race. Any allegation of ethnic or racist discrimination or bias within FIFA can derail the whole FIFA mission. Having wooed a world of multiple religions and ethnicities throughout his career, Blatter knows this, but is still capable of *faux pas* on the issue. It was his simplistic formula of the handshake as a means of countering and combating racism that led him to grant an unusually extended interview to the BBC's sports editor, David Bond.

Blatter has negotiated his way through his decade and a half in power with a mix of styles – buffoon one day, enforcer the next; he has been a gift to the media – traditional, social and new – in the time of speeded-up communication and instant news. The world media swooped on his naive statement on racism, after he had already been rendered increasingly vulnerable by the falling out with his rival for the presidency, Bin Hammam, and other ambitious careerists within the FIFA hierarchy, which had ushered in the most sustained crisis in FIFA's *annus horribilis*. Throughout Blatter's tenure as president, though, crisis management has been the order of the day. In the remainder of this chapter, I give two detailed examples, drawing on evidence from legal documents from Switzerland and the USA, that show how FIFA has responded to crises – perceived and real – in the courts: the first, from 2003, relates to the publication of my book *Badfellas: FIFA Family at War*;[15] the second to FIFA's conduct in its negotiations with MasterCard and Visa in 2006, in the tendering process to become a FIFA partner, or sponsor.

Court games 1: FIFA responses to critique

On 22 August 2003, the bailiff from the Brighton County Court (in England, UK) called at my personal residence to deliver some court papers. These were from Nobel and Hug solicitors, Zurich, on behalf of two plaintiffs, FIFA (Plaintiff 1), and Joseph S. Blatter (Plaintiff 2), and constituted an application for an injunction against the co-authored book *Badfellas: FIFA Family at War*. The request was to forbid the four named defendants – myself, my co-author, the publisher and Amazon Germany – from distributing the book for as long as seven specific passages, and the photograph of Sepp Blatter on the front cover, were included; the application was framed as a "petition" in regard to "injury to personal status" (with FIFA itself seen for legal purposes as a person, as well as Blatter). The petition requested "a so-called super-provisional injunction, e.g. order precautionary arrangements to be made immediately for the time being without hearing the opponents. This will be subject to *high urgency*. High urgency results in this case from the immediately pending the [sic] launch of the book ... in Switzerland" by the publisher and Amazon. The case for high urgency was based on the perceived threat that publication and distribution in Switzerland would make "another circle of persons ... aware of the accusations," and that the launch of the book would cause "injuries to someone's personality ... as with each additional delivery of a copy, more and more persons would be made aware of the false and slanderous allegations of corruption." Distribution of the book threatened to cause "a serious and irreversible injury to the personalities of the Plaintiffs. Any distribution of the book will daily increase this injury to their personalities due to more and more new purchasers being able to read the statements of Defendants 1–2," these latter being myself and my co-author. The injunction was refused. What were Sepp Blatter, and his legal representative Professor Dr Peter Nobel, so concerned about? What, more precisely, were the statements that prompted FIFA as an institution, and the FIFA president, to invest this amount of time and resource in seeking to silence a couple of academic researchers?

There is an air of indiscriminate panic in the petition. The claims move quickly from talking of a perceived threat to the personalities (image, or reputation, presumably) of FIFA and Blatter, to a harder, more certain assertion that publication "would" (not "might" or "may") have deleterious effects on the public personality of the organization and its president. In order to make the legal case, Professor Nobel and his team had to both contextualize the work, and engage in their own interpretive exercise:

> The material environment of the book may be assumed to be of judicial notice: In the summer of 1998, Plaintiff 2 was elected President of FIFA, the World Football Association, succeeding Havelange, his long-term predecessor. In June 2002 his appointment was approved by an overwhelming majority. Overall, the book "Badfellas – Fifa Family at War" is a "broadside" against FIFA, the World Football Association and its President Joseph S. Blatter. To the average reader, the title of the book "Badfellas – Fifa Family at War" creates a clear association to the Mafia and implies behaviour of a contemptible character of Plaintiff 2 and other functionaries of Plaintiff 1. In summary one may state that FIFA is portrayed as a corrupt organization, the exponents of which, under the cover of sports, allegedly have nothing else in mind than to enrich themselves and play power games. (See "Badfellas – FIFA at war", page 7, 33–35, 38, title and back pages.)

Not for the only time in the petition, the final reference to the book here gives the title incorrectly, or in abbreviated form, omitting the word "Family." And the word "corrupt" is also used, something the authors of the book never did – though two reviews excerpted on the front and back covers, from the *Independent* newspaper and *Total*

Football magazine, use the noun "corruption." Professor Nobel picked up on these reviews as the first two of the seven selected offending passages, arguing that "The Plaintiffs are discussed throughout the book, with the passages quoted in the petition only being the worst published to their disadvantage," and that "Portrayal of situations and persons in the book 'Badfellas – Fifa at war' is neither globally true nor in detail."

The other five items picked up on by FIFA's lawyers related to: the book's title; former General Secretary Michel Zen-Ruffinen's documentation of FIFA's organizational practices, in the wake of the ISL financial collapse of 2001 and in the build-up to the 2002 FIFA presidential election, as catalogued in the "Criminal Complaint" emanating from 11 members of the FIFA ExCo; a comparison with business practices in the corporate world; a comment on the leadership style of the FIFA president; and accusations of bribery for support that would have worked in Blatter's favour at the FIFA presidential election that took Blatter from the general secretary's office to the president's suite in Paris in 1998. I consider these five charges in turn.

First, the petition subjects the book's title to some sophisticated semantic deconstruction: "The meaning of the word 'Badfellas' is a colloquialism for 'bad boys' on the one hand and to the average reader, to [sic] combination of 'Bad' and 'Fellas' will clearly generate associations with the famous Mafia film 'GoodFellas' by Martin Scorsese." As members of the "Fifa family," the Plaintiffs' behaviour is therefore "put on an equal footing" with members of the Cosa Nostra, "given a Mafia-type aura." Evidence offered for this (Exhibit 8 in the petition) is an extract from the film from www.filmsite.org. No detail is given, on, say, which members of the FIFA family might best be compared to Robert de Niro or Joe Pesci. One wonders how business is really conducted in FIFA House or the Home of FIFA when its highly paid legal specialists are musing over Scorsese's back catalogue.

Second, the documentation delivered by hand to the public prosecutor's office in Zurich. This catalogued thirteen individual cases, listed in the "Blattergate" chapter in the book.[16] In the Criminal Complaint these were presented as "individual putative offences … in respect of which the prerequisites for the offence seem to the Complainants to be particularly clearly met."[17] They cover: payment to individuals for bogus services or unspecified advisory work, for information that might compromise others and for campaigning support and lobbying of national associations; gifting contracts for services to FIFA committee members or favoured providers; debt clearance for some confederations; and payment without rationale to national associations. More generally, Zen-Ruffinen described how Blatter was habitually bypassing, or suspending, committees; establishing his inner circle of advisers (his F-Crew, the *Führensgruppe* or leadership group); silencing potential witnesses; refusing to make files available for scrutiny; operating "again with the aim of *keeping secret* the financial situation of FIFA and his own financial machinations."[18] He summarized:

> FIFA is flawed by general mismanagement, disfunctions [sic] in the structures and financial irregularities. I therefore decided to stand up for the good of the game; it has been too long, that I was loyal to the president.
>
> Many FIFA representatives from places all over the world encouraged me with their full support to clarify matters in regard of the various harmful occurrences taking place in and outside the headquarters of FIFA. They felt embarrassed to be seen as "FIFA family members" after all the recent news which damaged the image of our organization.[19]

These FIFA representatives included 11 members of Blatter's Executive Committee. Only two of these, medical man Dr Michel D'Hooghe and Senes Erzik of Turkey, were still on Blatter's ExCo a decade on.[20] Zen-Ruffinen was to depart the scene soon after Blatter's re-election, succeeded by Urs Linsi, and then by Jérôme Valcke. Zen-Ruffinen had played for high stakes, contesting Blatter's "persistent, systematic *secrecy* tactics" and "equally persistent *stalling* tactics," claiming that according to FIFA statutes there is "no room for authoritarian, autocratic powers of leadership on the part of the FIFA President."[21] In other words, Blatter acts against the statutes, without transparency, as an autocratic, essentially unaccountable dictator. The petition for an injunction claimed that the complaints process had been "abated," though offered no evidence that the charges were without foundation, and ignored much of the case that complainants had made about the *modus operandi* of the FIFA president.

Third, the petition disputes a speculative statement about the consequences that might arise from a parallel "number and scale of charges,"[22] if such charges arose in the context of a multinational corporation. The possibility that someone of the FIFA president's status in such a context "would have lost his job and gone to jail"[23] is condemned as "a blatant infringement of the prohibition to be pre-sentenced." This of course is watertight in legal terms, though the speculative comparison holds in relation to numerous high-profile corporate cases across the world, and raises important issues in relation to the moral high ground so consistently claimed by FIFA in its mission statements and objectives.

Fourth, in reference to the concluding paragraph of the "Blattergate" chapter of the book, the petition objects to the statement that Blatter is "consolidated in power by a group of henchmen and sycophants; the family values and the dynasty, for the moment, are intact. FIFA House is like a court of the *ancien-régime*. Running FIFA is a matter of mastering not the football rulebook, more Machiavelli's *The Prince*."[24] The reference in *Badfellas* to Niccolò Machiavelli's classic manual on the art of political survival promoted an extraordinary response from FIFA's legal team:

> In addition, in a direct comparison with Machiavelli, the symbol for reckless and unlimited power politics that stop at nothing, Plaintiff 2 [Blatter] is portrayed as morally deficient and inferior. This comparison is even intensified by the malicious statement that the rules of football (and therefore the *central principle of fair play*) would not be applied. For the President of the most important sports association of football and the sports association as such this means derision and derogation. Calling the organization a court of the ancien régime, makes one imagine the picture of a Byzantine system, in which the ruler is above the law and any means of the system are fully available to him, associated with corruption, patronage and reckless power politics. This passage is solely directed at bringing FIFA and Joseph Blatter into disrepute.

On the contrary: the passage in question aims to summarize how FIFA's president has gained power, held on to power and adopted a particular leadership style in order so to do. Close colleagues and rivals of Joseph Blatter have provided testimony after testimony, cited not just in works by investigative researchers and investigative journalists, but increasingly across the world's media, confirming the accuracy of this portrayal.

Fifth, a passage on page 265 of *Badfellas* was challenged as untrue. In fact, this was a question relating to accusations, not an assertion of fact. But the petition concluded that none of the passages selected, and pored over in such forensic legalistic detail, "are true and appropriate":

> On the contrary, this is an actual defamatory construct, grouped – quasi in crescendo from passage to passage – around terms like "corruption", "Cosa Nostra", favouritism and mismanagement" [sic] and "vote-buying". These accusations are massive, both individually and globally.

Indeed they are, as agencies encountering FIFA in close-up for the first time – such as Transparency International, which at the end of 2011 withdrew from its advisory role in relation to FIFA's reform agenda, after FIFA appointed a specialist to chair the reform committee[25] – were increasingly to discover.

Court games 2: switching partners

MasterCard is a long-term sponsor of UEFA's Champions League, the annual European club competition, and of the UEFA European Championship, the four-yearly competition between Europe's national teams. It also used to be a FIFA World Cup sponsor, a partner of FIFA's for 16 years up to and including the 2006 World Cup. The story of how MasterCard lost this partnership to Visa is a telling one, revealing the dubious practices of central FIFA employees and officials. FIFA, at its ExCo meeting of 26 October 2005, had confirmed its commitment to keep working with MasterCard as its selected partner/sponsor for the forthcoming cycle, 2007–2014, and, as was stated in the decision of the United States District Court, Southern District of New York:

> At that point, FIFA never communicated or intimated that MasterCard was anything other than a respected and valued business partner. MasterCard, throughout the negotiations, remained positive towards concluding a deal and never displayed antagonistic actions, but instead simply acted in accordance with the Agreement and trademark statutes to enforce its invaluable intellectual property rights.[26]

But things were to turn sour.

MasterCard was the plaintiff in a legal action against FIFA. On 7 December 2006, Chief Judge of the U.S. District Court, Loretta Preska, signed off on a 125-page opinion that contained a wholesale condemnation of senior figures in the FIFA administration – employees, office holders and committee members – most prominently Jérôme Valcke, then marketing head, and Chuck Blazer, member of the ExCo and the marketing committee. Judge Preska's decision was that MasterCard could proceed with an injunction against FIFA preventing the implementation of any deal with Visa, and asserting its own rights to the sponsorship contract from 2007 onwards, also that all of MasterCard's costs could be awarded to the company. What was the evidence that led to such a conclusive opinion; and what led to the compromise-cum-resolution whereby MasterCard did not pursue this further in the courts, or push for its legal rights?

First, the evidence: here, the figures of Valcke and Blazer are the most prominent. Judge Preska pulled no punches in her introduction:

Section 9.2 of MasterCard's most recent sponsorship contract with FIFA gave MasterCard the first right to acquire the FIFA World Cup sponsorship for the next cycle. As is set out in detail below, FIFA breached its obligation under Swiss contract law to give MasterCard the first right to acquire the next round of sponsorship. In addition, FIFA's conduct in performing its obligation and in negotiating for the next sponsorship cycle was anything but "fair play" and violated the heightened obligation of good faith imposed by the applicable Swiss law (as well as FIFA's own notion of fair play as explained by its president).[27]

The report tells how FIFA's negotiators "lied repeatedly to MasterCard," assuring their long-term partner that, consistent with MasterCard's "first right to acquire," FIFA would sign no deal for post-2006 sponsorship rights with anyone else, unless it did not reach an agreement with MasterCard: "FIFA's negotiators lied to VISA when they repeatedly responded to the direct question of whether MasterCard had any incumbency rights by assuring VISA that MasterCard did not." FIFA's negotiators kept Visa up to date with detailed descriptions of where things were in negotiations with MasterCard, "while concealing from its long-time partner MasterCard both the fact of the FIFA–VISA negotiations as well as the status of those negotiations – an action FIFA's president admitted would not be 'fair play'."[28]

Valcke is personally damned at the beginning of the report: FIFA's marketing director lied both to MasterCard, FIFA's long-time partner, and to Visa, its negotiating counterparty, to both of which FIFA, under Swiss law, owed a duty of good faith. Who, then, didn't FIFA's negotiators lie to? CONCACAF general secretary Chuck Blazer was also picked out by the judge:

Chuck Blazer, a member of the FIFA Executive Committee and the FIFA Marketing & TV AG Board (Trial Tr. p. 230, l. 20–22), testified as to the March 14, 2006 FIFA Marketing & TV AG Board meeting. Mr. Blazer's testimony was generally without credibility based on his attitude and demeanor and on his evasive answers on cross-examination. ... [B]ased on his evasive answers and his attitude and demeanor, Mr. Blazer's testimony as to the March 14, 2006 Marketing & TV AG Board meeting is rejected as fabricated.[29]

The judgment conceded that some "portions of the FIFA witnesses' testimony were credible," but concluded that, overall:

their testimony was generally not credible, based on their attitude and demeanor and the varying degrees of impeachment they suffered. In contrast, the MasterCard witnesses were credible, based on their attitude and demeanor and all the other evidence in the case.[30]

Judge Preska painted the FIFA conduct in a far from flattering light. Valcke was encouraging Visa to find an extra US$30 million to equal the MasterCard bid while simultaneously reporting to FIFA committees that believed that they were in effect ratifying the MasterCard partnership:

> While the FIFA witnesses at trial boldly characterized their breaches as "white lies," "commercial lies," "bluffs," and, ironically, "the game," their internal emails discuss the "different excuses to give to MasterCard as to why the deal wasn't done with them," "how we (as FIFA) can still be seen as having at least some business ethics" and how to "make the whole f★★★-up look better for FIFA." They ultimately confessed, however, that "[I]t's clear somebody has it in for MC."[31]

MasterCard, recoiling from FIFA's shabby business dealings, accepted US$90 million in compensation and went away, leaving the World Cup to others more willing to negotiate with the mavericks from FIFA's administration and key committees. Temporarily shamed, Valcke left his post as head of marketing, soon re-emerging as general secretary, now number two to the FIFA president, in the latter's old job.

Crisis mismanagement

A decade on from the ISL crisis, and as the journalist Andrew Jennings[32] continued his dogged and relentless pursuit of evidence concerning FIFA's organizational practices and its "financial machinations," as Zen-Ruffinen described them from the inside, Blatter was becoming increasingly exposed, and unable to extricate himself from crisis after crisis simply by making hackneyed appeals to the "universality" of the game, and to the "immense social and cultural power of our game" rooted in "partnerships always based on respect, efficiency and solidarity."[33] "For the Game. For the World," the FIFA president reaffirmed at the end of his foreword to the 2010 financial report, delivered in Zurich in May 2011. Fewer and fewer people were being seduced by this idealistic rhetoric and humanistic hyperbole, and the power balance looked to be shifting, with a pledge being made by Blatter to strengthen the procedures whereby further malpractice might be bled from the infected arteries of the FIFA body. But the FIFA president had won his fourth term, and though he could no longer solve one crisis after another by inducements and rewards, he based his survival strategy on remaking his image and rebranding himself and his legacy as a reforming leader.[34] In the final chapters of this study, scenarios, solutions and futures (including the reform agenda) are considered, prior to a discussion of the theoretical frameworks that best account for the story of FIFA's political nature, sociological significance and cultural impact.

Notes

1 This vignette of the bidding process for the 2006 men's World Cup is drawn from Chapter 13 of John Sugden and Alan Tomlinson, *Badfellas: FIFA Family at War* (Edinburgh: Manistream Publishing, 2003), based on my observational fieldwork and interviews in London, Paris, Brisbane, Auckland, Cairo and Birmingham, from 1997 to 2002. For headlines on some of the episodes in the bidding narrative see also the BBC News website, for example "FIFA chief backs England 2006," March 11 1998, http://news.bbc.co.uk/1/hi/sport/football/64737.stm, consulted 7 July 2013.

2 Quoted in Alan Tomlinson, "A bid too far," *When Saturday Comes*, 162, August 2000, reproduced in "WSC Daily: A bid too far," 6 November 2008, http://www.wsc.co.uk/wsc-daily/944-November-2008/1340-a-bid-too-far, consulted 8 December 2013.

3 Michel Zen-Ruffinen, "STRICTLY CONFIDENTIAL – Presentation by the General Secretary (GS), Michel Zen-Ruffinen, FIFA EXCO – Meeting May 3, 2002, Zurich," 1121:Englpres.doc/2.5.02.

4 Personal correspondence from Blazer to the author, email, 25 May 2002. Blazer went on: "More meetings; more information; distribution of committee chairmanships and positions, including his opponents; financial information much more ample and available. However, his predecessor was a better politician."

This is an interesting use of the word "politician," and refers to the combination of charismatic presence, authoritative aura and diplomatic skill that characterized Havelange. This personal reputation was damaged irreparably in April 2013 when an internal FIFA report on ISL–FIFA dealings in Havelange's time damned the former president, not from a legal point of view, as the legal proceedings on ISL were closed, but from a "mere moral and ethical standpoint." Hans-Joachim Eckert, chairman of FIFA's new Adjudicatory Chamber, drew upon the report of the "investigatory chamber" of FIFA's Ethics Committee relating to the legal proceedings and ruling concerning ISL financial practices. Eckert's statement draws upon approximately 4200 pages of testimonies and documents and the report on the court case produced by Michael J. Garcia, chairman of the investigatory chamber. Eckert described ISL practices as "typical of a creative mixture of legal, i.e. contractually admissible activity, and deliberately fraudulent and disloyal conduct ... . From money that passed through the ISMM/ISL Group, it is certain that not inconsiderable amounts were channelled to former FIFA President Havelange and to his son-in-law Ricardo Teixeira as well as to Dr. Nicolás Leoz, whereby there is no indication that any form of service was given in return by them. These payments were apparently made via front companies in order to cover up the true recipient and are to be qualified as 'commissions', known today as 'bribes'. Known payments in this regard were made between 1992 and May 2000" ("Statement of the Chairman of the FIFA Adjudicatory Chamber, Hans-Joachim Eckert, on the examination of the ISL case, 29.04.2013," islreporteckert.29.04.13e.pdf, 3). Eckert confirms that no legal case can be made against recipients of such monies, as "the acceptance of bribe money by Havelange, Teixeira and Leoz was not punishable under Swiss criminal law at that time," but states that "the morally and ethically reproachable conduct" of Havelange and Teixeira remains undiminished by changes in legal procedures.

Havelange resigned from his honorary presidency of FIFA 11 days before the date of Eckert's statement. Leoz resigned from his ExCo and other committee positions and the CONMEBOL presidency, six days later. Blatter was FIFA general secretary at the time monies flowed between the bank accounts of ISL and the FIFA president, but Eckert notes that "President Blatter's conduct could not be classified in any way as misconduct with regard to any ethics rules. The conduct of President Blatter may have been clumsy because there could be an internal need for clarification, but this does not lead to any criminal or ethical misconduct" ("Statement of the Chairman," 5). It remains unclear whether Havelange and Teixeira, when paying 2.5 million Swiss francs into the ISL bankruptcy accounts in 2004, did so in association with Blatter: "It could not be determined with certainty whether the Swiss lawyer who helped coordinate the 2004 settlement had involved Mr Blatter in the deliberations and decisions," and, Eckert continued, it "cannot be established that President Blatter acted alone on his own authority when making any form of decisions to the detriment of FIFA and/or that the assets of the association were therefore at risk" ("Statement of the Chairman," 7). At the end of an epic narrative of corruption, Blatter could claim to be clear of any charges, and a champion of reform.

5 Zen-Ruffinen, "STRICTLY CONFIDENTIAL," 2.
6 Copies of the two sets of documents – Zen-Ruffinen's presentation to the ExCo (referenced in notes 2 and 4) and the Criminal Complaint – are in the possession of the author. For the Swiss Criminal Code, in an English translation without legal force, see http://www.admin.ch/ch/e/rs/311_0/a138.html, consulted 8 July 2013.
7 This account draws on Alan Tomlinson, "FIFA Family Fortunes," *Soccer Analyst*, 3/2, 2002: 7–9.
8 His 22 May 1998 letter is addressed to "all national associations of FIFA" and the confederations, but targeted at small, penniless national associations. A passage from it appears in Chapter 6. For the full text, see Sugden and Tomlinson, *Badfellas*, 150.
9 Zen-Ruffinen, "STRICTLY CONFIDENTIAL," 11.
10 Email from Blazer to the author (see note 4).
11 "Criminal Complaint" (see note 6), para. 57.
12 Marcus Christenson and Paul Kelso, "Soccer chief's plan to boost women's game? Hotpants," *Guardian*, 16 January 2004, http://www.guardian.co.uk/uk/2004/jan/16/football.gender, consulted 3 July 2013.
13 The letter was sent from the office of the FIFA president, and was headed "10 years of presidency." It was reproduced on Mohamed Bin Hammam's blog on 24 July 2011, the day after the FIFA Ethics Committee judged the Qatari to be guilty of offering bribes for votes earlier in the year, in his foiled attempt to win

the FIFA presidency, and banned him from football-related activities for life. It was downloaded from http://www.mohamedbinhammam.com/en/Blog/blog. php?bldx=1667.

Bin Hammam had been dealmaking for years in the football world, and in May 2009 he was elected to the FIFA ExCo by the AFC. In triumphal mode, the Qatari announced that this was "the perfect election ... . Our delegates have shown the world the meaning of democracy." During the campaign, 24 AFC national associations reported intimidation, corruption and vote-buying, and some revealed that they had been offered grants dependent upon votes. Bin Hammam threatened to "cut the heads off rivals," and sought to bar five associations from the election, for "procedural reasons." Long-term but soon-to-depart FIFA ExCo member and AFC rival Chung Mong-Joon offered his advice to Bin Hammam, saying that he was "like a mentally ill man ... . He needs to be in a hospital, not in FIFA" (David Hills, "Said & Done: FIFA: Another perfect election," *The Observer*, 10 May 2009).

14 For CONCACAF president Jack Warner's involvement in the bribery scandal surrounding Bin Hammam's aborted candidature for the FIFA presidency, see John Sugden and Alan Tomlinson, "Once upon a time in Fifaland," *M People Trinidad*, 2, June 2011: 62.

15 Jointly authored with John Sugden, *Badfellas* was published in 2003, despite the legal action and demands described here.

16 Sugden and Tomlinson, *Badfellas*, 33–35.

17 "Criminal Complaint" (see note 6), para. 27.

18 Sugden and Tomlinson, *Badfellas*, 33; "Criminal Complaint," para. 13c.

19 Sugden and Tomlinson, *Badfellas*, 29; Zen-Ruffinen, "STRICTLY CONFIDENTIAL," 1.

20 The papers were filed on behalf of: Lennart Johansson, Stockholm; David Will, Brechin, Angus, Scotland; Antonio Mattarese, Rome; Issa Hayatou, Cairo; Chung Mong-Joon, Seoul; Michel D'Hooghe, Bruges; Per Ravn Omdal, Eiksmarka, Norway; Amadou Diakité, Mali; Slim Aloulou, Tunisia; Ismael Bhanjee, Botswana; and Senes Erzik, Istanbul.

21 Sugden and Tomlinson, *Badfellas*, 33; "Criminal Complaint," para. 8.

22 Sugden and Tomlinson, *Badfellas*, 37.

23 Ibid.

24 Ibid., 38, reproduced verbatim in the petition.

25 BBC, "Transparency International cuts ties with Fifa," 2 December 2011, http://www.bbc.co.uk/news/world-europe-15996806, consulted 2 December 2011.

26 *MasterCard International Incorporated v. Fédération Internationale de Football Association*, No. 06 Civ. 3036 (LAP), 2006 United States District Court, Southern District of New York, 7 December 2006, 91, para. 263.

27 Ibid., 2–3.

28 Ibid., 3.

29 Ibid., 73–75, paras 213 and 214.

30 Ibid., 23, footnote 3, para. 56.

31 Ibid., 4.

32 Andrew Jennings has researched and presented several brilliantly illuminating BBC *Panorama* documentaries on what he called FIFA's "dirty secrets" and "beautiful bungs," and its collusion with individuals in some of the continental confederations. The episode entitled "FIFA and Coe" shows some reconstructions of the New York court case.

33 Words selected by Blatter for use in his foreword to the financial report presented to the FIFA Congress in May/June 2011, when referring to the South Africa World Cup of 2010 (FIFA, "FIFA Financial Report 2010: 61st FIFA Congress, Zurich, 31 May and 1 June 2011," (Zurich: FIFA, 2011), http://www.fifa.com/mm/document/affederation/administration/01/39/20/45/web_fifa_fr2010_eng[1].pdf, consulted 8 June 2011).

   He also added: "Thanks to the conservative and careful financial policies that we followed in the 2007–10 period, we have been able to considerably increase our investment in football development programmes, and in 2010, we were able to give each member association a total extraordinary FAP payment of USD 550,000 and each confederation USD 5 million." Such a strategy, amounting to a handout totalling around US$144.4 million, should not be underestimated in any assessment of the allegedly wavering but still sustained power and influence of the FIFA president.

34 PA, "Sepp Blatter wins Fifa president election," *Independent*, 1 June 2011, http://www.independent.co.uk/sport/football/news-and-comment/sepp-blatter-wins-fifa-president-election-2291733.html, consulted 3 July 2013.

8 Futures

FIFA has weathered many storms, to invoke FIFA president Blatter's favourite metaphor of survival, and has in many respects been a beneficiary of the phenomenon identified by Roman satirist Juvenal as *panem et circenses* ("bread and races," more commonly given as "bread and circuses"). Juvenal was referring to how public entertainment or spectacle can be associated with a decline in political spirit; the populace looks for fun and ignores wider social or political issues.[1] Indeed, when journalists or broadcasters turn their attention to the ethical problems of FIFA – endemic maladministration, little transparency, zero accountability, bogus idealism – they have habitually asked why all this matters, when the match goes on and the peoples' game prospers.[2] But the sheer scale, and increasing visibility, of the self-serving and ethically dubious practices of football's world governing body have come more consistently under the interrogative gaze of reforming networks and campaigning, investigative journalists.[3] This also tarnishes the product and the image of the product, and big corporate players are far from happy to be associated with a flawed body exposed as hypocritical, ethically dubious and routinely unaccountable. This does not, though, guarantee instant reform within the organization; FIFAcrats are highly skilled, many reciprocally dependent on the benefits provided by their positions, and ruthlessly survivalist. This is not a point at which to witness a crucial turning point, a Salt Lake City moment, in the complementary story of the Olympics, when widespread condemnation of corruption among IOC personnel led to serious reforms. But the claims from within FIFA that a "road to reform" is being travelled ensures that the critical gaze will now be sustained, more than ever before. And the corporate partners will keep asking questions. What, then, are the likely directions that FIFA will take in the future? In this penultimate chapter I consider the potential influence of the sets of interests that are sometimes said to be the sources of serious institutional reform at FIFA – clubs, sponsors and states or governments – and then outline five future directions or scenarios that might shape, or indeed reshape, FIFA's future.

Pressures, interest groups, stakeholders

Clubs[4]

In the context of Sepp Blatter's stated intent to push through reform of FIFA practices, various groups had been claiming to be the true voice of football, none more robustly than the European Club Association (ECA). This is the self-proclaimed "nuclear family of the football society," the successor to the elite G14 group established in 2000, expanded to 18 in 2002, and disbanded six years later. In its metamorphosis into a champion of the club-based game, the ECA now claims to represent the interests of more than 200 European clubs from 53 UEFA national associations – ordinary members (identified according to UEFA rankings of member associations) and "associated members." It campaigns for a more democratic governance model for the game, with clubs seeking equal rights with federations and associations, and calls for transparency in decision-making, not least in relation to UEFA and FIFA revenues.

The ECA appoints members to UEFA's Professional Football Strategy Council; in 2011 these were from AC Milan, Manchester United, AZ Alkmaar and Real Madrid. Its members also appear in the line-up of FIFA's Committee for Club Football. This committee has 25 members, drawn from 20 countries. In confederation terms, Europe provides eight of these countries, Africa, South America and Asia three apiece (though one of Asia's is Australia), Central and North America two, and Oceania just the one. France, Spain and Italy have double representation, as does the USA, though two of these representatives have observer or consultant status rather than full membership. It is arguable, therefore, that FIFA's forum for clubs reflects the global power relations of football politics, with 11 European members among the 25 committee members.

Who are these stakeholders, and what is their stake? In late 2011 there was England's representative on the FIFA clubs committee, Ivan Gazidis, chief executive at Arsenal; from France, there is Lyon's Jean-Michel Aulas, as well as UEFA president Michel Platini in the chair; Portugal's Porto sends Diogo Brandão; AC Milan's Umberto Gandini along with countryman Michele Centenaro, ECA general secretary, represent Italy's interests; FC Barcelona president Sandro Rosell and club director Raul Sannlehi comprise the Spanish contingent; Dynamo Kiev's Igor Sturkis represents Eastern European interests; John McClelland of Rangers was there too, though he resigned his position at the Scottish club in mid-October; but speaking up the profile of the ECA in the maelstrom of allegations and bribery revelations and condemnation of FIFA practices was its chairman, Germany's Karl-Heinz Rummenigge, of Bayern Munich; he had been pitching the ECA's line for some years, in tough talk in the corridors of power.

It's a new twist on the old tale of club versus country. The clubs claim that the international calendar disrupts their rhythms, that the investment of the clubs in the human capital of the game – the players – is not realistically acknowledged by the money-making machine FIFA, the men's World Cup in particular, and that a more transparent redistribution of these monies should compensate clubs for their release of players for international tournaments. A deal was struck on the formation of the ECA, UEFA allocating US$62.8 million to clubs for players participating in the Euro 2008 championship. And US$40 million from World Cup 2010 income was allocated by FIFA to the clubs providing the players at the tournament, to cover insurance and other costs. But this is seen as petty cash in relation to the billions of FIFA revenue during its World Cup cycles.

ECA creates networks of lobbyists. A meeting with European Commissioner for Education, Culture, Multilingualism and Youth, Cypriot Androulla Vassiliou, in July 2010, might focus upon mundane-sounding items like club licensing and financial fair play, but Rummenigge and his general secretary, a couple of other ECA colleagues billed as representatives on "social dialogue" and the ECA's European Union affairs adviser would be talking big issues here: the nature of European markets; the monopoly on global rights that FIFA has for the cash cow of the World Cup.

Within weeks of Blatter's unopposed re-election as FIFA president in 2011, Rummenigge was announcing that Blatter was unfit to hold the position, that FIFA lacked "serious and clean governance" and that any FIFA president needed to be "fair, serious and democratic." The ECA discusses "good governance" at its annual assembly, and disputes the historical model whereby UEFA and FIFA are based on the national associations alone; ECA insiders call this a "governance system of a bygone era." A more commercialized game demands fuller representation of the clubs, they insist. But of course the ECA really means the top clubs, and so Rummenigge also allows talk of a football revolution in which the UEFA Champions League might be threatened by a breakaway elite league. The ECA is raising the stakes here, though this breakaway route is far from likely. But the voice of the clubs will not be silenced, and, along with Platini, Rummenigge has the credibility of a former top player. As Blatter has continued to varnish his own image and legacy, perhaps Platini is en route to the Home of FIFA, over-looking Lake Zurich, and Rummenigge has his eyes on Platini's UEFA position down by Lac Léman. There is a long way to go in this football revolution though, as FIFA statutes can only be changed by a majority vote in Congress, and that's made up of the 209 national associations eligible to vote. The beneficiaries of the historical model of governance are hardly likely to accept the richest clubs as the proponents of an alternative, more streamlined approach. But even if the FIFA Committee for Club Football has no clear brief or agenda, the club bosses are in there, claiming to speak for the wider football world.

Sponsors

Along with the media's purchase of broadcasting rights, corporate sponsors have been the basis of FIFA's enrichment in the last quarter of the twentieth century and its recovery from a fragile economic position immediately following ISL's collapse in 2001. The huge sums from primary partners and others buying into marketing rights have constituted around 25 per cent of FIFA's income.

In Chapter 7 the contest between Visa and MasterCard was presented as a case of dubious, unethical business practice by FIFA in its dealings with its partners. It has not been common to see in such close-up the workings of the FIFA dealmakers. For the most part, sponsors have been happy to be guided by media audience and brand awareness figures – as demonstrated in Chapter 6 by Hyundai's response to its continuing World Cup sponsorship – rather than looking too closely at the ethics and morality of the conduct of some of FIFA's top figures. But in the 2010–2011 cycle of controversies, allegations and revelations, even the usually silent and sanguine sponsors began to produce murmurings of discontent, especially in the media glare surrounding the FIFA president's re-election fiasco.[5] Four of the six partner companies commented, Sony and Hyundai proving unreachable to the press pack hounding them for their views on the FIFA crises.[6] Coca-Cola and Adidas, the longest-term partners, issued FIFA a slap on the wrists. Coca-Cola commented that the "current allegations being raised are distressing and bad for the sport. We have every expectation that Fifa will resolve this situation in an expedient and thorough manner."[7] Adidas played to its historical pedigree:

> Adidas enjoys a long-term, close and successful partnership with Fifa that we are looking forward to continuing. Adidas will be an official sponsor of FIFA World Cup 2014 in Brazil. Having said that, the

negative tenor of the public debate around FIFA at the moment is neither good for football nor for Fifa and its partners.[8]

No intent to go then, but clean up the public image please. Visa observed that the "current situation is not good for the game and we ask that Fifa take all necessary steps to resolve the concerns that have been raised."[9] The sponsors were hauled into the media spotlight, all regretting allegations and debate, none actually blaming FIFA. How could they? Long-term partners have long-term understandings, and their corporate privileges at party-time are not too far removed from the luxury life-styles of the FIFA elite; Blatter himself, of course, knows this particular game from his time as an Adidas trainee, and as a product of the Horst Dassler school of corporate responsibility. Visa, experienced Olympic sponsor, reaffirmed its commitment to "the 2014 World Cup in Brazil and other tournaments before then," and stressed its distance from FIFA's processes and procedures:

> As a sponsor we are not involved in the bidding process or other administrative issues faced by the governing body. This matter does not concern or impact our sponsorship rights related to the 2014 World Cup in Brazil. ... As a matter of policy we do not speculate on business decisions or sponsorship renewals. Visa has nothing else to add on the matter.[10]

That's that then: roll on Rio 2014.

Only the Emirates, sponsor since 2006, linked the controversies to the nature of the FIFA administration, and to the global fan base of the game:

> Emirates, like all football fans around the world, is disappointed with the issues that are currently surrounding the administration of this sport. Emirates' sponsorship of all Fifa tournaments, including the Fifa World Cup, aims to help promote football and ensure that it is accessible to the billions of football fans; something Fifa has managed to do extremely well in recent years. We hope that these issues will be resolved as soon as possible and the outcome will be in the interest of the game and sport in general.[11]

Here, Emirates occupied the moral high ground. There's some old-fashioned regional rivalry in this response. The stained would-be challenger for Blatter's presidency, Mohamed Bin Hammam, isn't one of ours, it is implied, he is from Qatar, the place that a few months ago rustled up the votes for the 2022 World Cup. But there's nothing on us.

Thierry Weill, FIFA's marketing director, pushed aside *World Football Insider's* questions about how the allegations might impact in the short- or long-term on FIFA's marketing strategy, and insisted that there was no expectation that sponsors would desert FIFA, saying that he was "not concerned" about the top-tier sponsors' comments and responses to the bribery allegations.[12] This indifference – some might call it over-confidence or cockiness – rebounded on FIFA when Emirates, a parvenu among this select group of elite partners, intensified the tone of its comments later in the year, Boutros Boutros, senior vice-president for corporate communications, saying that the company had felt "overlooked" during the votes-for-money scandal preceding the FIFA presidential election: "We are seriously thinking about not renewing our partnership with FIFA beyond 2014," he said at the Melbourne Cup horse race.[13] But he also confirmed that discussions on renewal would be taking place.

The nearest any sponsor got, therefore, to an outright condemnation of FIFA practices, was an off-the-cuff remark on a day at the races. Sponsors will go ahead and support any potential organizational reform to FIFA, but they are unlikely to generate such change, and, as the Olympics have shown,[14] new sponsors – albeit increasingly short-term or region-specific ones – continue to queue to gain the rights to exposure via the most viewed sporting and cultural events in the world.

National associations

Sunder Katwala, with reference to democratic governments' mandates for the protection and promotion of the public interest, argues that the "potential power of governments over sporting bodies is frequently underestimated."[15] This is because, he adds, sporting bodies such as FIFA need the support of a government more than that government needs such bodies; not least for recognition and legitimation, and "licence to operate." The Swiss state is notoriously lax in its regulation of supra-national bodies, though, and of course it was the high-profile intervention of the USA's legal system that stimulated reform in the IOC,[16] not any legalistic or governmental initiative by the Swiss polity. FIFA is often talked of as a corporate entity – Transparency International calls it "a global company with huge revenues"[17] – but it is in fact "an association registered in the Commercial Register in accordance with art. 60 ff. of the Swiss Civil Code."[18]

States and governments, technically and legally, have no hold over FIFA, and this is because FIFA's statutes recognize representative national football associations and assert the independence of those associations. FIFA defines "country" as "an independent state recognised by the international community," and provides that, other than in exceptional cases, "only one Association shall be recognised in each Country."[19] Exceptions include the four British associations, granted recognition as separate members of FIFA, and a former territory or country that may have been integrated into another, as in the case of Hong Kong. Apart from this, the statutes avoid any engagement with the thorny problems of states, governments and political systems. They deal with national football associations conceived as independent entities.

This independence is emphatically reaffirmed in the statutes. Members of FIFA sign up to "manage their affairs independently and ensure that their own affairs are not influenced by any third parties."[20] It is stressed that "violations" of such obligations can lead to sanctions – suspension, for instance – even if the influence of the third party was not the member's fault. It is crystal clear in the statutes that: "Each Member shall manage its affairs independently and with no influence from third parties."[21]

What these stated principles allow FIFA to do is to pick and choose what constitutes "influence from third parties." Generally speaking, FIFA can let the national associations get on with their own affairs, on the assumption that national football associations are independent bodies, free from influence from, say, political institutions or regimes, or economic corporate interests. It is, of course, a mere conceit to seek to uphold this. Across the political spectrum of FIFA's global membership, economic interests of local corporations or multinational businesses and the policies of controlling or interventionist states frame the football spectacle. To illustrate this, we look in more detail at two cases involving FIFA interventions in the national operations of its member associations.

Kenya[22]

A report on maladministration and corruption in Kenyan football by Bob Munro identifies the source and core of the problem as the national association:

> A key problem in too many football and other sports organizations in Africa is that, once elected, the officials start handling the organization as if it was their private property, treat the athletes and members as if they are the enemy, marginalize the athletes and member clubs in key decision-making bodies and then ignore or change the statutes to perpetuate themselves in power.[23]

The challenge, Munro observes, is to make such national sports organizations more representative, to give teams, athletes, coaches and referees a clearer, expanded "role in making the policies and decisions about their sport off the field":

> our national football association, the Kenya Football Federation (KFF) which tried to re-brand and re-invent itself in late 2008 as Football Kenya Ltd (FKL), has been misled and mismanaged for over a decade by a small group of exceptionally selfish and incompetent officials who repeatedly put their personal interests and ambitions ahead of the best interests of their members, their sport and even their country.[24]

How could such a situation come about, and persist? The answer lies to some degree in the use that disingenuous and unscrupulous power-brokers can make of the FIFA principle of non-interference by third parties. This allowed such individuals and factions within the KFF to work towards "entrenching a culture of corruption," along the way stealing from FIFA and undermining the development of the game across the country, while using the world body as a protective screen and a front for its criminal activities.

In November/December 2006 the KFF was banned from FIFA; it was readmitted in March 2007. This was the culmination of a bitter row and sustained rivalries between competing sets of interests and factions in the Kenyan football world, and followed an earlier suspension of the association by FIFA. The tensions emanated from questions concerning both the legitimacy of people in authority and the destination of monies paid by FIFA to the national association. In 2004, the national association's chairman, secretary and treasurer were charged in court with the theft of more than 55 million Kenyan shillings (well over half a million US dollars), and were defended by their lawyer with the claim that "the money does not belong to the government or KFF but to FIFA." KFF officials even overlooked the election process for their own positions, and when Kenya's High Court, again in 2004, confirmed that these officials were no longer legally in office, "FIFA ignored that High Court ruling," branding the sports minister's attempt to establish a transitional caretaker committee as a form of "government interference in football." On these grounds, FIFA banned the association in June 2004, set up a normalization committee made up of the former officials and their friends, lifted the ban in August, and promoted new elections in December. FIFA president Sepp Blatter visited Kenya in 2005 and met with the Kenyan authorities; a new chairman took office for a short spell, and an implementation plan for reform was agreed at a meeting with FIFA and the African confederation (including Kenya's sports ministers) in Cairo in January 2006, but negligible change was accomplished. In October 2006 the old regime took back power in a boardroom coup, and factional disputes continued.

When the Kenyan sports minister disbanded the KFF in November 2006, FIFA again banned the country. Readmission was granted on the basis that third-party interference would cease. FIFA was effectively legitimating a corrupt administration. Factional rivalries continued unabated and in 2008 two KFF officials met with FIFA in Zurich and got approval to transform the federation into a private company, Football Kenya Ltd (FKL) with themselves and one other official as the only three directors; one of these officials, Mohammed Hatimy, charged with theft in 2004, was still leading the FIFA-recognized federation in 2010. Little was known about where annual FIFA funding of 20 million Kenyan shillings ($US217,640) went, beyond trips to Congresses, meetings and tournaments. But such officials play the powerbroker: FKL chairman Hatimy "even ... made a public statement on the FIFA Presidential candidates as if that was his personal decision and choice to make."[25]

Blatter had not included Nairobi on his campaign trail for the 2011 presidential election, sending long-established envoy for Africa Emmanuel Maradas to pitch the re-election manifesto. Hatimy was more impressed by the personal visit of Qatari Mohamed Bin Hammam, who was at the time positioning himself as a rival to Blatter for the FIFA presidency. Bin Hammam had promised to double the annual funding from FIFA, up to around half a million dollars, and also double the *Goal* programme funding to a million. Hatimy said: "Mohamed Bin Hammam is our choice since his manifesto is geared towards helping Third World countries like ours. Blatter is concentrating a lot in Europe and the big nations." He dismissed allegations of bribery for votes: "These are just malicious rumours by people who are out to get publicity. Personally, I have received no inducement."[26] With Hatimy's switch of affiliation from Blatter to Bin Hammam, proven to be corrupt, small wonder that FIFA was insistent into 2011 on independently monitored elections for the federation. But its vacillation in this case, and its implicit support for unconstitutional practices and financial criminality, were a consequence of the way in which the non-interference clause can be exploited by interested parties.

Football missionaries can be predictably idealistic, and Munro prefaces his narrative with the assertion that football development and administration is in the business of "creating new heroes, role models and leaders." Burdened with such expectation, it would not just be the Kenyan association that would fall short of these lofty ideals. But Munro's appeal to these values and aims allowed him to call on FIFA as the defender of institutional freedom and independence within the space of civil society. The non-interference clause, though, is as flexible and malleable as its users wish it to be. It potentially protects the weak (civil society) from the strong (the state). But more often it facilitates the alliance of sets of interests operating above and beyond the regulatory reach of the state. There is no constitutional place or role for the state in FIFA's organizational world; it defines the category of the national as it chooses, denigrates the notion of the political in its statutes, and as such creates a unique and self-perpetuating worldwide system of power without accountability, a pseudo-democracy of the hand-picked and self-selected.

Greece[27]

Greece's national association, the Hellenic Football Federation (HFF), has had a stormy relationship with FIFA during the years of Blatter's presidency. The champions of Europe in 2004, the country was suspended by FIFA in July 2006. The world body's Emergency Committee adjudged that a proposed new Greek law on professional football leagues undermined "the independence of members and decision-making," and "constitutes another example of interference from the government in football affairs." The government minister for sport, George Orfanos, alleged that the Greek FA lacked transparency in its procedures, and had spurned democratic voting rules: "The HFF does not observe the laws of the country. ... We want more democratic rules – rules that apply to all other sporting federations in Greece. If they insist, state protection will be withdrawn." The football federation responded with accusations that the government was legalizing state intervention, so sidelining the federation.

This issue had been running for some time; in April 2001 FIFA had produced a joint declaration, with the Greek federation and the Greek national government, stating that the three parties looked "to negotiate in good faith solutions to solve issues of common interest ... to bring the Greek FA's legal scope of action into line with the FIFA Statutes while at the same time taking into account the guidelines of the Greek Government for national sports policies." *BBC Sport* reported: "The domestic row centres around an amendment to the sports law in Greece which states that no sports official can hold office if he is accused of a serious crime. The vice-president of the Greek FA, Victor Mitropoulos, has been accused of embezzlement." In 2006, the FIFA president effectively lobbied the Greek minister to change the law so that the autonomy of the federation could be assured. The law was swiftly amended, the suspension soon lifted.

A veteran sport writer in Athens called this the "big secret" in Greece, and expanded on the context, linking FIFA's intervention to long-established betting scandals and match-fixing: "the referees in Greece are like second-class people … and take some money to fix a match – they take a lot of money for one match and then they stop."[28] This match-fixing was also seen as connected to the extraordinary dominance of the team from the port of Piraeus, Olympiakos, with its record of national championship titles up to 2008: in my respondent's words, "12 championships in 16 years, 12 championships. But when they go to the UEFA Champions League they don't go further because they have a good team in Greece" but the referees in Greece are not with them in European competition. Referees, then, in a national culture in which allegations of corruption across myriad spheres of public and private life are hardly unknown, are tempted by big pay-offs from bribes linked to the international as well as national gambling economy. On the European stage, in a UEFA Cup match, a Greek team was involved in a particular crooked-looking game and this was the perfect opportunity for those claiming to represent the integrity of the game to move against the authorities at club and national level implicated in the scandals. My source continued:

> The big secret in Greece is that the president of the national football federation was involved in this fixing story. The government was trying to replace him but couldn't do it, because you're not allowed to be involved. It's a FIFA rule. So when the president of the federation saw the danger of the government discovering these stories, he sent a letter to FIFA saying the government wants to get involved in Greek football, come here and attack them. And sometimes the FIFA say, well, no one government can get involved in the federations, and so you're in danger of being thrown out of the organization [FIFA]. Now okay they were right, but in Greece the big secret is that the national federation was … and the president, well he's out of the game now because they've had problems with the law.[29]

This testimony illustrates the extreme flexibility and ultimate absurdity of FIFA's third-party non-interference principle. If government or state interference is seen as contrary to the statutes, basically incompatible with the core principles of world football governance, then in the name of civic institutions' right to autonomy the most crooked and corrupt national association or federation can be handed *carte blanche* by FIFA to continue in its flawed and fraudulent ways. That is why FIFA most often seeks to mediate but not adjudicate in such matters, and one of the consequences of this *laissez faire* strategy is that morally dubious and

sometimes criminally culpable individuals are legitimated in their institutional positions and status. Greece is, albeit relatively recently in
modern historical terms, a working democracy. Speaking for the institutional freedom of its member associations, FIFA's actions or inactions
can potentially undermine the very freedoms for which it claims to
speak. In explicitly non-democratic contexts, such as theocratic dynasties
in Gulf states in which the institutions of civil society are no more than
the playthings or the birthright of a ruling elite,[30] the non-interference
principle is more absurd still.

Stasis or change?

The institutional actors discussed here have neither the collective
coherence nor the capacity or commitment to effect change and reform
in world football governance. Clubs, sponsors (and broadcasters) and
associations have too much at stake to consistently challenge FIFA and
its affiliated confederations. The Havelange manifesto reshaped the world
game, establishing a vulnerable yet self-sustaining interlocking system of
interests, bolstered by an idealistic and hyperbolic rhetoric that can be
reworked in the name of a universal movement or mission.

Roger Pielke, drawing upon Ruth Grant and Robert Keohane's
model of mechanisms of accountability in world politics, has asked the
question "How can FIFA be held accountable?"[31] Grant and Keohane
argue that non-governmental organizations must "be increasingly transparent if they are to remain credible."[32] But they also note that such
organizations operate, in effect, in a non-regulated space: "There is no
sociological global public ... only a very small minority of people in the
world identify and communicate with other people on a global basis, or
even follow world events very closely."[33] There is, they also observe, no
juridical public on a global level: no legal institutions define a public
over which they have the authority to act globally. Hopes for global
participatory institutions remain premature, they add, though "feasible
actions to improve accountability" might be possible in the realms of
standards, sanctions, information, delegation and participation.[34]

We have seen throughout this study that the FIFA leadership can
appeal to its Congress as the ultimate source of its accountability, and so
bypass or deflect debate about or movement towards these "feasible
actions." Pielke addresses directly the seven forms of accountability that
Grant and Keohane propose: hierarchical, supervisory, fiscal, legal,
market, peer and public reputational. On these levels, Pielke concludes,
FIFA falls short: "FIFA demonstrated time and again that it has essentially no hierarchical, supervisory, peer or public reputational

accountability, and minimal fiscal accountability. This means that efforts to reform FIFA from within or as a consequence of pressure from governments, the public, the media or watchdog organizations are unlikely to result directly in any significant change."[35] Essentially, FIFA has the capacity to resist wholesale or radical change and reform, remaining beyond the reach of any effective legal body in relation to its wider remit and operational brief, and deflecting market accountability through its institutional definition as a non-commercial body.

In this context, several scenarios can be projected for FIFA's possible future development. FIFA power-holders, primarily the president and close allies, have excelled at *scapegoating*: sacrificial lambs have been identified, often paid off in silence agreements and then business carries on as usual. This has become a well-established strategy for individuals' survival and institutional renewal. *Internal reform*, though placed on the agenda by Blatter himself, is unlikely to involve serious levels of accountability. This is considered in more detail in the final chapter of this book. *Dealmaking* with the most powerful allies is a pragmatic means of survival, and has been underway for some time, as testified to by observers and insiders and reported in this study; into his fourth presidential term, there was still talk of Blatter leaving office mid-term, so easing Michel Platini into the FIFA presidency. *Breakaway* moves could seriously threaten FIFA's authority, should clubs, through the ECA, or the most powerful and rich federations, particularly UEFA, propose a new world order or model of governance for football, effectively setting up alternative governance structures and contesting the traditional and historical hegemony of FIFA. *External pressure* is the most likely source of real reform, if a combination of national courts and international bodies – the UN for instance – could establish any acceptable form of jurisdiction over an organization afforded the autonomy and minimal accountability that it receives from the Swiss polity, and which is reaffirmed by its own impotent and collusive general membership. In the final chapter, the focus shifts from speculation about future trajectories to consideration of how we might best account for FIFA's capacity to survive in an essentially static form, and to reproduce itself in the wake of revelations, crises, critiques and calls for serious change and reform.

Notes

1 William Barr, "Introduction," in *Juvenal: The Satires*, Juvenal (Oxford: Oxford University Press, 1992), 10.81.
2 Examples include British broadcast journalist Rob Bonnett asking me this question during an in-depth interview on BBC World's *Talksport*, 2003.

3 Andrew Jennings is foremost among these investigative journalists. See http://transparencyinsport.com.

4 An earlier version of this discussion of emerging club power was published as "Balance of power – ECA challenges FIFA," *When Saturday Comes* 298, December 2011.

5 See IMR Sports Marketing & Sponsorship, "FIFA – He who pays the piper calls the tune" (IMR Publications, 1 June 2011), http://www.imrpublications.com/commentdetails.aspx?nid=34, consulted 16 November 2011.

   Business correspondents pounced on the story; see Louise Armitstead, "Fifa's sponsors kick up a fuss over corruption claims," *Telegraph*, 1 June 2011, http://www.telegraph.co.uk/finance/newsbysector/retailandconsumer/leisure/8548864/Fifas-sponsors-kick-up-a-fuss-over-corruption-claims.html, consulted 16 November 2011.

   Reuters relayed the Adidas and Coca-Cola responses; see Randsdell Pierson, "UPDATE 4: Coke, Adidas say FIFA allegations hurt soccer," Reuters, 30 May 2011, http://www.reuters.com/article/2011/05/30/soccer-fifa-sponsors-idUSN 3024865720110530, consulted 16 November 2011.

6 See *Telegraph*, "Fifa corruption claims: What the sponsors are saying," 1 June 2011, http://www.telegraph.co.uk/finance/newsbysector/retailandconsumer/leisure/8548440/Fifa-corruption-claims-What-the-sponsors-are-saying.html, consulted 16 November 2011.

7 Ibid.

8 Ibid.

9 Ibid.

10 *World Football Insider*, "Visa joins chorus of FIFA partners concerned by corruption scandals," 31 May 2011, http://worldfootballinsider.com/Story.aspx?id=34402, consulted 16 November 2011.

11 *Telegraph*, "Fifa corruption claims."

12 *World Football Insider*, "Visa joins chorus of FIFA partners."

13 Jack Atchinson, "Emirates not to renew FIFA sponsorship over corruption scandal," CaughtOffside, 2 November 2011, http://www.caughtoffside.com/2011/11/02/emirates-not-to-renew-fifa-sponsorship-over-corruption-scandal/, consulted 16 November 2011. See also Associated Press, "Fifa sponsor Emirates 'disappointed' by corruption scandal," *Guardian*, 31 May 2011, http://www.guardian.co.uk/football/2011/may/31/fifa-sponsor-emirates-corruption-scandal, consulted 16 November 2011.

14 See Alan Tomlinson, "The making – and unmaking? – of the Olympic corporate class," in *Palgrave Handbook of Olympic Studies*, eds. Helen Lensjky and Stephen Wagg (Basingstoke: Palgrave Macmillan, 2012).

15 Sunder Katwala, *Democratising Global Sport* (London: The Foreign Policy Centre, 2000), 93.

16 See Jean-Loup Chappelet and Brenda Kübler-Mabbott, *The International Olympic Committee and the Olympic System: The Governance of World Sport* (London: Routledge, 2008), 89.

17 Sylvia Schenk, "Safe Hands: Building Integrity and Transparency at FIFA," (Berlin: Transparency International, 16 August 2011), 2, http://www.transparency.org/whatwedo/pub/safe_hands_building_integrity_and_transparency_at_fifa, consulted 28 September 2011.

18 FIFA, *FIFA Statutes: July 2013 Edition* (Zurich: FIFA, 2013), http://www.fifa.com/mm/document/AFFederation/Generic/02/14/97/88/FIFAStatuten2013_E_Neutral.pdf, consulted 6 December 2013, s. 1, para. 1.

19 Ibid., "Definitions," no. 6 and s. 10, para. 1.

20 Ibid., s. 13, para 1(i).

21 Ibid., s. 17, para. 1.

22 The Kenyan case study is based on Bob Munro, "From grassroots to gold medals: Are stakeholder-led reforms and ownership a way forward for African football?" paper delivered at the African Football Executive Summit on *Leadership, Governance and 21st Century Marketing Strategies for the Development of the Game on the African Continent*, 26–27 May 2011, Accra, Ghana. Munro was presenting in his capacity as chairman of Mathare United FC, and Managing Director of XXCEL Africa Ltd; he was a founding director and former chair of the Kenyan Premier League Ltd.

    See also Paul Doyle, "Kenya leads way in ending blight of corruption in African football," *Guardian*, 11 July 2010, http://www.guardian.co.uk/football/2010/jul/11/kenyan-premier-league, consulted 18 November 2011.

23 Munro, "From grassroots to gold medals."

24 Ibid., 1.

25 Ibid., 7. See also Collins Okinyo, "Bin Hammam has more to offer – Hatimy," *SuperSport.com*, 11 May 2011, http://www.supersport.com/football/article.aspx?Id=417017, consulted 2 December 2011.

26 Quoted in Okinyo, "Bin Hammam has more to offer – Hatimy."

27 See *FIFA.com*, "Suspension of Greek FA averted after signature of Joint Declaration," 30 April 2001, http://www.fifa.com/newscentre/news/newsid=77442.html, consulted 18 November 2011; Daily Mail, "Football: Greece given stay of execution," *MailOnline*, undated, http://www.dailymail.co.uk/sport/article-42343/Football-Greece-given-stay-execution.html, consulted 18 November 2011; *BBC Sport*, "Greece given suspension by Fifa," 4 July 2006, http://news.bbc.co.uk/sport1/hi/football/internationals/5141866.stm, consulted 18 November 2011.

28 Interview with the author, Athens, Greece, April 2009.

29 Ibid.

30 See Alan Tomlinson, "Eastern promise: Football in the societies and cultures of the Middle and Far East," in *Sport and Leisure Cultures*, Alan Tomlinson (Minneapolis: University of Minnesota Press, 2005), 135–142.

31 Roger Pielke, "How can FIFA be held accountable?" *Sport Management Review*, 16/3, 2013: 255–267.

32 Ruth W. Grant and Robert O. Keohane, "Accountability and abuses of power in world politics," *American Political Science Review*, 99/1, 2005: 42.

33 Ibid., 34.

34 Ibid., 41.

35 Pielke, "How can FIFA be held accountable?"

9 Conclusion

This final chapter, prior to an overall theoretical and interpretive discussion and debate, summarizes the core themes of the analysis presented in the preceding chapters. This is not to tell a linear story of institutional growth, but to seek recurrent patterns and trajectories that reveal the scale and operational reach of FIFA as an organization at different points in its history; a reach that has had political, economic and cultural consequences and significance in and across an increasingly globalizing world.

In the introduction, FIFA's decision-making, from the technical level of the rules of the game through to its granting of World Cup Finals to Russia and Qatar, were shown to be a form of soap-operatic narrative of increasing interest to the global media, particularly in the focus on the organization's eighth president, Joseph "Sepp" Blatter. With the media spotlight on Blatter and the FIFA *modus operandi* intensifying, the period from the end of 2010 to the end of 2011 was presented as an *annus horribilis* in the contemporary history of FIFA under Blatter's stewardship.

Chapter 1 overviewed the origins of FIFA and its place as a symbol of early-twentieth-century globalizing forces, based on cultural, political and economic initiatives transcending the nation state and with some trans-continental dimensions, the first men's World Cup taking place in Uruguay in 1930. In Chapter 2, organizational and institutional functions of FIFA were considered, and the vulnerabilities of its practices and procedures illustrated, particularly in relation to ethical dimensions of the practices and conduct of FIFA committee members in recent decades.

Chapter 3 switched back to the history of the organization to explore the influence of the most prominent of FIFA's presidents, tracing the ways in which the values of particular leaders shaped the organization of the time, but also sharpened the contradictions and tensions that would characterize the organization's growth and expansion. In particular, the modest social roots of presidents Jules Rimet and Stanley Rous were illuminated, their origins marking out their careers as instances of social mobility in a world in which possibilities for sport–cultural development were opening up, in an expanding international context, preceding the hegemony of the business model under the seventh president, João Havelange.

Chapter 4 examined the career of the FIFA president of 1998 to the time of writing, FIFA employee from 1975, Sepp Blatter; it revealed his styles and strategies in surviving charges and allegations made throughout his administrative career as technical officer and general secretary, and in the presidential role. In Chapter 5, the clock was turned back to the point at which FIFA, alongside the IOC, was looking for economic partners with which to deliver more to the expectant emerging nations in the international post-colonial context.

Chapter 6 was dedicated to the FIFA portfolio: first, the men's FIFA World Cup, the event that has framed FIFA's expanding global profile, which in the late 1970s and early 1980s, and early 2000s reshaped and salvaged FIFA's economic health, and which is acknowledged by the FIFA president as the "motor" of the overall growth and development of the federation;[1] second, the less high-profile activities and initiatives supported by FIFA, all of which are essentially dependent on the continuing economic success of the men's World Cup.

Chapter 7 took a closer look at selected moments of crisis in the post-Havelange administration or regime, and at the way in which FIFA, Blatter, and some key close colleagues and allies have responded to and survived successive crises. Chapter 8 showed how other institutional actors might be seen as agents of social change or catalysts for reform, but are constrained by their continuing interests in the credibility and acceptability of FIFA.

In this final chapter, key analytical and theoretical themes and debates are drawn upon in order to account for the resilience of FIFA and explain its capacity to sustain its status and influence in the face of the torrents of critique and exposure that have characterized the period of Blatter's leadership.

Ignorance and (in)action

In two brilliantly insightful texts on the disequilibrium between state or governmental responsibilities and increasingly powerful and unaccountable international money markets, published during the period from the mid-1980s to the late 1990s, Susan Strange summarized her contributions to the formation of the academic field of international political economy. Combining her background in economic journalism with a grasp of historical and global trends, she produced dazzling and accessible syntheses in *Casino Capitalism* (1986) and *Mad Money* (1998). In her 1997 preface to a reissue of the first book, Strange reminded her readers of the social importance of money in the economy, whether a planned, market or mixed economy: "Money's fructifying, enabling power for good was matched by its terrible disruptive, destructive power for evil."[2] In this language there is a strong element of moral judgement as well as analysis; Strange was not a journalist for nothing. But her brand of political economy was also a call to arms. If we identify hypocrisy, exploitation, malpractice, political inadequacies and economic excesses, is there, she asked, "no chance at all of doing more than hoping for the best but expecting and preparing for the worst?" Her answer is a positive one, as she identifies the "doing more" as "the task for the future for officials, for journalists and especially for academics. They have more time than the journalists and more freedom than the officials to think about the feasible options of what might be done."[3]

There is a debate to be had here, of course, about the relative freedom of the academic; much depends upon the principles of his or her employer, and the funding basis for the research. But critical, independent, disinterested, non-aligned research is still possible, though not always easy to sustain with a focus upon organizations such as FIFA that have no public accountability, to states or governments, or to any obvious supra-national body. One thing that the independent academic researcher can do, though – as indeed can individuals or think-tanks – is to link investigative research and critical analysis to proposals for intervention, even reform. In many ways, the academic researcher and the campaigning investigative journalist are best-fitted to such a task, rooted as they should be in the accumulated evidence base, alongside an informed and realistic analytical account of the organizational and institutional flaws of the system they have studied. Such an account can also be complemented by a call for change, but first I introduce one of Strange's ideas that may help relevant parties in the world of sport and football governance see where and how flaws in the system have emerged, and why informed intervention is not merely an option but more than ever vital to the credibility of the administration of the game, at all of its levels across the world.

Referring to the expansion of international financial markets from 1970 to 1985, Strange commented that this "had opened up very large 'areas of significant ignorance' for governments. ... [T]here were more things that policy-makers needed to know but did not know about what was going on in the markets."[4] She expanded on this in Chapter 5 of *Casino Capitalism*, entitled "The Guessing Game," where she distinguished between "unavoidable ignorance," "insignificant ignorance" and "significant ignorance."[5] Unavoidable ignorance relates to the innumerable things we cannot know; insignificant ignorance refers to the very many things that we do not know, maybe do not need to know, and may well be indifferent towards or uninterested in knowing. And then there is the "large, undefined area" of significant ignorance: "in it there are all the things we ought to know and which we need to know, but do not know."

How might a working-through of Strange's categories illuminate not just the world of FIFA as an organization, based in one city in a European country, but also the wider world, embracing the other social actors and institutions that make up FIFA globally? The moment might come when an agency or actor of real influence finds it appropriate to see what has previously been considered to be insignificant ignorance as a case of significant ignorance. Take the case of the USA and the failed bids by the city of Chicago and the US soccer federation to host the 2016 Summer Olympics and the 2022 men's World Cup, respectively. One bit-player in both of these failed campaigns was Barack Obama.

In October 2009, the US president flew into Copenhagen on the day of the Olympic vote, looking to wow the IOC electorate. Among bedazzled bookmakers, odds shortened on Chicago winning the bid. But IOC members do not take to being preached to at the last minute, to being marooned in their rooms at the whim of the US secret service as the presidential couple arrives. Chicago went out in the first round of voting.[6] In Zurich in December 2010, the USA's loss to Qatar in the vote to host the 2022 World Cup may have surprised some, but after the IOC decision Obama hardly had international sporting events at the top of his agenda. The US president had written to the FIFA president before the IOC decision. "As a child, I played soccer on a dirt road in Jakarta, and the game brought the children of my neighborhood together," he wrote, before passing on the generational baton: "As a father, I saw that same spirit of unity alive on the fields and sidelines of my own daughters' soccer games in Chicago."[7] Hailing soccer as "truly the world's sport," and the World Cup as a promoter of friendly competition and camaraderie throughout the world, Obama added that the bid "was about much more than a game. It is about the United States of America inviting the world to gather all across our great country in celebration of our hopes and dreams." If President Obama or his letter-writer had known a little more about FIFA's preoccupations, commitments and intra-political dynamics – all of which were really spheres of insignificant ignorance for them in the context of rather bigger priorities – the language would have been different. FIFA invites the world to gather at its delegated host country for these events; and adding the adjective "great" into "our country" might irritate or provoke members of an organization in which US personnel make up a tiny minority. But the Chicago humiliation in October later that year ensured that there'd be little hope of the US soccer federation having White House support fourteen months later. Political ignorance had here proved a form of significant ignorance. Within months, the one US citizen on FIFA's ExCo, Chuck Blazer, was facing FBI probes into his financial dealings, and turned whistle-blower against his old boss and confidant Jack Warner of Trinidad and Tobago and announced that he would be leaving his CONCACAF general secretary's role in the very near future.

As media interest in the FIFA issue mushroomed throughout 2011, watchdog agencies called for reform, investigative journalists brought the story onto the front pages and previously emollient players in the FIFA game broke, or promised to break, their silences. In August the UK branch of Transparency International, the self-labelled "global coalition against corruption," produced "Safe Hands: Building Integrity and Transparency at FIFA."[8] By the next FIFA ExCo meeting, the author of the report found herself drawn upon as an expert, in the FIFA president's rearguard action to establish credible anti-corruption procedures.

Careful not to name a single individual, and even more careful to note that all information in the report was "believed to be correct" in April 2011 when the report went to press, "Safe Hands" plays nicely on the notion of the role of FIFA as the custodian of the world game. In effect, the report transplants its well-established principles and framework onto the FIFA case, arguing that some multi-stakeholder group or some other group with "solid reputations" should be assigned the task of clearing up past cases in FIFA of bribes and scandals, to ensure "a new era of openness and accountability,"[9] and that new procedures should be established for good governance and transparency.

The author, Sylvia Schenk, recognizes that FIFA's overall structure poses distinctive questions and problems, with no equivalent of company shareholders, and archaic "old-boys' networks" at the core of its practices and procedures. Decision-making processes should involve, she proposes, some form of outside scrutiny, in the form of "non-executive directors or supervisory boards in the private sector." Schenk has a sharp eye for the fault lines in the FIFA landscape, but the report has little feel for the scale of the task facing anyone who would challenge and seek to transform an organization so rooted in its statutes and Congress membership. The report concludes with an evangelical refrain, that FIFA, responsible for the world's most popular game, which is "a role model for youth everywhere," should recognize that "few bodies have such an opportunity for delivering a message of fair play, integrity and respect for the rule of law."[10] By December 2011, though, Transparency International had already distanced itself from FIFA's reform processes, expressing disapproval over the composition of the proposed task force.

Launching FIFA's centenary publication in 2004, Sepp Blatter posed four questions about what conclusions might be drawn from FIFA's first 100 years, appealing to history and the historians who authored the book, a less demanding forum than he would find his queue of interrogators to be six or seven years later:

> How great has FIFA's influence been? To what extent do the actions of FIFA's leaders and those of any of its many committees, having been faced by the vicissitudes of world history, economic challenges and humanitarian imperatives, stand up to a critical evaluation? Has FIFA been a true guardian of football's ideals? If so, does it still play this role?[11]

The previous chapters of this study have provided some answers to these questions, a task not comprehensively undertaken by the authors of the centennial book, despite their "unrestricted access" to FIFA's archive collection and the "total freedom which they ... enjoyed during the writing" of the book.[12] The first question is quite easy to answer. The historical achievements of FIFA have been immense. From a modest and stumbling start in the western and northern regions of Europe, FIFA grew into a globally recognized body genuinely representative of football's interests worldwide. It also established the men's World Cup, after a little over a quarter of a century of wrangling over amateur and professional status and the claim of the Olympic football tournament to be the quadrennial world championship. This is an extraordinary organizational trajectory, by any standards. The FIFA acronym is a global brand, and the brand's activities take place across all continents and in all societies, with cultural variations and adaptations of course, but still – for the most part – recognizable as the "Simplest Game," as some of the sport's first rule-makers and enthusiasts called it.[13] And once the continental confederations were recognized, FIFA could rightly claim to represent the sport in all corners of the earth.

How this extensive and sustained influence has been achieved, though, moves us on to the second question, which raises the issue of the critical evaluation of recent and contemporary leadership. Any informed and balanced evaluation can only conclude that the price paid for the immense influence of FIFA on the world game has been a high one. FIFA, establishing itself in Zurich, Switzerland in 1932, after the hasty removal of an official who had embezzled almost all the funds, recovered to survive in a modest fashion, then seriously internationalize after World War II and in the post-colonial period and negotiate the challenge of the growth of the television and media industries. But the pacts with partners were corrosive of independence and idealism. What Strange called the "fructifying" power of money was counterbalanced by the flaws and greed of those who saw the self-aggrandizing potential of involvement in the booming football economy. It is arguable – indeed, the mass of evidence from the last quarter of the twentieth century and the first decade of the current century points in only one direction – that the price of the survival and expansion of FIFA, and the escalating economic value of its main product, the men's World Cup, has been too high, in terms of the obdurate unaccountability of the world governing body and the opaque financial processes that have underpinned its survival and increasing wealth.

Has FIFA been a true guardian of football's ideals? Blatter's third question is on one level easy to answer. FIFA has made much of the principles of fair play and integrity, and the terms of its stated mission; of the 387 committee members in positions on FIFA committees in late 2011, many would be there for the good of the game – "For the Game. For the World" – and not for themselves. Dr Michel D'Hooghe was visibly dismayed at London's Park Hotel in May 2011, the week of the UEFA Champions League final, as the vote-buying scandals in the Caribbean were changing the landscape of FIFA's forthcoming pre-sidential election: "I am not one of them, I have nothing to do with a FIFA of corruption," the ExCo and multiple-committee veteran, and medical commission chair confirmed. And despite match-fixing and betting scandals, most football administrators believe in the fair play principle. Without that, there is really no sustainable moral base to sporting competition. It is highly likely, therefore, that the vast majority of committee men in FIFA believe themselves to be guardians of football's ideals, and their actions and inputs would support and justify such a sense of duty and mission.

But individual motivations, actions and ideals do not necessarily flow into collective values. If the leadership sets the precedent for how to conduct business, then the willing workhorses for the common good are tarnished by the example set at the top, and may even follow it. And if this example leads to unmonitored and undeclared remunerations, more and more luxury travel, and increasing compensation for your incon-venience, even the honourable man may become complicit in an endemic culture of excess and privilege. Such members may sit in committee after committee meeting thinking disapproving thoughts, but never expressing that disapproval. "Speak what we feel, not what we ought to say," Edgar said in the final lines of Shakespeare's *King Lear*. Speaking what we ought to say, or feel that others want to hear, is a recipe for autocracy. The silence of well-intentioned committee members renders such figures – intentionally or otherwise – guardians as much of their own status and self-interest as of refereeing development, or the work of the medical commission.

There is another dimension to FIFA's profile, created by the organization's employees. In 1997, experienced FIFA ExCo member David Will estimated that FIFA had around 200 employees. This would have astounded Stanley Rous, with his tiny administrative staff of no more than half a dozen or so full-time employees in 1974. In 2013 the number of employees at FIFA in Zurich was more than 500. The rewards are high, and bodies like FIFA attract the most ambitious of administrators. Little is known about the employee base of FIFA. It is certain, though, that the protection of football's ideals is not at the very top of their career concerns; as long as the World Cup spectacle continues to accrue audiences and profits, that's enough to confirm the extension of the contract, the continuing tax exemptions within the Swiss polity, the mega-luxurious lifestyle of the supra-national professional on the move. One can only conclude that the future of a different, changed, reformed FIFA lies in the hands, actions and visions of those institutional actors willing to trade what they see as insignificant ignorance for more informed action and intervention, based on a recognition of the flaws of FIFA, and a sense that action should be taken to understand such flaws as actionable. Only then will reform be generated by employees within the organization, or among actors (such as committee members) close enough to the centre of power to gain sufficient knowledge to redefine insignificant ignorance as significant. The answer to Blatter's question as to whether FIFA has been a "true guardian of football's ideals" can, on the balance of evidence, only be "to a seriously limited extent."

Bottom of the league

We have known of FIFA's practices and reputation for a long time. One World Trust's "2007 Global Accountability Report," measuring – or at least measuring perceptions – of transparency, participation, evaluation and complaint response mechanisms, placed FIFA at the bottom of its league table of INGOs.[14] The table for transnational corporations had Google at the bottom. Interpol was adrift at the bottom of the IGO table. The question for a critical social science and organizational analysis is in many ways no longer whether FIFA is corrupt. This study, citing a

senior football business figure in Europe as well as numerous other testimonies, has shown that in too many respects "FIFA's now so corrupt
that it no longer knows that it's being corrupt."[15] The serious question
is how FIFA has functioned so long when it is so widely perceived to be
corrupt; and, secondarily, what could be done to challenge corruption
by making FIFA more accountable.

On the first question, the One World Trust lists four possible strategies
for prompting the increased accountability of organizations such as
FIFA. First, one could "create a sense of urgency for accountability
reform" linked to a perceived risk to the organization. If such a sense of
urgency was created by principal partners such as media rights clients and
corporate sponsors, FIFA might have to change; its revenues could collapse.
But, as shown in previous chapters, such bodies are habitually happy
with cosmetic changes. Cleanse the house that Jack built, condemn the
Qatari scapegoat and carry on as usual, without probing too far into the
heart of the endemic malpractice and self-aggrandizement. The IOC is
often mentioned here as a precedent. It was the US courts and corporate
sponsors that leveraged the pressure for change after the Sydney and Salt
Lake City scandals: the law and the economy in a pincer movement.
But partners are often complicit in previous practices. Individuals can be
sacrificed in national courts without fatal damage to the institution.

The Trust's other strategies relate to desirable changes in vision and
leadership, echoing wider calls for the interrogation of the FIFA leadership's
style and the mission of the federation. In a general sense, the need for
reform has been accepted among commentators for some time; in 2000
Sunder Katwala concluded that: "Few would doubt that sporting governance needs reform – the bigger question is whether reform is possible."[16]
His most optimistic scenario was reform from within, by an emergent
generation of sport administrators more alert to what would best serve
their careers, taking perhaps a first step of collaboration to create an
"open and transparent multi-stakeholder forum on good sporting governance,"[17] so avoiding or overcoming those more self-serving interests
that have led to the ossification of organizational structures.

Katwala's "more likely" scenario was the intensification of pressures
for reform from outside, from governmental and corporate sources: the
former could make life harder for rogue sporting bodies to continue
their old ways, while the most prominent players among the latter could
simply pull the plug on the torrents of funding pouring into sport. For
Katwala, the least attractive scenario is no reform from within, and no
effective reform initiative from without. In the FIFA case, as we have
seen in considering stakeholders and their responses in the previous
chapter, there is no simple solution to the problem of finding a source of

reforming influence from without. Why should the richest football clubs be seen as flagbearers of a more democratic and open FIFA, when their own internal procedures are often veiled in secrecy and ruthless ambition? And sponsors are always happy, should some cosmetics be applied to the historical face and image of football governance, when the big match starts or the globally followed tournament kicks off. Katwala is right to observe that particular outside pressures – as in the case of the International Olympic Committee and the Olympics – may provide the key moment in a reform process. But we have seen that such moments arise quite rarely.

The most serious challenge to the Havelange–Blatter dynasty from within the broader world of football governance came from UEFA president Lennart Johansson in 1998; his strategy document "Vision" (reproduced in full in the Appendix) embraced democratic principles and, above all, a strengthening of the role of the continental federations in global football governance.[18] Johansson appealed to core democratic principles informing his challenge for the FIFA presidency: "The challenges that lie ahead cannot be tackled by one person alone, in his capacity as FIFA president. What is needed is an international, democratic network based on trust, transparency, loyalty and solidarity." But as we have seen, Blatter won his first presidential cycle not least by offering "tailor-made" solutions – of a financial kind, and through the targeted *Goal* programme – to the smaller nations that make up the majority of FIFA's 209 national associations (see Chapters 6 and 7). This cemented a power base that no candidate has come close to challenging.

As part of his strategy for holding onto power for the remainder of his fourth term, the FIFA president has allowed expert commentators into the debate. Mark Pieth, professor of criminal law at Basel University in Switzerland, has experience in the bribery working group of the Organisation for Economic Co-operation and Development, and a curriculum vitae that includes advising the World Bank and the United Nations; Pieth was appointed chair of FIFA's new Independent Governance Committee (IGC). At the end of November 2011, his concept paper "Governing FIFA" proposed the introduction of: term limits for the president and other officials; independent non-executives on the ExCo; a "lead director" that has the capacity to challenge the president through independently convened meetings; conflict of interest regulation enabling removal of individuals from official positions; a remuneration committee to set salaries for officials and staff; direct payment to member associations, and auditing processes and procedures; and restrictions on the overlaps between committees.[19] Pieth emphasized that "we are talking about serious stuff here," but also stressed that his task was not to investigate past wrongdoing but to look positively and optimistically "into the future." It was also recognized that a cooling-off period of a year would be necessary before the implementation of any identified and agreed changes, however these might be agreed. As the FIFA president introduced Pieth, he reaffirmed his commitment to necessary reforms: "I am happy and proud that you accepted the call, my call and the call of FIFA."

This appointment of a commissioned individual precipitated the withdrawal of the goodwill of Transparency International from FIFA's road map to reform. Pieth, talking of the acceptance of several reform measures by the May 2013 Congress, was upbeat about the reform process, claiming "quite spectacular" progress and success for the proposals of the IGC. These included the acceptance by the FIFA Congress of independent heads of the Investigatory and Adjudicatory Chambers of the Ethics Committee, and the return to Congress of the responsibility for deciding on World Cup host cities. But the FIFA chiefs have not agreed to age limits and limits on terms of office. The spectacular here looks more akin to the speculative.

Institutional reform does not transform automatically an organization's culture and practice. This book has shown the multiple ways in which time and again in its recent history FIFA has failed to follow practices and principles such as those proposed by Pieth's IGC, even though clear rules on conflict of interest, for example, have been conspicuously established in FIFA's Ethics Code. The question remains: how can FIFA be changed so that its practices really do match its own declared principles and values? The survival of FIFA has been based on its place within and above the supra-national institutional culture of our times. Its future will continue in large part to be shaped by this institutional culture and history.[20]

This study has focused on the internal workings of FIFA and its institutional culture, and the perennial question of the relationship of the actions of such organizations to their declared ideals. It concludes with a plea for sustained challenge to and continuing critique of elements of the practices and culture of FIFA, linked to proposals for feasible and ethical changes. In 2002, in the aftermath of the ISL collapse, with FIFA's leadership struggling for credibility, I suggested several directions for reform.[21] FIFA could seek to gain some credibility in the eyes of a sceptical public by opening its books to scrutiny, coming out from behind the veil of Swiss secrecy and banking laws that have protected world sports organizations, as well as hoarders of Nazi gold, for half a century and more. It could ask those national federations that have accepted huge and regular handouts to say precisely where the money has gone. It could look to use the profits from bonanzas such as the World Cup Finals to develop the game at the grassroots. It could review the membership and composition of key committees, so that henchmen of the president don't sell on media rights for FIFA events to their own cronies or even their own companies. It could give the Executive Committee proper and useful functions, such as setting the budget and advising and consulting on major contracts and genuine tenders. It could begin to act with integrity for the good of the game, rather than to support the egos of the FIFAcrats and the lifestyles of hangers-on. It could; FIFA could do all of these things. So why has it done so few of these things, unless under the glare of adverse publicity and an increasingly hostile world media? And how has its leadership survived so long with the revelation of so many fraudulent or corrupt activities occurring within the framework of its leaders' administration and authority?

In his essay on responses to organizational decline, in states, firms or voluntary associations, Albert O. Hirschman assesses the effects on institutional life of two core responses to organizational decline: "exit," a concept he takes from classical economics; and "voice," more associated with political science. Put at its crudest, the Hirschman argument is that organizational failings are found out by management when those they manage exercise either an exit option, whereby they leave, or a voice option, whereby dissatisfaction is expressed directly to management or some other appropriate authority.[22] Exit is neat, in that "one either exits or one does not," whereas voice is far more messy, and can include anything from "faint grumbling to violent protest."[23] In the FIFA context, the leadership has for the most part perfected its own version of these dynamics. People do leave, with severance packages and silence agreements; but the majority want to stay on the FIFA payroll and career path. And voices are rarely raised in any normal process or everyday context – only at times of outright conflict or internal rivalry, or potentially divisive crisis.

Hirschman also introduces the concept of loyalty into his argument:

> As a rule, then, loyalty holds exit at bay and activates voice. It is true that, in the face of discontent with the way things are going in an organization, an individual member can remain loyal without being influential himself, but hardly without the expectation that *someone* will act or *something* will happen to improve matters.[24]

In FIFA, though, activation of voice can lead to a precariousness of position. Individuals aware of the fault lines in the organization's structure stay silent, close to complicit, in the knowledge that almost no one will act, and nothing will happen, except where crisis resolution is required; FIFA does not act as a rational organization in its everyday *modus operandi*. The rewards of loyalty remain too high for individuals to channel an increasing awareness of significant ignorance into taking a voice option. FIFA works in such a way that it can manoeuvre individuals towards exit, and suppress any sense of voice. Framed as a modern organization, it in fact functions as an autocracy. Any feasible call for change must recognize this, and as a starting point question the nature of FIFA's compliance culture. In this context and light, the core foci of potential reform remain issues of ethics and accountability:

- Financial transparency – this demands more detailed exposition on the nature of financial categories in the FIFA accounts, particularly salaries of employees and officers, and expenses for committee members and delegates.
- Effective monitoring of FIFA initiatives, such as *Goal*, with adequate detail on what infrastructural football developments have been achieved and what they continue to accomplish.
- Declarations of interest and potential conflicts of interest for any individual aspiring to hold office on FIFA committees.
- A maximum number of committee positions to be held by any single individual.
- Stronger cooperative liaison with the six "continental" federations, in relation to representation within the FIFA committee structure.

Organizationally and institutionally, however, FIFA has remained beyond the reach of any process of accountability, the declared Supreme Leader accountable only to his Congress. In its *annus horribilis* of 2010–2011 and beyond, the organization looked more vulnerable than at any point in its history, but it still knew its brands – the teams were not boycotting the tournaments, there was no haemorrhaging of sponsors, the events in Brazil in 2013 notwithstanding. And there are good things that FIFA has done for the game, for the world: the Japanese women's team has taken the Women's World Cup away from Europe and North America for the first time; the men's World Cup has been to Africa. The Havelange dimension of the FIFA mission is for the most part accomplished. But the organization will remain vulnerable to exploitation by ambitious and self-serving individuals and unaccountable cabals unless voices are mobilized, and heard, within a more open climate of collaboration and development befitting the institution that claims to speak for the simplest game, the peoples' game.

Notes

1 Blatter was speaking at the FIFA building in Sonnenberg, Zurich, at the opening session of the symposium "The relevance and impact of FIFA World Cups, 1930–2010," 24–27 April 2013.

2 Susan Strange, *Casino Capitalism* (Manchester: Manchester University Press, 1997), vi–vii.

3 Susan Strange, *Mad Money* (Manchester: Manchester University Press, 1998), 188.

4 Strange, *Casino Capitalism*, vii.

5 Ibid., 121.

6 Alan Tomlinson, "Lording it: London and the getting of the Games," in *Watching the Olympics: Politics, Power and Representation*, eds. John Sugden and Alan Tomlinson (London: Routledge, 2012), 11–12.

7 These excerpts were released by the US soccer federation, reported by Ronald Blum, "Obama writes FIFA in support of US World Cup bid," *The Seattle Times*, 14 April 2009, http://seattletimes.nwsource.com/html/sports/200905 2543_apsocwcupusobama.html, consulted on 15 November 2011.

8 Sylvia Schenk, "Safe Hands: Building Integrity and Transparency at FIFA," (Berlin: Transparency International, 16 August 2011), http://www.transparency.org/ whatwedo/pub/safe_hands_building_integrity_and_transparency_at_fifa, consulted 28 September 2011.

9 Ibid., 3.

10 Ibid., 8.

11 Joseph S. Blatter, "100 years of FIFA: Foreword from the FIFA President," in *100 Years of Football: The FIFA Centennial Book*, Christiane Eisenberg, Pierre Lanfranchi, Tony Mason and Alfred Wahl (London: Weidenfeld and Nicolson, 2004), 7.

12 Ibid., 9.

13 Uncomplicated rules were recorded in a small pamphlet, "The Simplest Game," in 1862 by John Charles Thring, who was a contributor to the formulation of the Cambridge Rules in 1846/8, named after the university at which these footballers played and adapted the game they had brought from their various public schools. This simple set of rules formed the basis of the game as recognized and developed by the Football Association, inaugurated in 1863. See Alan Tomlinson, *A Dictionary of Sports Studies* (Oxford: Oxford University Press, 2010), 195.

14 One World Trust, "2007 Global Accountability Report: Accountability Profile, Fédération Internationale de Football Association." See http://www.oneworld trust.org.

15 Jürgen Lenz, interview with the author, Rome, 27 May 2009.

16 Sunder Katwala, *Democratising Global Sport* (London: The Foreign Policy Centre, 2000), 90.

17 Ibid., 92.

18 See John Sugden and Alan Tomlinson, *FIFA and the Contest for World Football: Who Rules the Peoples' Game?* (Cambridge: Polity Press, 1998), 250–254.

19 Matt Scott, "Blatter faces curbs on his power at Fifa," *Guardian*, 1 December 2011: 2; "Governance expert charged with bringing FIFA 'up to speed'," *Around the Rings*, 11 November 2011 (with reporting from Zurich by Marta Falconi).

20 A full theorization of FIFA and its place in contemporary global culture would require an interdisciplinary programme of related projects, exploring the degrees

and locales of globalization and the federation's contribution to that process; tracking the post-colonial contexts in which the hegemony of the FIFA leadership has been challenged and emergent parts of the Third World and global South empowered; and probing the practices through which sport development has been a form of the politics of the belly. These broader theoretical questions have been posed and in part answered in Sugden and Tomlinson, *FIFA and the Contest for World Football*. See also their "Power and resistance in the governance of world football: Theorising FIFA's transnational impact," *Journal of Sport and Social Issues*, 22/3: 299–316.

21 See Alan Tomlinson, "Must do better," *When Saturday Comes*, 183, May 2002.
22 Albert O. Hirschman, *Exit, Voice and Loyalty: Responses to Decline in Firms, Organizations, and States* (Cambridge: Harvard University Press, 1970), 4.
23 Ibid., 15 and 16.
24 Ibid., 78.

Afterword

On Myths, the Investigative and the Economic

The FIFA story, as this study has reaffirmed, is a high-profile soap-operatic narrative on the transnational stage. Every decision on World Cup hosting sparks allegations and counter-allegations, and as this book went to press the controversy over FIFA's granting of the 2022 men's World Cup Finals to Qatar showed no sign of abating; indeed it provided a recurrent backdrop for stories about UEFA president and potential FIFA presidential candidate Michel Platini, and about alternative pretenders to Blatter's position, such as Jérôme Champagne, former French diplomat and FIFA insider now calling for a cleansing of the FIFA stables.[1] This long-running story has to be understood, as argued in the opening chapter, through interdisciplinary and investigative approaches. Some of these approaches have been considered in the study, and here I add further comment. Also, the subtitle of the book refers to myths, and the way in which FIFA's documentation of its goals and ideals can be analysed as myth merits retrospective reflection.

The noun "myth" has two meanings, referring respectively to a fictitious narrative, and to a fictitious person or object.[2] FIFA may help create legends – of players, teams, nations, performances – but it does not invent explicitly imaginary histories or events. It may share the presentational principles of fictional dramas and narratives, but it is not fiction. It is not this aspect of the definition of "myth" that is evoked in the book's subtitle. Rather, the term here signposts the ways in which FIFA and its single product, football, have increasingly become framed as a source of myths, in the sense in which Roland Barthes talked about mass or popular cultural forms as myths in his groundbreaking essays of 1954–1956. He was interested in going beyond the dressed-up realities of the media, cultural producers and common sense of his time: "I wanted to track down, in the decorative display of *what-goes-without-saying*, the ideological abuse which, in my view, is hidden there."[3] He used the idea of myth, with examples from sport, food, cinema and advertising, to explain "the falsely obvious." And he linked the idea of myth to theories of language. Take the everyday statements and images of our culture, Barthes was saying, and recognize – he was paraphrasing Horace here – that things that are repeated are significant.[4] They are significant because they become taken for granted. FIFA mantras are then less contested: the good that the federation does for the game clouds over the bad. Everything can be a myth, Barthes further observes, "providing it is conveyed by a discourse."[5] The term "myth," then, can help direct attention to the way in which powerful institutions in an age of global communication have the capacity to relate their own histories, in their own time and in contexts of their own making, therefore introducing, in the selective retelling of their own narratives, elements of myth – as analyses of FIFA discourse in this study have shown.

The investigative imperative that has underpinned this study is an application of the principles and arguments articulated in earlier collaborative work, and work in recent years on aspects of global football governance.[6] Embracing the investigative project can be a long-haul commitment, unpredictable in accessing or securing sources, though here vital for posing key questions about the values, motivations and practices of those benefiting from FIFA's continued profile and the myth-making discourses by which the federation justifies itself to the world.

Interdisciplinarity generates its own challenges, and no doubt political scientists and economists, historians and sociologists, and other academic specialists could dispute the use of particular analytical frameworks or field-specific concepts; that is the excitement and the risk of a commitment to open-minded interdisciplinarity. In Chapter 6, it was claimed that "all the competitions listed in FIFA's event calendar, along with its redistributive initiatives and its CSR programmes, are loss leaders, made possible by the vast revenues that can be generated by the top event." In the absence of any seriously transparent presentation of FIFA's finances, the equilibrium achieved between the cash cow and the loss leader by the federation is a hugely successful strategy, satisfying major partners and constituencies. As such – and I make no claim here to analytical economic expertise in this framing of FIFA's finances – these essentially economic terms act as an overarching metaphorical framework for the understanding of FIFA's economic *modus vivendi*.[7] It would be an unadventurous interdisciplinary framework indeed, and a half-baked investigative approach, that did not at least attempt to locate the FIFA story within a broader frame of political economy and economics.

Notes

1 See Owen Gibson, "Is Jérôme Champagne the man Fifa needs to change direction at the top?" *Guardian*, 12 November 2013, http://www.theguardian. com/football/blog/2013/nov/12/jerome-champagne-fifa-change-direction, consulted 18 November 2013.

2 *The Compact Edition of the Oxford English Dictionary, Complete Text Reproduced Micrographically, Volume 1 A–O* (London: Book Club Associates by arrangement with Oxford University Press, 1979), 1889.

3 Roland Barthes, *Mythologies* (London: Paladin, 1972), 11.

4 Ibid., 12.

5 Ibid., 109.

6 John Sugden and Alan Tomlinson, "Digging the dirt and staying clean: Retrieving the investigative tradition for a critical sociology of sport," *International Review for the Sociology of Sport*, 34/4, 1999: 385–397. See also Alan Tomlinson, "'Lord don't stop the carnival': Trinidad and Tobago at the 2006 FIFA World Cup," *Journal of Sport and Social Issues*, 31/3, 2007: 259–282, note 3.

7 See John Black, Nigar Hashimzade and Gareth Myles, *A Dictionary of Economics*, 4th edition (Oxford: Oxford University Press, 2013), 191 on the "loss leader," a good priced so low so as to attract customers who are then expected to purchase other goods. "Cash cow" is widely understood to refer to a product with exceptionally high profit margins, with excess used for other purposes. FIFA is not technically a profit-making business, but its finances make sense in terms of the cash cow–loss leader balance.

Appendix

VISION for the Future Governance of Football[1]

Lennart Johansson

Preface

> "Football can only maintain its leading role if our world-wide movement retains its spirit of solidarity"

It is my firm belief that, in the future, football will be challenged in several different ways. Many steps have to be taken to guide the world-wide football movement towards modern structures. Football has a glorious past and a wonderful present, but the success stories of the past are of little relevance to the problems of tomorrow. The challenges that lie ahead cannot be tackled by one person alone, in his capacity as FIFA president. What is needed is an international, democratic network based on trust, transparency, loyalty and solidarity. These fundamental elements will lead our sport successfully into the next century.

The world football movement is a community. For this reason, FIFA has to further strengthen its democratic governance, as the United Nations of world football. In order to strengthen the democratic spirit and establish a fair system of balance between FIFA, the confederations and the associations, a revised structure must be openly discussed and then implemented.

Besides democratic governance, the professional management of the world-wide football movement is also of paramount importance.

It is for this reason that I am presenting this VISION paper, with the following five fields of action and the key objectives:

1. Football at Grassroots Level
   Strengthen the entire world-wide football movement
2. Football at Professional Level
   Define clear objectives and monitor the development of top-class football

3. Football at Management Level
   Involve the representatives of the national associations and the confederations in all FIFA activities
4. FIFA and the Confederations
   Redefine the role and functions of the confederations in the FIFA
   statutes
5. FIFA and the National Associations
   Strengthen the national associations politically, financially and structurally

In this VISION paper, FIFA's tasks are defined as those of a global
nature, whereas the Confederations would assume all functions which
can be better dealt with at a continental level, taking into account the
growing importance of the Confederations since their foundation, and
the associations would assume all functions which can be better dealt
with at national or even regional level.

This VISION paper describes the most important criteria to which I
intend to lead world football's governing body FIFA into the next century. I will be able to fulfil this task with the help of all those who
support the ideals of solidarity and democracy within the family of
football.

Lennart Johansson

VISION for the Future Governance of Football

1. Football at Grassroots Level

Strengthen the entire world-wide football movement

- Increase participation in every country and in all sectors and levels
- Facilitate access to football for everyone, regardless of sex, ability and age
- Launch world-wide grassroots programmes in co-operation with the
  associations, clubs, schools, communities, sponsors and media
- Improve educational standards of coaches, referees and officials at all levels
- Increase awareness of the social importance and responsibility of
  football in every single country

2. Football at Professional Level

Define clear objectives and monitor the development of top-class football

- Establish, promote and enforce a detailed code of conduct for all
  participants in the game

- Define the legal structure of professional clubs and leagues and their relationship with the national associations, confederations and FIFA
- Ensure a fair share for the confederations in organizing final rounds of FIFA competitions
- Implement a fixed match calendar for qualifying competitions in co-operation with the confederations. The present World Cup format remains unchanged, i.e. 32 teams
- Ensure co-operation with the Olympic Movement
- Create an Under-20 competition for women at world level
- Create the logistical and financial base to permit inter-continental competitions for national and club teams

3. Football at Management Level

Involve the representatives of the national associations and the confederations in all FIFA activities

- Ensure a fair share of leadership within FIFA. The number of presidential terms to be limited by a statutory amendment. The maximum duration of the presidency to be set by the FIFA congress
- Meetings between the FIFA president and the presidents of the confederations will take place at least four times per year
- The presidents of the confederations will automatically become members of the FIFA Executive Committee and vice-presidents of FIFA
- FIFA Executive Committee members will chair a FIFA committee in accordance with their specific capacities
- Members of FIFA committees will be proposed by the national associations to their confederation, which will then propose them to FIFA
- All committee member appointments will be approved by the FIFA Executive Committee
- The chairmen of committees within the confederations should automatically be members of the respective FIFA committees
- Development of a long-term financial and marketing plan for FIFA by the Executive Committee
- The general secretaries of the confederations will attend FIFA Executive Committee meetings in a consultative capacity

4. FIFA and the Confederations

Redefine the role and functions of the confederations in the FIFA statutes

- FIFA president to have regular meetings with the Confederations

- Allocate an appropriate contribution from the World Cup to the confederations, to strengthen each of them in their aim to promote football by investing in sporting, technical and administrative matters
- Support the confederations to complete and train their full-time staff in the following sectors:

  - management
  - technical development/coaching
  - development programmes
  - marketing/PR
  - medical services

  - competitions
  - refereeing
  - legal matters
  - media services

- FIFA to delegate all areas where the confederations can act independently, namely in all continental-related business matters
- FIFA to support the confederations to set up their own development programmes
- FIFA to entrust the confederations with the task of ensuring that the higher income from the World Cup will be used by the national associations for increased investment in grassroots and other development programmes

5. FIFA and the National Associations

Strengthen the national associations politically, financially and structurally

- FIFA to maintain the "one country–one vote" system
- Defend the integrity, authority and independence of national associations from external interference
- Strengthen the position of the national teams of the member associations
- Defend the principles of ethics and fair play in the game, and strengthen the social importance of football within society
- Reserve a substantial part of World Cup income for distribution in equal parts to all member associations. This allocation will not be less than one million US dollars per association and is to be used for concrete projects, grassroots programmes, participation in competitions, education and technical equipment. The projects will be defined in co-operation with the confederations according to the needs of each association.

Commentary

Reform

FIFA's road to reform is hardly newly mapped terrain. The *Vision* document in this appendix emphasized core principles of transparency and solidarity, implemented within a democratic framework. In the weeks leading up to the 1998 presidential election, Swedish UEFA president Lennart Johansson reaffirmed these values. Looking for support from Asian delegates, in Kuala Lumpur, he instanced his leadership of UEFA as a model for the future "where everybody is allowed to have his opinion but … has to bow to the majority. This is not common in FIFA today. It is more a dictatorship". Johansson also attacked outgoing president Havelange for putting "words and actions, let's say, in my mouth, which is wrong. He is not using the truth".[2] Johansson's team plugged his key messages over the following weeks: "It's time for a change", said a 24 May press release: *"Lennart Johansson stands for Integrity and Sincerity* he will guide FIFA with *moral leadership* by strengthening world football through *democracy, transparency and solidarity"*. Trust and loyalty would be at the heart of Johansson's commitment to a fairer distribution of power, money and events, within an international democratic network. The press release accused Blatter of copying Johansson's *Vision,* but claimed too that if elected Blatter would try everything, with the help of the FIFA administration, to prevent "implementation of Johansson's *Vision* that today is uncontested in the entire World of Football".[3] There was an air of anxiety to the press release, as Blatter was known in his campaign to be giving "promises on private bases and on FIFA bases", and playing around with promises "just for election reasons". The Johansson team exuded misplaced electoral confidence though, predicting that in the election the Swede would gain double the amount of votes of Blatter – 120 to 60 – come 8 June in Paris. In fact, of 191 votes cast – Johansson's team had been anticipating the total votes to amount to 183 – Johansson secured only 80, and, visibly shaken, conceded defeat. Close to 16 years later Blatter was approaching FIFA's 64th Congress in São Paulo with glib assurances of the success of the reform agenda and an ominous eye on a possible fifth term of presidential office. In mid-January 2014, he told L'Equipe 21 TV: "Let me repeat what I have been saying. I am not yet tired enough to decide that I will retire."[4] "Having said that, everything is open. I will certainly take a stand before this year's Congress," he added. A further period from 2015 would take Blatter well into his 80s, no doubt pledging to keep the reform agenda firmly on the road, though apparently not prioritising any principle of fixed presidential terms of office.

Lobbying

Any organization based upon a purportedly representative and demo-cratic structure with decision-making and accountability anchored in the statutes and the Congress – and in FIFA's case the single vote of each member/national association – will generate intense forms of lobbying. Johansson himself travelled widely, attending the congresses of the continental confederations, in his 1998 campaign. But he sought to be consistent and transparent in addressing delegates and representatives. His clarion call was to democratic channels of accountability. In his *Vision* pledges he offered financial support to all national associations, and increased involvement in the business of FIFA for individuals. There would have been no guarantee that as president Johansson could have succeeded in implementing institutional and procedural changes that would have accomplished his reformist and transformative goals. But there is no doubt at all that he would have introduced processes and procedures, and forms of monitoring, that would have made the organization more open and transparent. Blatter's lack of such a commitment has rendered FIFA still more vulnerable to abuse and exploitation, at the same time as the interests of the majority of national associations and Congress members have coalesced with his own, as manifest in the record vote of 186 that secured his fourth term of office. In January 2014, former FIFA employee, French diplomat Jerome Champagne, declared his intent to run for the presidency in 2015, on a ticket of bringing change to FIFA: "We need a different FIFA, more democratic, more respected, which behaves better and which does more." In a tone of resigned realism, though, he noted too that it was unlikely that he could defeat Blatter if the current president chose to seek a fifth term.[5] As part of his reformist vision, Champagne looked to involve and empower national associations, with less influence for the continental confederations, a bold divide and rule strategy, though when he talked of Blatter as "someone of relevance" who was unlikely to be unseated, the *realpolitik* of FIFA dynamics resurfaced, and there was little to suggest that a Champagne manifesto and campaign would fare any better than had Johansson's proposals the year that Blatter took the presidential position and the reins of power at FIFA.

Notes

1 Reproduced from John Sugden and Alan Tomlinson, *FIFA and the Contest for World Football: Who Rules the Peoples' Game?* (Cambridge: Polity Press, 1998), 250–254. Released by Lennart Johansson/UEFA in the build up to the FIFA presidential election of 1998.

2 Nelson Graves, "Johansson says he has votes to win the FIFA job", Thursday 14 May 1:33 PM EDT, 1998, Reuters.

3 Press Release, *KEY MESSAGES for the last two weeks of the "ELECTION CAMPAIGN '98"*, Nyon, 24 May 1998.

4 Mark Bisson, "Blatter Blasts Sochi Boycotts, Considers Run for FIFA Presidency", *Around the Rings*, 17 January 2014, http://www.aroundtherings.com/

site/A__45660/Title__Blatter-Blasts-Sochi-Boycotts-Considers-Run-for-FIFA-Presidency/292/Articles, consulted 27 January 2014.
5 Martyn Ziegler, "Sin bins and caps on foreign players: Champagne reveals manifesto in bid to replace Blatter as FIFA president", MailOnline, 20 January 2014, http://www.dailymail.co.uk/sport/football/article-2542647/Champagne-bid-replace-Blatter-FIFA-president.html, consulted 27 January 2014.

Index

Entries in **bold** denote references to tables; entries in *italics* denote references to figures.